First World War
and Army of Occupation
War Diary
France, Belgium and Germany

3 DIVISION
Divisional Troops
40 Brigade Royal Field Artillery
5 August 1914 - 28 February 1919

WO95/1400

The Naval & Military Press Ltd
www.nmarchive.com
Published in association with The National Archives

Published by

The Naval & Military Press Ltd

Unit 10 Ridgewood Industrial Park,

Uckfield, East Sussex,

TN22 5QE England

Tel: +44 (0) 1825 749494

www.naval-military-press.com

www.nmarchive.com

This diary has been reprinted in facsimile from the original. Any imperfections are inevitably reproduced and the quality may fall short of modern type and cartographic standards.

© Crown Copyright
Images reproduced by permission of The National Archives, London, England, 2015.

Contents

Document type	Place/Title	Date From	Date To
Heading	3rd Division Divl. Artillery 40th Brigade R.F.A. Jan-Dec 1916		
Heading	3rd Divisional Artillery. 40th Brigade R.F.A. January 1916.		
War Diary	Boeschepe	01/01/1916	31/01/1916
Heading	3rd Divisional Artillery. 40th Brigade R.F.A. February 1916.		
War Diary	Dickebusch	01/02/1916	09/02/1916
War Diary	Dehtezeele	10/02/1916	10/02/1916
War Diary	Audenfort	11/02/1916	19/02/1916
War Diary	Poperinghe	20/10/1916	29/10/1916
Heading	3rd Divisional Artillery. 40th Brigade R.F.A. March 1916.		
War Diary	Poperinghe	01/03/1916	31/03/1916
Heading	3rd Divisional Artillery. 40th Brigade R.F.A. April 1916		
Heading	D.A.G. 3rd Echelon G.H.Q. Vol 21		
War Diary		01/04/1916	30/04/1916
Heading	3rd Divisional Artillery. 40th Brigade R.F.A. May 1916.		
War Diary		01/05/1916	31/05/1916
Heading	3rd Divisional Artillery. 40th Brigade R.F.A. June 1916.		
Miscellaneous	A Form. Messages And Signals.		
War Diary		01/06/1916	30/06/1916
Heading	3rd Divisional Artillery. 40th Brigade R.F.A. July 1916.		
Miscellaneous	A Form. Messages And Signals.		
War Diary		01/07/1916	31/07/1916
Heading	3rd Divisional Artillery. 40th Brigade Royal Field Artillery August 1916.		
Miscellaneous	Staff Captain 3rd D.A.	31/08/1916	31/08/1916
War Diary		01/08/1916	31/08/1916
Heading	3rd Divisional Artillery. 40th Brigade R.F.A. September 1916.		
Miscellaneous	Staff Capt 3rd D.A.	30/09/1916	30/09/1916
War Diary	Talus Bois Valley Carnoy	01/09/1916	06/09/1916
War Diary	Bray	07/09/1916	07/09/1916
War Diary	Montigny	08/09/1916	08/09/1916
War Diary	Hem	09/09/1916	09/09/1916
War Diary	Conchy	10/09/1916	10/09/1916
War Diary	Bavaval	11/09/1916	11/09/1916
War Diary	Labeuvriere	12/09/1916	13/09/1916
War Diary	Mazingarbe	14/09/1916	23/09/1916
War Diary	Labeuvriere	23/09/1916	24/09/1916
War Diary	Martes & Ham	25/09/1916	30/09/1916
Heading	3rd Divisional Artillery. 40th Brigade R.F.A. October 1916.		
Miscellaneous	Brigade Major 3 DA	27/01/1916	27/01/1916
War Diary	Marthes	01/10/1916	07/10/1916
War Diary	Colincamps	08/10/1916	08/10/1916

War Diary	Hebuterne	09/10/1916	30/10/1916
Heading	3rd Divisional Artillery. 40th Brigade R.F.A. November 1916.		
Miscellaneous	Brigade Major 3rd D.A.	01/12/1916	01/12/1916
War Diary	Hebuterne	01/11/1916	30/11/1916
Heading	3rd Divisional Artillery. 40th Brigade R.F.A. December 1916.		
Miscellaneous	Brigade Major 3rd DA	01/01/1917	01/01/1917
War Diary	Hebuterne	01/12/1916	31/12/1916
Heading	3rd Division Divl Artillery 40th Brigade R.F.A. Aug-Dec 1914		
Heading	3rd Divisional Artillery. 40th Brigade R.F.A. August 1914.		
War Diary		05/08/1914	31/08/1914
Miscellaneous	Major R.A. Australian D.S.O. Ca to R.F.A.	16/02/1923	16/02/1923
War Diary		20/08/1914	05/09/1914
Heading	3rd Divisional Artillery. 40th Brigade R.F.A. September 1914		
War Diary		06/09/1914	16/01/1915
War Diary		01/09/1914	30/09/1914
Heading	3rd Divisional Artillery. 40th Brigade R.F.A. October 1914.		
War Diary		01/10/1914	11/10/1914
Diagram etc	Shows Move of Sections		
War Diary		12/10/1914	13/10/1914
Diagram etc	Moves of Sections		
War Diary		14/10/1914	31/10/1914
War Diary		14/10/1914	02/11/1914
Heading	3rd Divisional Artillery. 40th Brigade R.F.A. November 1914.		
War Diary		01/11/1914	07/11/1914
Diagram etc	Dotted line shows telephone wire		
War Diary		08/11/1914	16/11/1914
Diagram etc	1/2 Mile & 28 Bde H.Q. R.A.		
War Diary		16/11/1914	30/11/1914
Heading	3rd Divisional Artillery. 40th Brigade R.F.A. December 1914.		
War Diary		01/12/1914	03/12/1914
Diagram etc	Battery Observing Station		
War Diary		04/12/1914	17/12/1914
Diagram etc	Second position		
War Diary		18/12/1914	31/12/1914
Miscellaneous	Cairnie Colinsburgh Fife	10/04/1923	10/04/1923
Heading	3rd Div. R.F.A. 40th Brigade. War Diary, Jan-Dec 1915		
Heading	3rd Division 40th Bde. R.F.A. Vol VI 1-31.1.15		
Diagram etc	Battery Observing Station		
War Diary		01/01/1915	08/01/1915
Diagram etc	Map A.2 R.F. 1/40000		
War Diary		09/01/1915	31/01/1915
Heading	3rd Division 40th Bde. R.F.A. Vol VII 1-28.2.15		
Diagram etc	Sketch Map		
War Diary		01/02/1915	28/02/1915
Heading	3rd Division 40th Bde. R.F.A. Vol VIII 1-31.3.15		
Diagram etc	Sketch Map		
War Diary		01/03/1915	31/03/1915

Type	Description	From	To
Heading	3rd Division 40th Bde R.F.A. Vol IX 1-30.4.15		
War Diary		01/04/1915	30/04/1915
Diagram etc	Positions of Batteries 40th Bde R.F.A. on Fields		
Heading	3rd Division 40th Bde R.F.A. Vol X 1-31.5.15		
War Diary		01/05/1915	31/05/1915
Diagram etc	Trace For Use With Artillery Maps.		
Heading	3rd Division 40th Bde RFA. Vol XI 1-30.6.15		
Diagram etc	Ypres		
War Diary		01/06/1915	30/06/1915
Heading	3rd Division 40th Bde R.F.A. Vol XII 1-31.7.15		
Diagram etc	Position Occupied on night of 7/8 July by 23rd Btty and 49th Betty R.F.A. in red Positions taken up by Bde on 14th Shewn shaded in Ink.		
War Diary		01/07/1915	31/07/1915
Heading	3rd Division 40th Bde R.F.A. Vol XIV Sep 15		
Diagram etc	Ref: Belgium Sheet 28 NW		
Diagram etc	Tracing From Map Belgium Sheet 28 1/20000		
War Diary		01/09/1915	30/09/1915
Heading	3rd Division 40th Bde R.F.A. Oct 15 Vol XV		
War Diary		15/08/1915	31/08/1915
War Diary		01/08/1915	14/08/1915
Diagram etc	Map Belgium Sheet 28 1/20000		
Diagram etc	Ypres		
Heading	3rd Division 40th Bde R.F.A. Nov to Dec. 1915 Vol XV		
War Diary		01/10/1915	31/10/1915
War Diary		24/11/1915	30/11/1915
War Diary		01/11/1915	23/11/1915
War Diary	Dickebusch	01/12/1915	24/12/1915
War Diary	Boeschepe	28/12/1915	31/12/1915
Diagram etc	28 Belgium		
Diagram etc	4th Bde R.F.A.		
Heading	3rd Div R.F.A. 6th Battery War Diary Oct-Dec 1915		
Heading	3rd Div 6th Batty R.F.A. 40th Bde. Oct To Nov. 15 Vol I		
War Diary		01/10/1915	30/11/1915
Miscellaneous	3rd Division Summary Of Intelligence. No. 40	28/11/1915	28/11/1915
Miscellaneous	3rd Division Summary Of Intelligence. No.41.	00/11/1915	00/11/1915
Heading	6 Bty. RFA. Dec Vol. II		
War Diary		01/12/1915	31/01/1916
Heading	3 Division. Troops. 40 Brigade Royal Field Artillery. 1914 Aug To 1919 Feb.		
Heading	B E F 3 Div Troops 40 Bde R F A 1917 Jan-1917 Dec		
Heading	War Diary. 40th Brigade R.F.A. 3rd. Division. January. 1917.		
War Diary	Hebuterne	01/01/1917	17/01/1917
War Diary	St Oven	18/01/1917	28/01/1917
War Diary	Sarton	29/01/1917	29/01/1917
War Diary	Aubrometz	30/01/1917	31/01/1917
Heading	War Diary. 40th. Brigade. R.F.A. 3rd. Division. February. 1917.		
War Diary	La Comte	01/02/1917	07/02/1917
War Diary	Etree Wamin	08/02/1917	20/02/1917
War Diary	Wanquentin	21/02/1917	28/02/1917
Heading	War Diary. 40th. Brigade. R.F.A. 3rd. Division. March. 1917.		

War Diary	Wanquetin	01/03/1917	07/03/1917
War Diary	Arras	08/03/1917	31/03/1917
Heading	War Diary. 40th. Brigade. R.F.A. 3rd. Division. April. 1917.		
War Diary	Arras	01/04/1917	11/04/1917
War Diary	Tilloy	12/04/1917	12/04/1917
War Diary	Wancourt	13/04/1917	30/04/1917
Heading	War Diary. 40th. Brigade. R.F.A. 3rd. Division May 1917		
War Diary	Wancourt	01/05/1917	31/05/1917
Heading	War Diary. 40th. Brigade R.F.A. 3rd. Division. June. 1917.		
War Diary		01/06/1917	30/06/1917
Heading	War Diary. 40th. Brigade R.F.A. 3rd. Division. July. 1917.		
War Diary	Bapaume	01/07/1917	31/07/1917
Heading	War Diary. 40th Brigade. R.F.A. 3rd. Division. August. 1917.		
War Diary	Beaumetz	01/08/1917	31/08/1917
Heading	War Diary. 40th. Brigade R.F.A. 3rd. Division. September 1917.		
War Diary	Beaumetz	01/09/1917	22/09/1917
War Diary	Potijze	23/09/1914	30/09/1914
Heading	War Diary. 40th. Brigade R.F.A. 3rd. Division. October. 1917.		
War Diary	Ypres	01/10/1917	31/10/1917
Heading	War Diary. 40th. Brigade. R.F.A. 3rd. Division. November 1917.		
War Diary	Vaux	01/11/1917	30/11/1917
Heading	War Diary. 40th. Brigade. R.F.A. 3rd. Division. December. 1917.		
War Diary		01/12/1917	31/12/1917
Heading	3rd Division Divl. Artillery. 40th Brigade. R.F.A. 1918 Jan-1919 Feb		
War Diary	Hendecourt Special Sheet Parts 51B S.W. S.E. 57C NW, N.E.	01/01/1918	29/01/1918
War Diary	Vaulx	01/02/1918	28/02/1918
Heading	3rd Divisional Artillery. 40th Brigade R.F.A. March 1918		
War Diary	Ficheux	01/03/1918	31/03/1918
Operation(al) Order(s)	Centre Group Order No. 127.	17/03/1918	17/03/1918
Miscellaneous	Artillery Programme.		
Miscellaneous	Reference Centre Group Order No. 127 of to-days	17/03/1918	17/03/1918
Heading	3rd Divisional Artillery War Diary 40th Brigade R.F.A. April 1918		
War Diary	Gouy En Artois	01/04/1918	01/04/1918
War Diary	Gauchin Verloingt	02/04/1918	02/04/1918
War Diary	Marles-Les Mines	03/04/1918	04/04/1918
War Diary	Barlin	05/04/1918	09/04/1918
War Diary	La Bourse	10/04/1918	12/04/1918
War Diary	Bellerive	13/04/1918	30/04/1918
Miscellaneous	6th 23rd 49th C/250 Batteries	20/04/1918	20/04/1918
War Diary		01/05/1918	31/05/1918
Operation(al) Order(s)	Left Group Order No. 162	03/05/1918	03/05/1918
Operation(al) Order(s)	Left Group Order No. 186	23/05/1918	23/05/1918
Miscellaneous	Reference Left Group Order No. 194 of 29/5/18	31/05/1918	31/05/1918

Miscellaneous	Field Artillery Co-Operation.		
War Diary		01/06/1918	30/06/1918
Operation(al) Order(s)	Left Group Order No. 209	11/06/1918	11/06/1918
Miscellaneous	Left Group Time Table For 18-pdrs. Table "A", 1st Phase.		
Miscellaneous	Left Group Time Table For 4.5" Hows. Table "C"		
Miscellaneous	Left Group Time Table For 18-pdrs. 331st Bde. R.F.A. Table "B".		
War Diary		01/07/1918	31/07/1918
War Diary	Hinges	01/08/1918	07/08/1918
War Diary	Bailleul-Lez-Pernes	07/08/1918	13/08/1918
War Diary	Rebruvriette.	14/08/1918	14/08/1918
War Diary	Hombercourt	15/08/1918	19/08/1918
War Diary	La Cauchie	20/08/1918	20/08/1918
War Diary	Douchy	21/08/1918	09/09/1918
War Diary	Vaulx	10/09/1918	11/09/1918
War Diary	Hermies	11/09/1918	09/10/1918
War Diary	Crevecoeur	10/10/1918	18/10/1918
War Diary	Quievy	19/10/1918	20/10/1918
War Diary	St Python	21/10/1918	22/10/1918
War Diary	Solesmes	23/10/1918	25/10/1918
War Diary	Ruesnes	26/10/1918	11/11/1918
War Diary	Le Cheval Blanc	12/11/1918	21/11/1918
War Diary	Marpent	22/11/1918	30/11/1918
War Diary	Purnode	01/12/1918	03/12/1918
War Diary	Spontin	04/12/1918	04/12/1918
War Diary	Scoville	05/12/1918	05/12/1918
War Diary	Grande Eineille	06/12/1918	06/12/1918
War Diary	Hotton	07/12/1918	08/12/1918
War Diary	Vaux Chavaine	09/12/1918	10/12/1918
War Diary	Regne	11/12/1918	11/12/1918
War Diary	Bovigny Germany	12/12/1918	12/12/1918
War Diary	Aldringen	13/12/1918	13/12/1918
War Diary	Nidigen	14/12/1918	14/12/1918
War Diary	Bertrath	15/12/1918	15/12/1918
War Diary	Dahlem	16/12/1918	16/12/1918
War Diary	Frohngan	17/12/1918	17/12/1918
War Diary	Kommern	18/12/1918	18/12/1918
War Diary	Embren Pissenheim	19/12/1918	19/12/1918
War Diary	Kreuzau and Drove	20/12/1918	28/02/1919

3RD DIVISION
DIVL. ARTILLERY

40TH BRIGADE R.F.A.

JAN-DEC 1916

3rd Divisional Artillery.

40TH BRIGADE R.F.A.

JANUARY 1916.

3rd Divisional Artillery.

WAR DIARY
or
INTELLIGENCE-SUMMARY.
(Erase heading not required.)

Army Form C. 2118

Map Reference BELGIUM Sheet 28 1/40000
Within 8 thumbnail SELLA

40th Brigade RFA.

Place	Date	Hour	Summary of Events and Information	Remarks and references to Appendices
BOESCHEPE	1st		JANUARY 1916.	
	to 6th		IN RESERVE NEAR BOESCHEPE	
	7th		Major E.S. ALLSUP rejoin from Hospital and Command Brigade.	
	8th 10 15th		No change	
	16th		1 Section 2 B: Battery relieves 1 section 6/7: Belgian Battery at H24 B4.2.	
	17th		1 Section 2 B: Battery relieves remaining section 6/7: Belgian Battery and comes under orders of DECHESNE'S GROUP	
	18th		No change	
	19th		1 Section 6: Battery relieves 1 section 3/7 Belgian Battery at H23 D5.4.	
	20th		1 Section 6: Battery relieves remaining section 3/7 Belgian Battery and comes under orders of DESCHESNE'S GROUP	
	21st		2/L GARSIDE joins Brigade and is posted to 23: Battery.	
	22nd to 25th		No change.	
	26th		Capt LUCAS 23: Battery posted to command 107 Battery R.F.A.	
	27th 29th		No change	

Army Form C. 2118.

WAR DIARY
or
INTELLIGENCE SUMMARY.
(Erase heading not required.)

Instructions regarding War Diaries and Intelligence Summaries are contained in F. S. Regs., Part II. and the Staff Manual respectively. Title pages will be prepared in manuscript.

Place	Date	Hour	Summary of Events and Information	Remarks and references to Appendices
BOESCHEPE.			JANUARY 1916 (continued)	
			40 Brigade RFA.	
	30.		1 Section 40' Battery returns 1 Section 1/7 Belgian Battery at H24C27 and come under orders	Movement BELGIUM Sheet 28 1/20000 Stated.
			1 Section 4/4 Belgian Battery at H30A03	of DESCHESNES GROUP.
			1 Section 6' Battery returns 1 Section 1/4 Belgian Battery at H30A3.6 and come under orders of CENTRE GROUP	
			Lt Col T.M. ARCHDALE rejoins brigade from Hospl.	
			Lt F.B. PERKINS 23" Battery wounded and to Hospl.	
	31st		1 Section 40' Battery returns 1 Section 1/7 Battery (Belgian) at H24C27.	
			40' Brigade HQ returns DESCHESNES GROUP HQ and assumes command of LEFT GROUP at BELGIAN C.Ho.se at H23B55	

W. Reigh.
Lt Col 40 Bde RFA

3rd Divisional Artillery.

40TH BRIGADE R. F. A.

FEBRUARY 1916.

WAR DIARY
or
INTELLIGENCE SUMMARY.

Army Form C. 2118.

Map reference BELGIUM Sheet 28 1/20,000 unless otherwise stated.

(Erase heading not required.)

Place	Date	Hour	Summary of Events and Information	Remarks and references to Appendices
			40 Brigade R.F.A.	
			FEBRUARY 1916.	
DICKEBUSCH.	1st		23rd Battery bring their remaining 2 guns into action on left of their other two at H.24.B.4.2	
			2nd Lieut GARSIDE wounded accidentally	
	2nd		No change	
	3rd		No change	
	4th		2nd Lt. R.E.V. BUCHAN joins Brigade and is posted to 23rd Battery.	
	5th		2nd Lt. C.M.R. SHIELL joins Brigade and is posted to 6th Battery.	
	6th		Gun position (2 guns) of 49th Battery at H.24.C.2.7 heavily shelled by enemy and 2 guns destroyed and remain withdrawn. Remaining 2 guns withdrawn and put into action at H.24.C.1.5.	
	7th		Advance parties of 17th D.A. arrive	
	8th	6 P.M.	Remainder of First Advanced Section (less detachments officers & specialists) march to DE HTEZEELE by (ST-OMER Sheet 4).	
		6 P.M.	1 Section 6th Battery at H.23.D.8.4 relieved by 1 Section A/78 Battery 17th D.A.	
			1 Section 23rd Battery at H.24.B.4.2 relieved by 1 Section C/78 Battery 17th D.A.	

WAR DIARY or INTELLIGENCE SUMMARY.

Army Form C. 2118.

Map references BELGIUM Sheet 28 1/20000 unless otherwise stated.

Place	Date	Hour	Summary of Events and Information	Remarks and references to Appendices
			FEBUARY 1916 (cont.)	
DICKEBUSCH	9th	5AM	40 Brigade R.F.A. Remainder of 40 Brigade details (less Officers detachments & specialists) march to	
	8th	6PM	1 Section 23rd Battery at H24 B4.2 relieved by one section of B/78 Battery 17th D.A. Detachments and officers of these sections move by Bus to OEHTEZEELE after relief.	
	9th	8AM	Remainder of 40th Brigade (less Officers detachments & specialists) march to OEHTEZEELE via STEENVOORDE.	
		6.30PM	1 Section 6th Battery relieved at H23 D 8.4 by one section 17/78 Battery 17th D.A.	
			do 23 do do H24 B4.2 do do C/78 do	
			do 49 do do H30 A0.3 do do D/78 do	
			do 49 do do H24 C1.5 do do B/78 do	
			40 Bde H.Q. relieved at BELGIAN CHateaU by 78 Bde H.Q. and Command of "LEFT GROUP" hands to O.C. 78 Bde R.F.A.	
			Officers specialists and detachments of above move by motor bus to OEHTEZEELE and billet.	
			(Reference Map ST OMER Sheet 4.)	

Army Form C. 2118

WAR DIARY
or
INTELLIGENCE SUMMARY.
(Erase heading not required.)

Instructions regarding War Diaries and Intelligence Summaries are contained in F. S. Regs., Part II. and the Staff Manual respectively. Title pages will be prepared in manuscript.

Place	Date	Hour	Summary of Events and Information	Remarks and references to Appendices
				Map reference ST-OMER Sheet 4
DEHTEZEELE			FEBUARY 1916 (Cont-)	
			40 Brigade R.F.A	
	10th	9am	Brigade marches (units at 10 minutes interval) to rest area via WATTEN — BAYENGHEM lez EPERLECQUES — NORDAUSQUES — TOURNEHEM — BONNINGUES — to rest billets as under	
			Bde H.Q. . . . . . AUDENFORT.	
			6 Battery . . . . . LE POIRET.	
			49 Battery . . . . . CAHEN and COURTEBOURNE	
			23 . . . . . HAMEL & CLERCQUES. Bde F.C. . . AUDREHEM.	
			Arriving at about 5 P.M.	
AUDENFORT.	11th		2nd Lt HARKER 23 Battery posted to Bde A.C.	
	12th		Lt EMPSON posted to 23 Battery from 6th Battery with temporary rank of Captain	
	13th		Lt PERKINS rejoins from Hosp	
	14		No change	
	15		No change	
	16		No change	
	17		No change	

WAR DIARY
or
INTELLIGENCE SUMMARY.
(Erase heading not required.)

Army Form C. 2118.

Place	Date	Hour	Summary of Events and Information	Remarks and references to Appendices
AUDENFORT.	18th	A.M. 1.45.	FEBUARY 1916 (Cont)	
			Map.reference ST-OMER Sheet 4. 40 Brigade R.F.A.	
			Orders received for 40 Brigade to move to reinforce V Corps.	
		9.0	March via BONNINGUES – TOURNEHEM – NORDAUSQUES – WATTEN	
			– WEMARSCAPPEL to billets near HARDIFORT arriving about 6 p.m.	
	19th	A.M. 12.20	Recon order to move to reinforce front of 17th Div'n	
		9.0	Move via CASSEL – STEENVORDE – ABEELE – to Billets as under	
			Bde HQ. 15 Rue de BOESCHEPE POPERINGHE	
			6" Battery M.6.B.3.3 (map BELGIUM Sheet 28)	
			23 Battery R.4.9.6.C Sheet 27	
			40 Battery N.1.A.8.9.C Sheet 28	
			Bde A.C. R.Q.B.2.8.C Sheet 27	
			Brigade comes under orders of 17th D.A.	
			6 guns 6" Battery going into action at H.3 & C.O.2 (Belgium Sheet 28) } and come under	
			4 guns 40 N.5.A.2.8.C } orders of Rt.Group 17 D.A.	
POPERINGHE	20th			
	21st		No Change	
	22nd		No Change	

WAR DIARY
or
INTELLIGENCE SUMMARY.
(Erase heading not required.)

Army Form C. 2118

Place	Date	Hour	Summary of Events and Information	Remarks and references to Appendices
POPERINGHE			FEBUARY 1916 (Cont) 40th Brigade R.F.A. (map Ypres & BELGIUM sheet 28)	
	22		No change	
	23		No change.	
	24		1 Section 28 Battery goes into action at I.31.B.3.5. and come under orders of Left group 17 D.A.	
			1 Section 23 Battery goes into action at H.26.B.9.2 to relieve 1 section 9D/76 Bty of Left group 17 D.A.	
	25		No change	
	26		No change	
	27		No change	
	28		No change	
	29		No change.	

Warner
Major
for O.C. 40 Brigade R.F.A.

3rd Divisional Artillery.

40TH BRIGADE R.F.A.

M A R C H 1916.

Army Form C. 2118

WAR DIARY
or
INTELLIGENCE SUMMARY.
(Erase heading not required.)

Place	Date	Hour	Summary of Events and Information	Remarks and references to Appendices
			40 Brigade RFA. (Map between BELGIUM sheet-28)	
	MARCH 1916.			
POPERINGHE.	1st	P.M. 4.30 to 5.45	Bombardment of the enemy position from ST ELOI to the YPRES– COMMINES Railway in which 4 guns 4.7, 4 guns 6" & 4 guns 2.3" take part.	
	2nd	A.M. 4.30	Assault on enemy "BLUFF" position N. of YPRES-COMMINES CANAL by 76" Infantry Bde.	
		4.32	Bombardment of enemy support line to form a Barrage.	
			Result:- All our lost trenches retaken and part of enemy salient. (THE BEAN) taken. 250 men 4 officers taken prisoners by us.	
	3		No change	
	4		No change	
	5		No change	
	6		No change	
	7		No change	
	8		No change	
			No change	
			No change	

WAR DIARY or INTELLIGENCE SUMMARY.

Place	Date	Hour	Summary of Events and Information	Remarks and references to Appendices
			MARCH 1916 (Cont)	
POPERINGHE.			40 Brigade R.F.A. (Map reference BELGIUM Sheet 28).	
	9th	1 pm.	One section 2/3: Battery relieves one section D/78 Battery at H.24.B.9.2	
	10th		One section 6: Bde & one section 49: Battery relieved by Canadian & proceed to W.L.	
			Remaining sections 6 & 49: Withdraw guns & personnel to W.L. on relief by Canadian.	
	11th	6 pm.	1 Section 6: Battery relieves one section A/78 Battery at H.23.D.9.4	
			49: B/78 H.24.C.0.7	
			49: C/78 H.24.B.3.8	
	12th	12 Noon	40 Bde HQ relieves 78 Bde HQ and takes over Command of LEFT GROUP.	
			W.Ls all occupied as under :-	
			6: Battery H.21.D.9.5 23 Battery H.26.C.6.6	
			49 Battery H.15.D.9.0 A.C. B.11.9.1.5 (Shot 27)	
			Shared by 49 & 23" H.26.C.1.9	
		6pm		
		6 pm	1 Section 6: Battery relieves one section A/78 Battery at H.23.D.9.4	
			6 B/78 H.24.C.0.7	
			49 C/78 H.24.B.3.8	
	13th		Lt. FORMAN. (23rd) proc to 108 Bty R.F.A. to act as Captain. 2/Lt HARKER (A.C) attached to 23rd Bty	
			2/Lt LEFROY (6) attached to A.C.	

WAR DIARY or INTELLIGENCE SUMMARY

Place	Date	Hour	Summary of Events and Information	Remarks and references to Appendices
			MARCH 1916 (Contd)	
	13th		40 Brigade R.F.A. (Map wherever BELGIUM Sheet 28).	
			Battery positions are re-adjusted and are occupied as under.	
			6" Battery 4 guns at I.23.D.9.4 2 guns at I.24.B.3.8	
			23 Battery 4 guns at I.24.B.9.2 2 guns at I.24.B.8.4	
			49 Battery 2 guns at I.24.C.0.2. 2 guns at I.24.C.2.4 2 guns at I.31.B.3.5.	
			There are also in the Group.	
			4 guns D/108 Battery at I.24.C.8.8 4 guns C/104 Battery at I.26.B.5.6	
			4 guns D/106 Battery at I.26.B.2.2 4 Hows 129 Battery at H.30.A.9.9	
			Group Zone. CANAL – Bay 15 – Trench 36 (just short of YPRES–COMMINES Railway)	
		7pm	2 guns D/106 Bty go out of action and are not replaced.	
	14th		No change.	
	15th	12 noon	Batteries vacate their W.Ls to make room for Belgians and	
			move to W.Ls as under. (Belgian Sheet 27)	
			6" Battery R.5.A.4.1 23 Battery R.5.A.6.2 49 B.Ty R.11.A.6.2 + R.11.A.1.7	
			B.A.C. does not move.	

Army Form C. 2118.

WAR DIARY
or
INTELLIGENCE SUMMARY.
(Erase heading not required.)

Instructions regarding War Diaries and Intelligence Summaries are contained in F. S. Regs., Part II. and the Staff Manual respectively. Title pages will be prepared in manuscript.

Place	Date	Hour	Summary of Events and Information	Remarks and references to Appendices
			March 1916 cont.	
	16th		40 Bde RFA. (Map when BELGIUM Sheet 28)	
			1st Group 7th Regt Belgian Artillery came under orders of Left Group.	
			6th Bty put in one section in action at FRENCH HOUSE I27A8.6	
			23 Bty put one section in action at I19A2.5	
	17th		2Lt LANDON and 2Lt WILLIAMS are attached to 6 & 49 respectively from DAC.	
	18th		No Change	
	19th	1 pm	Belgian cease to be under command of Left Group & come under command of Rt Group.	
	20		No change	
	21		No change	
	22		No change	
	23		No change	
	24		No change	
	25		No change	
	26		No change	
	27	4.15 pm	6 mines exploded by us under MOUND and along enemy front line west of ST ELOI immediately followed by Infantry assault	

T2134. Wt. W708—770. 500000. 4/15. Sir J. C. & S.

Army Form C. 2118.

WAR DIARY
or
INTELLIGENCE SUMMARY
(Erase heading not required.)

Instructions regarding War Diaries and Intelligence Summaries are contained in F. S. Regs., Part II. and the Staff Manual respectively. Title pages will be prepared in manuscript.

Place	Date	Hour	Summary of Events and Information	Remarks and references to Appendices
			March 1916 Cont.	
40 Pole Rd.	27 (cont)		(Map with BELGIUM sheet 28) and took up the had notice of spins in which attacked section of 4a' Bty. 6" Bty and 4 Hows of 129 Bty take part. Result: mine craters 120' in diameter 5 Offs & 19 S.O.R. Prisoners taken. 3rd Div an auth troops take Enemy first line trenches on a front of 600' and Enemy 2nd line trenches on a front of 300'. 23rd Battery section at I.19.A.2.5 carry out counter battery work and are shelled heavily. 2Lt. R.E.V. BUCHAN (23") Killed in Action. 3 O.R. (23) Killed in Action. 1 O.R. (23) Seriously wounded. Enemy put up a barrage through ST.ELOI and from time to time bombarded our position immediately on counter attack without result. Enemy turn have to time fire upon our new position but make no counter attack.	
	28"			
	29"		No Change.	

WAR DIARY
or
INTELLIGENCE SUMMARY.

(Erase heading not required.)

Place	Date	Hour	Summary of Events and Information	Remarks and references to Appendices
			March 1916 cont. 40 Bde RFA	
	30.		The Enemy bombing attacks repulsed near ST ELOI	
	31		Enemy bombing attacks succeeds in retaking a portion of the trenches won by us at ST ELOI	

1/4/16.

[signature]
Lt Col RA
Acting OC 40 Bde RFA

for OC. 40 Bde RFA.

3rd Divisional Artillery.

40TH BRIGADE R.F.A.

A P R I L. 1916.

Officer i/c
D.A.G.
3rd Echelon
G.H.Q.

Vol 204
21
3

Herewith War Diary
(duplicate copy) for April &
~~May~~ of the 40th Brigade R.F.A.

Brigadier Lieut Colonel
O.C. 40th Bde. R.F.A.

13/6/16

WAR DIARY
or
INTELLIGENCE SUMMARY.
(Erase heading not required.)

40th Bde RFA

Place	Date	Hour	Summary of Events and Information	Remarks and references to Appendices
	1st		No change.	
	2nd		No change	
	3rd	Early morn	216 F/Bde attack and take part of German front & support line inclusive. Cmdr No's 6 just E of ST ELOI.	
	4th		1 Sec/6 Bty at H25D94 where M/Sec H24B8.3 9/3 M/Sec CFA	
			— 2/3 — H24B8.3 11/3	
			— 4/9 — H24C2.4 10/3	
			— 4/4 — I31b4.5 12/3	
	5th		1 Sec/6 Bty at H25D94 relieved by 1 Sec 9/3 Bty CFA.	
			— 6 — I27A7.7 2/1	
			— 23 — H24B8.3 11/3	
			— 23 — H24B7 12/3	
			— 4/9 — H24c3.4 10/3	
			HQ 3" Bde CFA relieves HQ 40 Bde & assumes command of group.	

WAR DIARY
or
INTELLIGENCE SUMMARY.
(Erase heading not required.)

Army Form C. 2118.

Place	Date	Hour	Summary of Events and Information	Remarks and references to Appendices
			April 1916 Cont	
			L.O. Bott RFA	
	6th	Early morning	German attack at ST ELOI Succeeded in taking almost all ground won by us. L.O. Bde ordered into action as in order to fire on St Eloi front and accordingly into action in Priory Camp & trenches.	
			B was 4 RA lynch (Lt Col Denaford RA)	
			HQ Lo Bde at H.28.c 7½.8½	
			4 Gun 6 Battery at H.28.a 7½	
			2 Gun 29 Battery at H.29.c 5.7	
			L Trench Battery at H.33.c 1½	
	7th		Batteries do Barrage work all night	
			Batteries on Barrage work all day & night.	
			6 Bty 1st day 1 Gun fr. R 109 Battery 1 shrapnel 1 fuse at 10 m	
			23 " 2 " " 108 " " 2 fuse damaged	
			44 " 2 " " 29 " " 2 " at 10 m	
	8th		Batteries work all day & night.	
			23 BG had over 1 gun by 104th Shrapnel 2 gun damaged	

WAR DIARY
INTELLIGENCE SUMMARY

Place	Date	Hour	Summary of Events and Information	Remarks and references to Appendices
	APRIL 1916 (cont)		40 Bde RFA	
	9th		One Battalion B¹ Bty relieved by one subsection 27 R¹S CFA } and march down to rest area	
			2 B	
			4 G	
	10th		Remaining Section 23 Bty relieved by one subsection 26 R¹S CFA & 23 Bty march down to rest area to ECKE area	
			One Subsection B¹ Bty relieved by one subsect 27 R¹S CFA & march down to rest area	
			49	25
	11		One subsection B¹ Bty relieved by one subsect 27 R¹S CFA & march down to rest area	
			49	25
	12		One subsect 6 Bty relieved by one subsect 27 R¹S CFA	
			49	25
			Remainder of 40 Bde marches down to ECKE area	
			HQ 40 Bde relieved by 7¹ Bde CFA	
	13th		Will Billets - HQ W ECKE, B¹ Cavalier D.A. b¹(Sht27)Q1ad 5.7; 23(Sht27)Q13b61	
			49(Sht27) Q 31b2.7; B 6 (Sht27) P30d56.	

WAR DIARY
or
INTELLIGENCE SUMMARY.
(Erase heading not required.)

Army Form C. 2118.

Place	Date	Hour	Summary of Events and Information	Remarks and references to Appendices
			April 1916 (cont)	
	14		Lt LOVE (DAC) to attend a L of R.F.A	4 of R. R.F.A
	15		No change	
	16		—	
	17		—	
	18		2Lt Lauder (6") proceeded on a T.M. Course	
	19.		No Change.	
	20		—	
	21		—	
	22		—	
	23		Major H.A.L ROSE 6 Battery posted to q'Dn" on Bde Major R.A.	
	24		Capt V.C. DAVIES (47") to Command 6 Battery	
	25		No change	
	26		No change	
	27		No change	
	28		Lt Lacey 6 Bty to Hosp.	

WAR DIARY
or
INTELLIGENCE SUMMARY.

Army Form C. 2118.

Place	Date	Hour	Summary of Events and Information	Remarks and references to Appendices
			APRIL 1916 (cont)	
	29th		No change	40th Bde RFA BELGIUM sheet 28 NW.
	30		1 Sec 1st ER Battery 50th Div (N16c4.4) + 1 sec; 9] 2 -- ER Battery (N15b3.2) relieved by 1 sec 23rd + 6th batteries respectively; Gas attack on E.1 + E.2 trenches unsuccessful	

Ch J Booth Lt RFA
B/14/46th Bde

30/4/16

3rd Divisional Artillery.

40TH BRIGADE R. F. A.

MAY 1916.

Army Form C. 2118.

WAR DIARY
or
INTELLIGENCE SUMMARY.
(Erase heading not required.)

40th Bde RFA   BELGIUM Sheet 28 NW

Place	Date	Hour	Summary of Events and Information	Remarks and references to Appendices
MAY	MAY 1916			
	1st		Remaining Section of 6th Battery relieved by 2 Secs of 6th Battery and remaining Section of N.R. Battery (N 3 & 4 & 4.5") relieved by 4 guns of 23rd M.A.B Battery	
			49th Battery " " "	
			130th Battery " " "	
			Right Group — no (initial)	
			No change	
	2nd		" " " "	
	3rd 4th 5th 6th		were Couloire Group to Y & T.M. Battery and Y 3 T.M. Battery come under	
	7th		Col Carlisle proceeded to rejoin 1st Bde RHA 2nd Div.	
			Major Robinson 130th Bty taking temporary command.	
			2/Lieut) J.O. Mannay warned to England.	

WAR DIARY or INTELLIGENCE SUMMARY

Army Form C. 2118

Place	Date	Hour	Summary of Events and Information	Remarks and references to Appendices
	MAY (cont) 1916		40th Bde BFA.	
	9th		No change.	
	10th		40th Bde Column details on south. Becomes No 2 sec D.A.C.	
	11th		No change.	
	12th		2nd Lt. J. Ireton - sick - to hospital.	
	13th		Lt. Col. G.T. Main DSO assumes command of R⁺ GROUP. J/Lt A.L.Hammant to 107th	(Temp Capt.)
	14th	11am	30th Hour Bde split up. 130th Battery comes up in 40th Bde.	
	15th		No change	
	16th		"	
	17th		"	
	18th		"	
	19th			
	20th		2nd Lt. F.A. Buchan (49th) att. 63 Bty. 2nd Lt S.P.Williams (23rd) att. 49 Bty.	
	21st		2nd Lt. Corbutt att. 63 Bty from D.A.C. 2nd Lt. Davidson att. 23rd Bty from D.A.C.	
	22nd		No change.	
	23rd			

WAR DIARY
or
INTELLIGENCE SUMMARY.
(Erase heading not required.)

Army Form C. 2118

Instructions regarding War Diaries and Intelligence Summaries are contained in F. S. Regs., Part II. and the Staff Manual respectively. Title pages will be prepared in manuscript.

Place	Date	Hour	Summary of Events and Information	Remarks and references to Appendices
			MAY 1916 (cont)	
			40th Bde RFA	
	24th		No change.	
	25th		"	
	26th			
	27th		1 Gun handed over to 130th Battery, 4 D/251 35th Goes to Artillery School TILQUES	
	28th		2nd Lt Taylor att: A/135. 2nd Lt from DAC. 2nd Lt Whittaker att: C/35 from DAC	
	29th		1 Sec of 251st Bde (Northumbrian) relieves 1 sec RF Group at N15D2.2. N34a9.7. and N26c8.7. Relieved sections proceed to EECKE. Guns exchanged.	
	30 to 31st		Remaining sections relieved & Bdes are proceed to concentrate Brigade in rest.	

W. Smith Bgn
Lt Col RFA

3rd Divisional Artillery.

40TH BRIGADE R.F.A.

J U N E 1 9 1 6.

3rd Divisional Artillery.

"A" Form.
MESSAGES AND SIGNALS.
Army Form C. 2121.

| TO | 3⟨ D A |

Sender's Number	Day of Month	In reply to Number	
DO 21	13	—	AAA

Herewith War Diary of
40th Brigade for month of June
1916. It is regretted that owing
to an oversight it has not
been forwarded before.

Sd ??? ??? Lt Col
OC. 40th Bde R.F.A.

3 Dw Q   Forwarded.

From
Place 7
Time 13 T 6.

G.T. H. E????? Capt
for CRA 3rd Dw

40 Bde RFA
Vol 22

WAR DIARY
or
INTELLIGENCE SUMMARY.
(Erase heading not required.)

Army Form C. 2118

Place	Date	Hour	Summary of Events and Information	Remarks and references to Appendices
	JUNE 1916		40th Bde R.F.A. BELGIUM Sheet 28 N.W.	
June	1st		Brigade in rest at EECKE.	
	2d		No change	
	3d		Brigade moves into action to cover G.H.Q lines in YPRES salient. Positions finally taken up as follows:—	
			23 By H24c29 – 49th By H22c25 – 130th By H22central	
			Bde HQ H28 a 6.9. (130 By shelled out twice) 1st Battery once in	
			Bde HQ twice)	
	4th		No change	
	5th		107th By moved into action at H12b57 after having been shelled out near YPRES Convent. 4 other ranks wounded	
			in 107 Battery.	
	6th		Sh/L covers Q HQ lines from I.14c7.8 – I.19c54	
			6th Battery had 1 man killed & 1 wounded	
	7th		No change	
	8th		No change	

WAR DIARY
or
INTELLIGENCE SUMMARY.
(Erase heading not required.)

Army Form C. 2118

Place	Date	Hour	Summary of Events and Information	Remarks and references to Appendices
			JUNE 1916 (cont) 40th Bde RFA BELGIUM Sheet 28 N.W. & 5A HAZEBROUCK.	
	8th 9th		130th Battery comes under KOEBEL's Group and moves into position in YPRES (I.7.a.4.4.). Capt H.S. Browne joins 130 Bty	
	10th 11th		No change. No change	
	12th		Bombardment of German trenches in vicinity of ARMAGH WOOD and SANCTUARY WOOD. A certain amount of ground retaken, but situation not clear	
	13th		A fairly quiet day. Bombardment in of HOOGE trench begun about midnight.	
	14th 15th 16th		Our Artillery active all day. Quiet day. 6th Battery relieved by E Battery RHA . 49th Battery relieved by I Battery RHA. Notify they over from 23rd to 107th Bttrn. 130 Battery relieved by D/47 of 8th Division. III Battery moved to rest were marching all night	
	17th		40th Bde at EBBLINGHEM. 107 Battery again back 1/23 Bde	

WAR DIARY
or
INTELLIGENCE SUMMARY.

Army Form C. 2118

Place	Date	Hour	Summary of Events and Information	Remarks and references to Appendices
	June 1st		40th Bde. ST OMER	
			JUNE 1916 cont	
			Bde. leaves EBBLINGHEM at 8.0 a.m. Bde HQ goes to BAYENGHEM-lez-SENINGHEM. 49th KATFRINGUES, 6th KLART, 23rd & 13th to BAYENGHEM-lez-SENINGHEM.	
	19th		No change	
	20th		"	
	21st		"	
	22nd		Bde HQ moves to HALLINES the newer training area. 6th to ESQUERDES, 23rd & 13th to WIZERNES, 49th to HALLINES. Training. No change.	
	23rd		"	
	24th		"	
	25th		"	
	26th		"	
	27th		"	
	28th		"	
	29th		"	
	30th		"	

3rd Divisional Artillery.

40TH BRIGADE R.F.A.

J U L Y 1 9 1 6.

"A" Form.   Army Form C. 2121.
MESSAGES AND SIGNALS.   No. of Message............

Prefix......... Code.........m.	Words	Charge	This message is on a/c of :	Recd. at............m.
Office of Origin and Service Instructions.				Date............
....	Sent		............Service.	From............
....	At............m.			By............
....	To............		(Signature of "Franking Officer.")	
....	By............			

TO { **Staff Captain 3rd D.A.**

| * Sender's Number | Day of Month | In reply to Number | AAA |

Herewith War Diary of 40th
Brigade R.F.A. for the month
of July 1916 —

                [signature]
                O.C. 40th Bde R.F.A.

From
Place
Time

WAR DIARY
or
INTELLIGENCE SUMMARY

40 Bde R ArmyForm C. 2118
Vol 23

Place	Date	Hour	Summary of Events and Information	Remarks and references to Appendices
	July 1916		40th Bde RFA	
5A HAZEBROUCK	1st	5am	Orders from 4th Army Corps. Lt MUNT + 1 NCO leave on advance billeting party	1 appendix
	2nd	11am	6th Battery leaves by train from WIZERNES. Capt EMPSON detailed to act RTO	
		2pm	" " " "	
		5pm	" " " "	
		8pm	Bde HQ + 13S " " " "	
	3rd		Brigade detrains at CANDAS and marches under battery arrangements to HEUZECOURT.	
		11am	Brigade marches from S to NAOURS area. Brigade halts at Rd - HEUZECOURT - BERNAVILLE - CANAPLES - HALLOY - CANAPLES. No room in NAOURS. Billets for the night found at HALLOY. (Group system of billeting - no 2 Sec DAC joins 40 Bde (billets) and marching orders)	
	4th	9pm	Brigade leaves HALLOY marching under CRA's orders and proceeds to DAOURS. Route:- HALLOY - VIGNACOURT - ST VAST - AMIENS - RIVERY - DAOURS. Group system allotted - no 2 Sec DAC rejoins DAC at VIGNACOURT.	

WAR DIARY
or
INTELLIGENCE SUMMARY.
(Erase heading not required.)

Army Form C. 2118

Place	Date	Hour	Summary of Events and Information	Remarks and references to Appendices
	5th	4:30am	Brigade moved at DAOURS	
	6th	9am	Brigade battery commenced with 2 Echelons per battery going up to gun & reconnoitre positions (when) MONTAUBAN.	
		10am	Whole of 3rd DA moves to VAUX-SUR-SOMME and bivouacs in fields by the river.	
		1pm	3rd DA moves up to W.ld of BRAY area (BOIS DES TAILLES)	
		1pm	See new battery grounds after reporting: —	
			6th Battery Shed MONTAUBAN A3a 7.3	
			23" " A3a 5.5	
			49" " A3a 3.6	
			130" " A3c 5.6	
			BkHQ Shot 62c N.W. A 13b 7.2	
			Remaining batteries were into action. Bn HQ moves to F18c 4.9. Registration of enemy's wire in BAZENTIN-LONGUEVAL front begins.	
	7th	9am		

WAR DIARY
or
INTELLIGENCE SUMMARY.
(Erase heading not required.)

Army Form C. 2118

Place	Date	Hour	Summary of Events and Information	Remarks and references to Appendices
			40th Bde RFA MONTAUBAN (indiv. chuts)	
	July 1916 (cont)			
	8th		Brigade fired not less than 200 rounds a day at enemy wire on front S17c8,6 to S16c central (49°, 25°, 6") & around W.L. shelters near BRAY. Firing continues as yesterday.	
	9th		Firing continues at same rate & on same objective. Capt V.C. Davies and 2nd Lt L.M. Buchan wounded. (Capt Davies subsequently died of wounds). Dumps at guns worked up to 700 a gun for 18 pdr. and 400 for 4.5 Howr.	
	10th		Firing as yesterday. Capt H.C. Smith 6th Battery slightly wounded.	
	11th		Firing as yesterday. Capt Empson 23rd Battery temply commands 6th Bdy	
	12th		" " "	
	13th		2nd Lt Spoor joins 6th Bdy from D.A.C.	
	14th		3rd Division attacks line BAZENTIN-LE-GRAND to S. 16 central	
			9th Division attacks " situated to E of DELVILLE WOOD.	
		3.15am	Bombardment to the North commences.	
		3.20am	Our Bombardment commences. 40th Bde under orders of 9th D.A.	
			Tange S17c 8.6 to S16 c 0.3 main calling at B.P. 2". 130 Bdy Supported via B.P 5"	

WAR DIARY or INTELLIGENCE SUMMARY

Army Form C. 2118

Place: 40th Bde RFA

MONTAUBAN (Sheet)

Date	Hour	Summary of Events and Information	Remarks
JULY 1916 (cont)			
14(?)	3.25	Infantry assault line LONGUEVAL – BAZENTIN. 40th Bde lift onto support line.	
	3.30am	40th Bde lengthens range by 300 yds. Infantry sweep 2nd line trench.	
	4.10am	40th Bde lifts to objective S11c9.1 to S10d0.1	
	4.55am	40th Bde cones [covers?] advance of 3rd Div. Lengthen range by 100 yds.	
	5.5am	Bde fires on objective S10d5.4 to S9d6.4	
		Report the objective had been gained	
	5.35	Cavalry assemble in TALUS BOISÉE valley.	
	6.23am	Batteries cease firing and stand by.	
	8.35	HIGH WOOD BARRAGE S4D.1.4 to S4c.2.4	
	10.50	Enemy counter attack N of LONGUEVAL. Barrage fire from S11 central to S10 central.	
	12.10	Cease fire. Fire to prevent enemy being [?] halt.	
	1.15pm	Cavalry report enemy leaving main point S3a5. Opened fire	

WAR DIARY
or
INTELLIGENCE SUMMARY.
(Erase heading not required.)

Army Form C. 2118.

Place	Date	Hour	Summary of Events and Information	Remarks and references to Appendices
			JULY 14th (cont)	
			40th Bde RFA MONTAUBAN	
	(14th)	2.10p	Cease fire.	
		4.30p	HIGH WOOD shelled intermittently	
		6pm	BARRAGE fires from S5a03 to S5c3.2	
		6.30p	Cavalry and Field Artillery move forward W of CARNOY - MONTAUBAN road	
		10pm	Bn moved to covering right half of 8th & 9th Bde shell hole from S.14 c.4½ 9½ to S.16 b.0.7	
		11.15p	Cavalry reported being enfiladed from right. BARRAGE found around S.4.d central	
	15th	10.15a	Attack on BAZENTIN - WOOD	
		12.15p	DELVILLE WOOD and WATERLOT FARM reported captured by us.	
		1.30p	Enemy reported to be advancing from FLERS. BARRAGE formed from S.6 central to S.6 b 9.1	
		2.40p	Enemy reported counter-attacking HIGH DELVILLE WOOD	
		3.50p	DELVILLE BARRAGE formed (T.7 c.9.1 to T.7 c.1.9)	

WAR DIARY
or
INTELLIGENCE SUMMARY.
(Erase heading not required.)

Place	Date	Hour	Summary of Events and Information	Remarks and references to Appendices
			40th Bde RFA MONTAUBAN SHEET	
			JULY 1916 (cont)	
	15th	5.20p	HIGH WOOD reports retaken by us	
		5.35p	Whole of DELVILLE WOOD reported captured.	
		6.50p	"Cease fire"	
	16th	2.45am	3rd DA instructs barrage E of HIGH WOOD to be fired from 3.30 to 5.30 am.	
		9am	HIGH WOOD reports evacuated.	
		1.0pm	Enemy reported digging trench from S43.37 SE to S.44.08 and from there NE towards S.Sa.3.2. Batteries engaged.	
		2.30p	Positions in S.22.c & d reconnoitred by General Bde commander & BCs. Positions selected but not occupied.	
	17	10.15p	Bde area heavily shelled until 11pm. gas shell. Gas helmets worn.	
		10.40p	SOS LONGUEVAL received from 3rd DA.	
		midnight	"Cease fire"	
	18th	4am	S.O.S. received.	
		5am	"Cease fire"	

WAR DIARY
or
INTELLIGENCE SUMMARY
(Erase heading not required.)

Army Form C. 2118

Place	Date	Hour	Summary of Events and Information	Remarks and references to Appendices
MONTAUBAN column sheet			JULY 1916 (cont) 40th Bde RFA	
	18(cont)	10.45a	Northern portion of LONGUEVAL reported taken during the night	
		1.0p	SOS BARRAGE.	
		1.30p	Our infantry worried by machine gun fire. Bde searches and sweeps in S.11 a + b.	
		3 pm	Enemy strong points reported at S.11.d.17½ and S.11.d.3.8.	
		2.15p	Gas shell barrage S.of MONTAUBAN.	
		4.30p	Enemy reported to have attempted to advance about S.5.c+d but were retiring.	
		5.40p	Enemy reported advancing from S.5.k.5.9. Battenen switches up to B.t 10".	
	19.	8.15a	I DA reports enemy attacking DELVILLE WOOD. All batteries turn onto SOS BARRAGE.	
		12.45p	3rd DA opens intense barrage (DFSG) from S.11.S.8.3 to S.11 central.	
		9pm	"Leave fire" — intermittent harassing resumed.	
	20.	1.30a	S.O.S. from 3rdDA	

WAR DIARY or INTELLIGENCE SUMMARY

Army Form C. 2118.

Place	Date	Hour	Summary of Events and Information	Remarks and references to Appendices
MONTAUBAN Enclosed SHEET			40th Bde RFA	
	July 1916 (cont)			
	20th (cont)	2 am	"Cease fire"	
		11.40 am	3rd D.A. orders barrage S.11.d.9.9 to S.11 central. (BF 10")	
		12.15 pm	3rd D.A. report no infantry holding line S.11.D.0.8 westwards.	
		5.20 pm	2nd Lt WILKIE (49th) and Lt LONDON (6) wounded while patrolling SP00	
		5.40 pm	5th D.A. came into action in hostile battery positions	
		7.20 pm	"Cease fire" on barrage S.11.d.9.9 to S.11 central	
		9 pm	23rd & 49th Batteries move to trenches in A.4.a	
	21st	2.40 pm	Intense barrage ordered by 3rd D.A. on 6th Bde. (S.11.c.4.5 to S.12.b.0.5)	
		3.0 pm	6th Bde cease fire. 21st LODGE (E.49) and LANHAM (T.4") join from DAC	
		10.15 pm	SOS LONGUEVAL from 3rd Dn Batteries open fire (BF 5")	
		11.0 pm	Batteries cease fire	
	22nd	2 am	Heavy firing to the East	
		9.50 pm	13th Bde 5th Division attacks HIGH WOOD and SWITCH TRENCH	
		10.15 pm	SOS LONGUEVAL from 3rd DA	

WAR DIARY
or
INTELLIGENCE SUMMARY.
(Erase heading not required.)

Army Form C. 2118.

Place	Date	Hour	Summary of Events and Information	Remarks and references to Appendices
			JULY 1916 (cont) 40th Bde R.F.A	MONTAUBAN enlarged SHEET
	22nd(cont)	10.30p	3" D.A close BF 30" on T.7.c.9.2. & T.13.a.4.0.	
	23rd	12.20am	Heavy bombardment on our left	
		3.40am	Bombardment of DELVILLE WOOD & GUILLEMONT commenced. Attack on DELVILLE WOOD by us.	
	24th	2.25p	Bombardment of DELVILLE WOOD.	
		9.30p	S.O.S. LONGUEVAL received.	
		11.0pm	Batteries shelled the trenches on line on Bernay S.12.d.9.2 & S.12.c.0.2	
	25th		Heavy shelling during the afternoon in valley behind MONTAUBAN	
	26th	2.15am	S.O.S. LONGUEVAL	
		2.40am	Cease fire	
		3 am	Bombardment of DELVILLE WOOD.	
	27th	6.10am	Attack by 2nd & 5th Divisions on LONGUEVAL & DELVILLE WOOD. 3" D.A. shot the creeping barrage. Dvs reported reaching first objective relying through S.11 A + B. Enemy reported counter-attacking. Batteries reported independent rate.	
		12.30p		
		1.0p		

WAR DIARY
or
INTELLIGENCE SUMMARY.
(Erase heading not required.)

Army Form C. 2118.

Place	Date	Hour	Summary of Events and Information	Remarks and references to Appendices
MONTAUBAN	JULY 1916 (cont)		40th Bde RFA	
	27th	1.20pm	SOS LONGUEVAL. All batteries opened fire	
	28th	10.35pm	"	
	29th		28th & 49th Divisions took over line in front of GUILLEMONT. 6 Btys of old Divn. being sent to 28th & 49th Divns. Fire drawn from 5.30 a.central GUILLEMONT.	
	30th	4.30pm	Bombardment for attack on GUILLEMONT. Heavy wet Balloon from barrage on GINCHY. Our infantry reach GUILLEMONT but have to retire. Attack is not successful at any point.	
		10pm	Enemy reports attacking WATERLOT FARM. Barrage fired.	
	31st	11am	6" Bty relieved detachments of I.5 Bty. who to proceed to W.L.	
		10.30pm	Heavy fire in direction of GUILLEMONT. Batteries opened on SOS BARRAGE.	

Wm Cockell Major RFA
RA 40th Bde
31/7/16

3rd Divisional Artillery

40th BRIGADE.

ROYAL FIELD ARTILLERY

AUGUST 1 9 1 6

D.O. 47

Staff Captain
3rd D.A.

Herewith War Diary for the month of August 1916.

31/8/16

[signature]
O.C. 40th B.H.R.A.

Army Form C. 2118.

WAR DIARY
or
INTELLIGENCE SUMMARY.
(Erase heading not required.)

Place	Date	Hour	Summary of Events and Information	Remarks and references to Appendices
40th Bde RFA	AUGUST 1916		SHEETS LONGUEVAL and MARICOURT	
	1st	2 am	Relief commenced by 35th D.A. One section of 130 Battery relieved by 1 section of D/1/163 Battery. Billets patrols proved trenches.	
	2nd	8 am	Remaining section of 130 Battery relieved by battery section of D/1/163 Battery fell in at 6th & 4th Sjt the order (no guns of action). Batteries & wagons under battery management, to VILLE-SUR-ANCRE. Route Cross-roads. T.25.g.4 – MERICOURT – thence S of river ANCRE.	
		11 am	Brigade in next dense to find there.	
	3rd		No change.	
	4th		"	
	5th		"	
	6th		"	
	7th		"	
	8th		"	
	9th		"	
	10th		"	
	11th		"	

WAR DIARY or INTELLIGENCE SUMMARY

Army Form C. 2118

Place	Date	Hour	Summary of Events and Information	Remarks and references to Appendices
40th Bde R.F.A.			AUGUST 1916 (cont)	SHEETS LONGUEVAL & MARICOURT
	12th		No change	
	13th		No change	
	14th	8am	Bde & Btty commanders go up to reconnoitre Batty positions near MARICOURT.	
		3.40p	Wagon lines move up to BRAY area via MEAULTE. Bde HQ remains at VILLE-SUR-ANCRE	
	15th	4am	Relief of 27th Bde SS=DA commences.	
			A/276 personnel returned by 23rd Battery to 40 Bde at A15.5.1	A15.8.4
			B/276 " " " " 6 "	A15.6.1.3
			C/276 " " " " A)	
			D/276 " " " " 130	A15.0.3.8
			Conversion on and use taken over by personnel of 40 Bde. 2 additional sub blg constructed at each position putting in 40 Bde gun, to make up to guns at each position. 27th Bde leaves over to 23rd Bde.	

WAR DIARY or INTELLIGENCE SUMMARY

Army Form C. 2118.

Place	Date	Hour	Summary of Events and Information	Remarks and references to Appendices
40th Bde R.F.A.			LONGUEVAL and MARICOURT SHEETS	
	AUGUST 1916 (cont)			
		5 pm	55th DA prepare a position at A15c 4.6 for B/176 Battery which comes under 40th Bde. 40th Bde HQ taken over from 27th Bde (Col TOPPING) at A14.4.3. Batteries barrage line B10.a.2.0 to B10.a.5.7 to T25.c.5.0. 1000 rounds per gun. 18 pr. 200 rounds per gun, 4.5 How. 130 Battery fires on T25.c.9.5 to B10.8.8.	
	16th		3rd Division in conjunction with 24th Division on the left and the 153rd Fnd Division on the right attack the German line between B10.2.0 and B30b 7.2. 40th Bde cover 76th Inf Bde and new front — 6th + 23rd Batteries provide FOO (to 2nd Suffolks, 4/9" + B/176 Batteries provide FOO to 1st King's Own Royal Lancasters	
		5:10 p	Barrage went commenced	
		5:40 p	Zero hour	
		5:55 p	French aeroplane drops light signal, indicating that the French	

Army Form C. 2118.

WAR DIARY
or
INTELLIGENCE SUMMARY.
(Erase heading not required.)

Place	Date	Hour	Summary of Events and Information	Remarks and references to Appendices
			SHEETS	
			90.B.&R.F.A. LONGUEVAL and MARICOURT	
	AUGUST 1916 (cont)		have taken the MALTZ HORN RAVINE	
	18(a)	6.20p	Infantry call for intense rate of fire on final objective	
		6.35p	Rate of fire reduced to B.F. Speed.	
		7.0p	"	
		7.15p	B.F. 10 sec.	
			Trench report that our infantry have gained their next objective	
			-B1a 3.0 G.t 5.30 G.7.2. F.O.O reports intermediate objective taken	
		7.30p	LIAISON officer reports. 1 Coy of Suffolks in touch to B1a 9.2 but King's Own hung up on left. In touch on same in close touch	
		8.35p	F.O.O with King's Own reports they have infantry temporarily held up they have now gained their objective.	
		9.15p	LIAISON Officer reports that French have captured the RAVINE and also to the ANGLE WOOD. Right battalion report having advanced 200 yds but left held up.	
		9.35p	R.A report situation at 8.15pm was as follows - we hold line T 25 c 4.6 G.T 25 c 6.7 G.T 25 c 2.1 to B1c 4.6 to B1c 4.3 to B1a 9.0 to B1a 3.6 to B1b 6.8 to B8a 6.8.	

WAR DIARY
INTELLIGENCE SUMMARY

LONGUEVAL SHEETS
LONGUEVAL and MARICOURT

Date	Hour	Summary of Events and Information	Remarks
		AUGUST 1916 (cont) 40th Bde RFA	
17th		Batteries firing a barrage T25D 4.1 to B1 s.t 9½ during night to time they are ready to register LONELY TRENCH 25° 445° where	
	10pm	infantry attack LONELY TRENCH.	
18th	12-2am	LIAISON OFFICER reports situation not clear but right coy approx have gained objective and left coy have been held up by machine gun fire	
	1.14am	Situation still obscure — West Yorks on right have gained objective but Welsh Fusiliers have been held up by machine gun fire. 1.5 yds from LONELY TRENCH	
	7.35am	LIAISON officer reports both attacks failed and that we have on original front line	
	9.17am	trench attack for 5 minutes	
	9.30am	Batteries remain on barrage B10 4.3 to B16.6.10 until commencement of operations	
	2.44pm	Bombardment begins on T25c 5.1 to B16 2.2	

Army Form C. 2118.

WAR DIARY
or
INTELLIGENCE SUMMARY.
(Erase heading not required.)

Place	Date	Hour	Summary of Events and Information	Remarks and references to Appendices
40th Bde RFA			MARICOURT and LONGUEVAL SHEETS	
	August 1916			
	18th (cont)	2.45p	The 3rd Division in conjunction with the 24th Division on its left and the French 153rd Division on its right attacks the enemy's trench system between GUILLEMONT and ANGLE WOOD, exclusive.	
		3.40p	LIAISON Officer reports 1st Guards have gained 1st Objective (B1c28 to T25c6.3) fairly easily. 4 known prisoners taken.	
		4.5p	Guards and French reported taking 1st Objective.	
		4.45p	Artillery preparation for 2nd Phase commenced. (B1t.1.1 to B1b9.8)	
		8.0p	LIAISON Officer reports that infantry did not start on 2nd objective owing to situation not being clear.	
		11.30p	Report that strong counter-attack on French forced latter to retire taking our right with them.	
		11.40p	Group barrage changes to T25c6.0 to B1a3.1 with flanks on B1c8½.8½	
		midnight	Phases 3 & 4 of attack cancelled.	
	19th	5.15am	R.A reports line held from B1c2.8 to distance of 400 yrs up the road (B1a4.4). Barrage lifted accordingly to B1a9.0 (=T25½.0.0	

WAR DIARY or INTELLIGENCE SUMMARY

Army Form C. 2118.

Place	Date	Hour	Summary of Events and Information	Remarks and references to Appendices
40th B de RFA			AUGUST 1916 (cont)	LONGUEVAL — MARICOURT SHEETS
	19th	10AM	76th Inf Bde report that they are in possession of 1st objective and consolidating — French in touch with own right. Barrage changes to B10 9.2.0 to T25 3.0.0	
		11.50AM	Barrage changes to B10 7.8 & T25 5.23.0. Enemy to south of infantry retiring slowly.	
		4.10PM	LIAISON Officer reports line as follows:— S30 d 8.9 — T25c 2.3 — S30 d 8.2 — A6 b 8.8 — A6 b 6.2 — A6 b 9.1 — A6 b 9.4	
		7.20PM	Infantry report that they have captured parts of LONELY TRENCH (B10.4.6 to B10 2.8)	
		8.50PM	Infantry occupy the whole of LONELY TRENCH.	
		9.0PM	Batteries barrage as follows:— T25 c 9.0 to B11 3.0 at BP / 130th Battery barrage, for hour at German trench FALFEMONT FARM & WEDGE WOOD. 104th Bde 35th Div relieve 76th Bde 3rd Div.	
		9.45PM	Infantry report LONELY TRENCH firmly established.	
	20th	6.25AM	Our line reported to run as follows:— S30 D 9.8 — T25 c 2.3	

WAR DIARY
or
INTELLIGENCE SUMMARY

Army Form C. 2118.

40th Bde RFA

SHEETS LONGUEVAL and MARICOURT

Date	Hour	Summary of Events and Information	Remarks
AUGUST 1916 (cont)			
20(cont)	9.30am	RA report on line & line as follows :- B19c28 - B19a7.1 - S end of LONELY TRENCH - LONELY TRENCH - joining original frontline at T25c1.5 - S30D8.1 - S30D5.6 - S30b51 - S30b4.6 - also map T25c 1.5 & T25c 0.7	
	11.57am	Infantry report that in future shall be put W of line T25c central & B1 central so they have patrols along road through T25c and B1a.	
	12 noon	Batteries barrage as follows :- B16 g1.0 up road and thence N.westwards to German trench running from WEDGEWOOD B11 82.6.	
	6.15pm	Situation unchanged. Infantry lately using same line interpretate from B1a 5.5 & T25c 6.4	
	1pm	6" & 8"/16 guns rate of fire 1.30 Battery guns fire on FALFEMONT FARM and WEDGEWOOD.	
	8.30pm 9.0pm	49" and 23" Batteries have positions in HAPPY VALLEY at about S22 B8.7 and come under 24th DA for more cutting	

WAR DIARY or INTELLIGENCE SUMMARY

Army Form C. 2118

Place	Date	Hour	Summary of Events and Information	Remarks and references to Appendices
			46th Bde RFA	SHEETS LONGUEVAL — MARICOURT
	AUGUST 1916 (cont)			
	20 (cont)	9 pm	front of GUILLEMONT Infantry attempt to occupy strong point at S30 b 7.2 but fail.	
		10.10 pm	R.A. report as follows:— One Sports appears to run as follows:— French from ANGLE WOOD to B13.2.8 thence British N.W. to B13.a.8.4. Thence N. to T25.c.4.5. Which if found empty will be occupied.	
	21st	8.30 am	Infantry report no enemy within 200 yds SP near trench in front of LONELY TRENCH.	
		9.45 am	Received from R.A.:— French hold ANGLE WOOD and S.P. at B13.2.8. Their line runs through B.1 central B1 a 4.6 and 150 yds E of LONELY TRENCH — Have lack to this line at T25.c.0.8.	
		4.30 pm	24th Division attack Northern portion of GUILLEMONT. 35th Div. attack S.P. at S30 b 7.2.	
			130th Battery cooperated by firing on trench from T25 b 3.7 to 3.2 at 20 rounds an hour. (Spasmodic retaliation to B.F. 20 rds...)	

40th Bde RFA   (For A.F. "C" 2118).

W A R . . . . D I A R Y.   SHEETS

AUGUST 1916 (cont)   LONGUEVAL & HARICOURT

Date.	Hour.	Summary of events and information.
21st	7.5pm	All Batteries reduce rate of fire to B.P. 1 min.
	8.25pm	Infantry patrols out. No fire W of line GUILLEMONT — FALFEMONT FARM between 9pm and midnight
	9.5pm	Barrage as follows:- B2a1.8 to T26c0.4
	midnight	" " " :- B1b4.8 to T25d3.3. 130th Bty WEDGE WOOD to T26a0.5.
22nd	3pm	Forward positions as under reconnoitred.— 6th Battery A11b 8.1½ 25th Battery A12a0.0 49th Bty A5b4.4½ B/?/Bty A5b3½.2½
	10pm	104th Bde 35th Div: take over ANGLE WOOD from the French. Barrage for night as follows:- B16b8.5 to T25d5.5 12 salvoes an hour resting one battery. 130th Bty fires 4 salvoes an hour on trench running S.W. from WEDGE WOOD.
23rd	10.45am	R.A. orders 130th Bty to register T25d0.0 to T25c9.3
	3.30pm	FOO reports that DLI are going to attempt to establish an S.P. at T25c 6.4 after dark — also that they occupy BANTAM TRENCH (B1a5.5 to B1b3.2)
24th	9am	Work on new positions started. 6" + B/?/? working parties shelled causing casualties to the extent of 2 killed and 8 wounded.
	3.10pm	Programme re bombardment cancelled.
	3.50pm	Rates of fire for new programme changed

40th Bde R.F.A.   (For A.F. "C" 2118)

W A R .... D I A R Y.   SHEETS

AUGUST 1916 (cont)   LONGUEVAL and MARICOURT

Date.	Hour.	Summary of events and information.
24th	4.0pm	Amended programme cancelled. Original programme to take place.
	4.19pm	Final Barrage altered to that laid down in amended programme.
	5.40pm	Attack by the whole of the 4th Army in conjunction with the French. 104th Bde to pivot on Northern point of ANGLEWOOD and swing forward its left, keeping touch with 106th Bde on its left, to the line of the ANGLEWOOD – GUILLEMONT ROAD where they are to immediately dig themselves in. Infantry advance (104th Bde) cancelled but artillery programme of lifts takes place. R.T Battalion of 104th Bde to keep touch with the French.
	6pm	R.T Battalion 104th Bde gains objective and establishes posts from B 20 37 to original front line.
	8pm	Night firing commences on T 25 7. 130th B.G. 30 rounds per hour on WEDGEWOOD.
	10pm	RA report that the French have gained the whole of their objective and that it is thought that we occupy FALFEMONT FARM.
25th	25'	Our infantry reported to have dug in on

40th Bde RFA

WAR DIARY

(For A.F. "C" 2118)

AUGUST 1916 (cont)   SHEETS LONGUEVAL and MARICOURT

Date.	Hour.	Summary of events and information.
25th/25th	2.40pm	French report Germans massing in SAVERNACKE WOOD
	7.55pm	Squares B1b and B2a added for night and day firing to areas already allotted.
	8.15pm	S.O.S received from Inf Bde.
	9.45pm	LIAISON Officer reports no signs of Infantry attack, but enemy shelling C.Ts heavily
	10.15pm	All reported quiet.
26th/26th	3pm	Continuous shelling reported on front line and C.Ts by 4.2s and 5.9s.
	3.45pm	Retaliation by Heavy Artillery asked for and obtained. 13th Bde 5th Div relieves 104th Bde 35th Div
27th/27th	3.15am	Barrage changed to B1c 8½-8½ to B1b 7-7 to B2a 2-9 on account of digging party.
	5.57pm	Infantry report they have standing patrol at B2c 6 9
	9.40pm	Infantry ask for us shelling 400yds SW of WEDGE WOOD as Infantry are digging party out.
28th/28th	9.40am	RA reports on shelling of trench B1b 3.5 to B1b 0.8 as Infantry think it empty and wish to occupy it.
	5.30pm	130th Battery ordered to register supposed MG emplacements at B1b 4.2, B1b 5.7 and

40' Bde RFA (For A.F. "C" 2118).

WAR DIARY

SHEETS

AUGUST 1916 (cont)   LONGUEVAL and MARICOURT

Date.	Hour.	Summary of events and information.
28th		and B1c87.
29th	8 am	Preliminary bombardment for attack by 30th Div on left and 5th Div in conjunction with French on right, commences. Steady rate of fire maintained by battery during the whole day with occasional bursts of rapid fire in the form of Chinese attacks.
	12 noon	130" Bty engages hostile machine gun at B16 5.2 and also sunken road from B16 5.2 to 3.7.
	3.5 pm	Bombardment postponed. Batteries ordered to search area T26c and c.
	4.30 pm	Heavy thunderstorm and rain.
	11.55 pm	Infantry report that they hold old gun pits at B16 5.2
30th		Firing continues as yesterday.
	7.50 pm	Infantry attempt occupy line B16 5.8, 5.7, 8 and B1c 3.7
	9.10 pm	Our line reported as follows GORDON TRENCH from B1c 7.0 northwards B1c 9.1 to B1d 3.7 SP B11 5.1 (doubtful)
31st	12 noon	Infantry report occupation by us of X roads B16 8½ 4½. Continuous shelling with gas shell of CHIMPANZEE VALLEY
	8 pm	Our line now reported as follows :— GORDON TRENCH – B16 0.0 – B1 24.7 – B16 8.0 – B2a 1.3 – B2a 4.0 – B2 b 0.2 SP s at B16 5.2 and B16 9.4. Infantry digging at these points and hope to join B16 9.a to B2a 1.3. Germans digging trench from T26 c 0.2 – B16 7c.6 – B16 5.3 Shell holes at the present they hold. 13th Inf Bde relieved.

31/8/16   Lt Col RFA
                                                     Off'g 40 Bde

3rd Divisional Artillery.

40TH BRIGADE R.F.A.

SEPTEMBER 1916.

Sept 30th 1916

To Staff Capt
   3rd DA
From Col maor
   OC 40 Bde RFA

Herewith WAR DIARY for September 1916.

30/9/16   [signature] Lieut Colonel
                              OC 40th Bde RFA

3rd Army
Army Form C. 2118
40° Bde RFA
Vol 25

WAR DIARY or INTELLIGENCE SUMMARY
(Erase heading not required.)

SHEETS LONGUEVAL & MARICOURT 1/10,000

Place	Date	Hour	Summary of Events and Information	Remarks and references to Appendices
TALUS BOIS VALLEY CARNOY	Sept 1/1916	10 AM	Col. & B.C.'s of morning Brigade (180 Bde RFA) go on to meet opposite numbers of Relieving Brigade (150 Bde RFA)	
		11 AM	Digging party goes up to prepare one gun pit of B/276 Bty for howitzer which is to go up tonight. One 18 pdr of 180 Bde to go into each of the forward 6 gun positions tonight.	
		2:10 PM	R.A. order no shooting after 8.30 pm on line between T.25.c B.1.a & S.1.8. and in square B.16 and no shooting between 8.30 pm & 12 midnight on line between WEDGEWOOD & B > E 4.8. both inclusive	
		7 PM	All reported quiet on our front.	
		7:45 PM	First gun of all groups shot at 7 pm at about B.1.d.7.8.	
		8:15 PM	R.A. inform that programme of preliminary bombardment commences at 8 am 2nd inst. Target group on trench E of line GUILLEMONT — FALFMONT FARM.	
	Sept 2/16	6.45 am	R.A. reports all patrols in. Preliminary bombardment commences.	
		8 am		
		10.30 am	Liaison officer reports Infantry made no advance last night. Patrols were fired on from 2 machine guns from W corner of FALFMONT FARM (13.a.a.7.5) but by one from B.2.a S.8.4 Machine gun also reported at T.26.c 7.5. causing a great deal of trouble. Patrols report, in follow. Patrols proceeded to S corner of FALFMONT FARM and got within 25 yards without being seen and saw into mine at S corner of the farm.	

WAR DIARY or INTELLIGENCE SUMMARY

Army Form C. 2118

40th Bde R.F.A.

SHEETS LONGUEVAL & MARICOURT

Place	Date	Hour	Summary of Events and Information	Remarks and references to Appendices
TALUS BOIS VALLEY	Sept 2/9/16		Main item is army Wurtte + Wurtte. Patrols unable to pass S.W. corner of the farm & were seen when 50 yards away and windpiped on by M.G. about the centre of the farm. 3 sides of the farm stay suspect up anything I who left found no wire. The trench lines roughly half moon shape. Knew F.I. E. long line of wire stretching S.E. along a line of knubs.	
CARNOY		8 pm	15th Bde Order received by 13th Bty Bde	
		7.30 pm	Amendment to operation order received	
		12 midnight	sent to Battery	
	Sept 3/1916	6 AM	Preliminary Bombardment commence	
		9 AM	Attack on FALFMONT FARM begins	
		9.45 AM	LT MUNT reports from observation it appears that the 2nd K.O Scottish Bord.s have not finished their objective. All forward communication cut.	
		9.55 AM	2nd KOSB report having gained their objective but nowhere (FALFMONT FARM)	
		10.25 AM	Machine Gun still firing from N + S of FALFMONT FARM apparently none of our infantry now in objective	
		10.30 AM	Machine gun located at T.25.d.8.6. 130th Bty turned on.	

WAR DIARY or INTELLIGENCE SUMMARY

Army Form C. 2118

40th Bde RFA

SHEETS LONGUEVAL & MARICOURT

Place	Date	Hour	Summary of Events and Information	Remarks and references to Appendices
TALUS BOIS VALLEY.	Sept 3/9/16 Cont.	12.42 pm	Reports that several distant drone rays we held apart trench of FALFMONT FARM when our infantry are in pitch black in No-Mans-Land.	
CARNOY.		1.59 pm	2nd KOSB state that they are in German trenches. A few prisoners taken. Request that barrage shall we pushed to WEDGEWOOD.	
		2.10 pm	Received from R.A. Barrage group programme from now onwards from all gun groups W to S & E edge of WEDGEWOOD down hence line to B2a77. Including hour an section fire 30 secs. Intention to have 5th objective trench to have within...	
		2.14 pm	20th Div reports to have gained first objective to trench E to N to SAVERNAKE WOOD.	
		2.30 pm	C.R.A. rings up & orders intense rate of fire from 2.35pm – 2.45pm & then dp 200 yds. Enemy to remain at 2.45 pm. Batteries informed but too late to make all batteries to engage target.	
		2.50 pm	LT MUNT reports artillery co-operation not obtained in time & arrvl vn-reported to 3.15pm. R.A. gave the same information to keep their to line B2a 7.6 to WEDGEWOOD NBF 20 seen till 3 PM. Many Guns at intense rate till 3.15 pm and then dp 200 yds in NE direction. Then minutes were transmitted to batteries.	
		3 PM	Capt. EMPSON reports 3rd flares from GUINCHY seen by two officers at O.P. also signal support to indicate the capture of GUINCHY.	
		3.10 PM	95th Inf Bde reports as follows:– Situation believed to be as follows:– 95th Inf Bde have reached 2nd objective. Are now supporting companies 1st E Surrey Regt and 1st DEVON Regt not advanced again. 1st GLOUCESTER Regt have been ordered to assist 13th Inf Bde in attack on WEDGEWOOD & machine gun fire 1st DCLI have moved forward to 2nd objective.	

WAR DIARY or INTELLIGENCE SUMMARY

Army Form C. 2118

40' Bde RFA

SHEETS LONGUEVAL & MARICOURT

Place	Date	Hour	Summary of Events and Information	Remarks and references to Appendices
TALUS BOIS FAVIEY CARNOY	3rd Sept 1916	3.35 pm	Observing officer of 6" Bty reports:- Our infantry seen advancing & passing T.26.D.3.1. First attack succeeded without second attack approved enough.	
		3.40 pm	LIAISON OFFICER reports as follows: - 1st Royal WEST KENTS were not going enough to attack - 1st BEDFORD REGT made attack later but a heavy bombardment on trench WEDGEWOOD - B.2.a 7.6 is required from. All guns were firing rapidly + time exp.	
		3.45 pm	F.O.O reports enemy in machine guns active at T.26.b.9.5 & T.26.a.6.8. Shelter barrage necessary. Our infantry now on line FALFMONT FARM – WEDGEWOOD. Our infantry are advancing towards LEUZE WOOD. Trench 3/pm	
		4.50 pm	A large force of Germans is reported to be advancing on FALFMONT FARM in a westerly direction but is in places kept up by our barrage. Batteries ordered to open fire up to BYF 10 area.	
		5.5 pm	95th Bty report seeing seen on line T.26.c.0.3 – T.26.c.1.9 but they were too present to notice techniel owing to our barrage. Reports made out left + BDE on left advised exp. WEDGEWOOD measured to B.2.a 7.6 according W	
		5.9 pm	RA order the firing longer to be engaged. Rate of fire from 6.10 pm – 6.30 pm to be minimum Rate corner of tr from. Down to be minimal. Three other ammunition batteries. H.E. only to be used. up to 6.30 pm. action 30 secs	
		5.20/m	RA order that firing shall cease at 6.30 pm	
		6 pm	RA order that barrage shall creep 100 yds N.E. at 6.30 pm and then cease fire. orders sent to batteries. SP much RA report seen dropping beyond the French line. All batteries ordered to keep 100 yds.	
		7.50/m	RA order:- SOS barrage of guns. T.26.c.5.5. - B.2.a 6.4. W of FALFMONT FARM - B.2.a 6.2	

Army Form C. 2118

40th Bde RFA

WAR DIARY
or
INTELLIGENCE SUMMARY
(Erase heading not required.)

Summary of Events and Information SHEETS LONGUEVAL & MARICOURT
1/10,000

Instructions regarding War Diaries and Intelligence Summaries are contained in F. S. Regs., Part II. and the Staff Manual respectively. Title Pages will be prepared in manuscript.

Place	Date	Hour	Summary of Events and Information	Remarks and references to Appendices
TALUS BOIS VALLEY, CARNOY	Sepr 3/1916	8.12 am	LIEUT MUNT reports:- "Infantry attack was driven back by heavy fire almost as soon as it left our trenches. From message received from 1st BEDFORD REGT it seems that they could not attack in line. G.O.C. 13th INF BDE is recommending that no further attack takes place tonight."	
		8.22 pm	G.O.C. 13th INF BDE informed of our S.O.S. lines & approx.	
		11.15 pm	C.R.A. rang telephone re "Bombardment to be carried out tomorrow". All batteries ordered to register T.26 & 4.1. to NW corner of FALFMONT FARM inclusive before 10 am. 4 rnds where live from T.26 & 4.1. to point 48 to be bombarded. Situation vague but from all accounts in which GUINCHY, GUILLEMONT possibly WEDGEWOOD but not FALFMONT FARM. The French are reported to have taken SAVERNAKE WOOD.	
	Sepr 4/1916	7.15 am	18 Pdrs reduce rate of fire at Sessons 6 per hour.	
		8.55 am	F.O.O. reports "Hostile barrage much lighter. Observation difficult".	
		9.45 am	Officer patrol reports an German :- Prussia inf to numb at S.E. corner of FALFMONT FARM. Enemy have received machine guns in position there & handed SE of FALFMONT FARM by companies of 1st CHESHIRE REGT & 15th ROYAL WARWICKSHIRES are changing sides which by companies of men relieved up by reserve guns from	
		10.10 am	CAPT EMPSON reports that when he gained FALFMONT FARM observation of hump running NW from FARM unpracticable. Range found to be 50 yds over.	
		10.20 am	C.R.A. rang up about registration. Make aware from not shell not go over much.	
		10.30 am	Ulster reported sweeping short in and around WEDGWOOD. Batteries informed and damage dept late 200 yds	

1875 Wt. W593/826 1,000,000 1/15 T.R.C. & A. A.D.S.S./Forms/C. 2118.

Army Form C. 2118

40th Bde RFA

WAR DIARY
or
INTELLIGENCE SUMMARY
(Erase heading not required.)

SHEETS LONGUEVAL & MARICOURT 1/10000

Place	Date	Hour	Summary of Events and Information	Remarks and references to Appendices
Happy Valley TALUS BOIS	Sept 4/16	11am	Preliminary orders received re bombardment — these orders re bombardment received	
		12.50 pm		
		1.10 pm	Adjutant went to orders meeting (noise of fire)	
VALLEY CARNOY		1.55 pm	Barrage ordered to cease at 3.40 pm to line T.26.c.77 — T.26.d.21.6 sent to Battalions on O.O.	
		2.10 pm	Barrage ordered to cease at 3.40 pm to line T.26.c.77 — T.26.d.21.6 sent to Battalions received	
		2.20 pm	C.R.A. orders Barrage to lift 200 yds in a N direction on front at about T.26.c.77 — T.26.d.1.6. Sent to Battalion by wire.	
		3.10 pm	Gunner allied trenches at FALFMONT FARM and trenches immediately NW & SE of it and probably also the trench from T.26.c.4.5 to T.26.a.7&4 at the same line 15th Corps at GUINCHY. Return fire at intense rate on line B.2.a.3.7 to B.2.a.5.31. Fire kept up sweeping at present approximately as follows T.20.d.1.0 along road to T.26.c.1.0 — T.26.c.14 through WEDGEWOOD to T.26.c.1.42 — B.2.a.12.6 — B.2.a.18.32 — B.2.c.47. B.2.d.0.51 — B.2.a.24.41. We also held a line of camp holes and posts about 100-150 yds in front of our B.2.a.12.32 to B.2.d.5.1. No information obtained as to direction N.M.T.20.d.1.0 except that we don't hold QUINCHY.	
		3 pm	R.A return group to cease fire at 6.30 pm	
		4.15 pm	LIAISON OFFICER reports that he saw our infantry into FALFMONT FARM. Division still uncertain. Germans reported to be massing in QUARRY at T.26.d.2.2.	
		6.35 pm	H. Metcalfe reports night company held up by MG at B.2.c.5.8. 130° 3TY a 23rd BTY. ravined on	
		6.20 pm	Infantry reported digging in front ahead of sunken road in T.2.6.c. Division at FALFMONT FARM still uncertain	
		7.10 pm	Lt. STAGG reports yellow flares seen at T.26.d.4.8.	
		7.17 pm	F.O.O reports our infantry entering Western side of LEUZEWOOD at T.A.l.c.2.4.	

Army Form C. 2118

40' Bde RFA

WAR DIARY
or
INTELLIGENCE SUMMARY
(Erase heading not required.)

Instructions regarding War Diaries and Intelligence Summaries are contained in F.S. Regs., Part II. and the Staff Manual respectively. Title Pages will be prepared in manuscript.

Summary of Events and Information SHEETS. LONGUEVAL & MARICOURT. 1/10,000

Place	Date	Hour	Summary of Events and Information	Remarks and references to Appendices
TALUS BOIS VALLEY.	Sept 4th 1916	7.35 pm	Our infantry reported to be held up by M.G. fire S. Eastern of FALFMONT FARM, but making progress slowly.	
GUILLEMONT.		8.55 pm	RA orders SOS lines as follows B2 & 4.64 to T17.c.0.5 at B.F. 1 min. raking 2 batteries.	
		9.5 pm	Lt WHITRIDGE reports that our infantry are digging in from LEFT of to N.W. corner of LEUZE WOOD but the enemy still have a footing in FALFMONT FARM and in trenches immediately S.E. of it.	
		9.10 pm	RA reports aeroplane reports our frame lines as follows at about 7.10 pm. "Road between T26.c.8.5 – T26.c.1.9. NW corner of LEUZE WOOD and in QUARRY T.30.D – GNE of it directly north signs.	
	Sept 5th 1916	8.15 am	LIAISON OFFICER reports that infantry have now reoccupied the whole of FALFMONT FARM.	
		8.25 am	Infantry not seen from FARM down to B2d.4.8 while we stopped as they would be bombing back from FARM in that point.	
		8.40 am	LIAISON OFFICER reports "not in support to be in possession of whole ridge to LEUZE WOOD. Heavy guns and 18 pdrs will report to be shelling this area but barrage lifted 100 yds further up the road from FALFMONT FARM.	
		9.10 am	Report received from infantry that shelling of FARM should be stopped.	
		9.50 am	RA reports that his trench was advancing from our line between OAKHANGER & SAVERNAKE WOODS. No shells to fall S of line FALFMONT FARM & T28 C.1.2.	
		9.55 pm	Shells falling short on FALFMONT reply reported to be coming from direction of CHIMPANZEE TRENCH. Our F.O.O. referred by F.O.O. of ASKWITH GROUP. LIAISON OFFICER returned by officer of REYNOLDS GROUP.	
		10 am	Lt WHITRIDGE reports situation at 10 am to be as follows. Then FALFMONT FARM our line runs N along road to T26.c.8.5. Our french is linked back and runs in NW direction to FALFEY TRENCH about T.26.5.3. We also hold from T.26.c.8.7 to T.26a.8.1.	
		4 pm	Lt WHITRIDGE relieved by REYNOLDS GROUP. CRA rings up and orders reconnaissance of VALLEY instead of ANGUS WOOD with a view to pushing guns there.	

Army Form C. 2118

40th Bde RFA

WAR DIARY
or
INTELLIGENCE SUMMARY
(Erase heading not required.)

Instructions regarding War Diaries and Intelligence Summaries are contained in F. S. Regs., Part II. and the Staff Manual respectively. Title Pages will be prepared in manuscript.

SHEETS LONGUEVAL & MARICOURT 1/10,000

Place	Date	Hour	Summary of Events and Information	Remarks and references to Appendices
TALUS BOIS VALLEY CARNOY.	Sept 5th 1916.	4:30pm	Col. & Adjt. start for ANGLE WOOD. Divide positions for 2 Bde's ANGLE WOOD and valley in front during to stoppage of recent by FALFEMONT FARM. Sullivan would have to some Bde action to hang up the attempt so as to make him to clear the crest. Not a great deal of shelling going on except at about 5:30 pm - 10 pm. When the enemy started a stiff barrage in the front of FALFEMONT FARM two red lying stars - S.O.S. lights. Rockets were sent up and the enemy opened heavy rifle and MG fire. TROTTE TRO? going up and the north between LEUZE WOOD & BOULEAUX WOOD. Trouble appeared to be on the outskirts of COMBLES. Colonel reaching Hqrs at 9:15 pm.	
		9:30pm	R.A. report turnt to be in COMBLES	
	Sept 6th 1916.	6am	Col. takes up Col. Thomas to 16.94 to ANGLE WOOD to show him positions reconnoitred on previous day.	
		7:50am	Division reported as follows:- Last night in our right and enemy public to reach their objective. We are to hands in T27a + T27c central. They were held up by MG fire and rifle. MG's located at T27a.6.7 T27b.6.7 T27c.9.7.? Were very much on the left of their infantry who are well through the wood and any there was further of their whole about the open to the rear. They are in touch with troops on the left but not on right. There was news of trouble which turned down into SSE to COMBLES.) no further news about heavy bombardment during afternoon + evening.	
		3pm	B/76 @ TY moves out and came to be under command of 40th Bde.	
		6pm	All Batteries withdrawn to Wagon Lines. Ammunition handed over to 160th Bde. Bde Hqrs remain at TALUS BOIS VALLEY for the night.	

Army Form C. 2118

40 Bde RFA

WAR DIARY
or
INTELLIGENCE SUMMARY
(Erase heading not required.)

Instructions regarding War Diaries and Intelligence Summaries are contained in F.S. Regs., Part II. and the Staff Manual respectively. Title Pages will be prepared in manuscript.

AMIENS / LENS   1/100,000

Place	Date	Hour	Summary of Events and Information	Remarks and references to Appendices
BRAY.	7.9.16	9 am	The Brigade marched from Wagon Lines at BRAY via MEAULTE, VILLE, BUIRE, HEILLY, FRANVILLERS to MONTIGNY.	
MONTIGNY.	8.9.16		To HEM via CONTAY, TOUTENCOURT, RAINCHEVAL & MARIEUX.	
HEM.	9.9.16		CONCHY SUR CANCHE via BARLY, BOWNIÈRES, FORTEL, VACQUERIE.	
CONCHY	10.9.16		BAYAVAL via FLERS, CROISETTE, PIERREMONT, ANVIN, EPS.	
BAYAVAL	11.9.16		LABEUVIERE via CAUCHY A LA TOUR, AUCHEL, MARLES LES MINES, LAPUGNOY.	
LABEUVIERE	12.9.16		Remained at LABEUVIERE. (2nd C.I.B.M. inspected the guns of the brigade & the ammunition in the elements).	
	13.9.16	9 am	Received BC's met by MT. ST MARINGARBE preparatory to taking over from 3rd (Comp) DA 14th BIS GROUP, the brigade to occupy lines at NOEUX LES MINES, PLACE A BRUAY.	
		3 pm	The brigade marched via MARLE LES MINES.	
			after dark. 2 guns of 6" Bty returned A/169 Bty 31st Div	
			2 - 23 - C/306 - 61st	
			2 - 49 - C/307 - 61st	
			2 - 130 - D/169 - 31st	
			All battery positions were in the vicinity of FOSSE 7.	
MAZINGARBE	14.9.16	12 noon	Command of 14 BIS GROUP passed from the group of the 3rd DA (Comps) to 40th BDE RFA and the command of the batteries passed to the batteries of 40th BDE. Reliefs of the intervening batteries after dark, one section (no part of the batteries of the 40th BDE completed the relief) the 31st & 61st DIV.	
dutto	15.9.16		Batteries continued registration. 23rd Bty cooperated with TM's in cutting wire in front of hostile trenches in front of 14 B16.	
			after dark one section { 2 gun 106 Bty } 23rd Bde relieved { 1 section C/176 } in 14 BIS GROUP D.23 - { 2 gun 108 Bty } { D/178 }	
dutto	16.9.16		Batteries continued registration 2 2 108 Bty employment TM's and no power dug after dark. Position 108 Bty } completed relief of { C/178 } D/23 { D/178 }	

Army Form C. 2118

WAR DIARY
or
INTELLIGENCE SUMMARY
(Erase heading not required.)

40th Bde RFA

Place	Date	Hour	Summary of Events and Information	Remarks and references to Appendices
MAZINGARBE	17.9.16		No change. All batteries fired a few rounds the retaliation or remain quiet at report of hostile batteries or of 76th Bde de front line	HAZEBROUCK SP 1/100,000 LENS 1/10,000
ditto	18.9.16		"	
ditto	19.9.16		"	Also 2/Lt "H" Bty comp. wk TMS appointed 14-17/9.
ditto	20.9.16		Orders received from 2nd DA that 14th Bde GROUP will be relieved by 176 BDE of 40th DA on the 27/23. 23/24 Sept. 2nd Lt N. HUNT - 23rd Bty sent to FIELD AMBULANCE (SICK)	
ditto	21.9.16		Lt.-Col. GILL. O.C. 176 BDE RFA taken normal Bty position + OP's of O.C. 176 BDE	A Bty - 6 Bty
ditto	22.9.16		No change.	C " - 176 BDE 176 DE" relieved
"	"		After dark relief commenced	D " - 176 BDE C/161 Bty/32nd DA
ditto	23.9.16	12 noon	at 12 noon command handed over of 176 BDE + BC's relieving batteries	
			after dark relief completed	
LABEUVRIERE		3 pm	BDE HQRS Marched to LA BEUVRIERE	
ditto		9 pm	Batteries " " LABEUVRIERE	
ditto	24.9.16		Brigade remained in LABEUVRIERE	
MARTHES & HAM	25.9.16		Bde Brigade marched to MARTHES & HAM. via MARLE LES MINES. AUCHEL. CAUCHY A LA TOUR. BELLERY	
			ESTRÉE BLANCHE. BLESSY ↑ HAM.	
ditto	26.9.16		Training commences	
ditto	29.9.16		ditto continues	
ditto	30.9.16		ditto ditto	

3rd Divisional Artillery.

40TH BRIGADE R.F.A.

OCTOBER 1916.

Brigade Major
3' D.A.

Herewith War Diary for the
month of October 1916.

Sinclair Benstol
OC 40th Bde R.F.A.

2*/16

40 Bde R.F.A.
Vol 26

Army Form C. 2118

WAR DIARY
or
INTELLIGENCE SUMMARY

40ᵗʰ Bde R.F.A.

(Erase heading not required.)

Place	Date	Hour	Summary of Events and Information	Remarks and references to Appendices
				HAZEBROUCK & LENS 1/100,000 — HEBUTERNE TRENCH MAP 10,000
MARTHES	1-10-16		Training continues.	
ditto	2-10-16	9.30 am	Inspection of Batteries at training by G.O.C. Division & C.R.A.	
	3-10-16		Training continues. Orders for moving received. Marched to Battalion.	
	4-10-16		Training continues.	
	5-10-16		The Brigade marched to WAVRANS via ESTREE BLANCHE, FLECHINELLE, CUHEM, FEBIN FALFART, FOUNTAINS LES BOULANS, BERGUENEUSE.	
	6-10-16		The Brigade marched to LE CAUROY via ST POL, HERLIN LE SEC, BUNEVILLE, ESTREE WAMIN.	
	7-10-16		The Brigade marched to BERTRANCOURT via BEAUDRICOURT, LUCHEUX, MOYOICOURT, PAS, AUTHIE, LOUVENCOURT.	
COLINCAMPS	8-10-16		Bde Hqrs at BEAUSSART. Batteries in position in SERRE sector K27 c & d (HEBUTERNE Trench map 10000) commences K2 d 79 – K29 c 18.	
HEBUTERNE	9-10-16	9.30 pm	All guns in action. None cutting the opposite front line.	
HEBUTERNE	10-10-16		Wire cutting continues on 2nd & 3rd lines.	
ditto	11-10-16		Wire cutting continues. Firing at night to keep gaps open.	
ditto	12-10-16	2.15 pm	Wire cutting continues. 3rd B.A. – 2nd D. 4th Infantry to learn whether by the Trench mortar.	
ditto	13-10-16		Wire cutting continues also not demonstrations to draw concentrations. 6" Battery shelled at 2.15.	
ditto	14-10-16		Wire cutting continues. Smoke attack in front of 3rd Div at 3.17 pm. 6"-25 Batteries shelled intermittently.	
ditto	15-10-16	7.15 pm	Raid by 10th Northumberland Fusiliers successful. Point of entry K29 c 37.60. 1 prisoner captured. 6"-23 Battery shelled.	
ditto	16-10-16		Wire cutting keeps continues. 6"-23 Btry ditto.	
ditto	17-10-16		Wire cutting continues. Bde Hqrs moved COURCELLES. Bde temporarily taking over the position of the 315 Bde.	
	18-10-16		Additional wire cutting from K24 C 42 to K29 B 51.6 accorded to the Brigade. Wire cutting continues. 6" B'dy O.P. shelled.	

Army Form C. 2118

WAR DIARY
or
INTELLIGENCE SUMMARY
(Erase heading not required.)

40th Bde
R.F.A.

HEBUTERNE TRENCH MAP 10.S.22.D.

Place	Date	Hour	Summary of Events and Information	Remarks and references to Appendices
HEBUTERNE	19.10.16	2.7 pm	Rain. Wire cutting continues. Relief of 9" By 126 by 76 By Bde completed. Barrage fired when heavy guns attack STUFF & REGINA TRENCHES.	
ditto	20.10.16		Wire cutting continues.	
ditto	21.10.16		Wire cutting continues. 130° By shelled with 7.7s 4.2 5.9s.	
ditto	22.10.16		Wire cutting continues. 49° By neighbourhood gas received.	
ditto	23.10.16		Wire cutting continues. Enemy preliminary bombardment carried thro. several carried. Rain.	
		7 pm – 10 pm	Barrage for 3rd Army movement of TANKS.	
ditto	24.10.16		Wire cutting continues. Rain.	
ditto	25.10.16		Wire cutting continues. Rain.	
ditto	26.10.16		Wire cutting continues. Rain. 93 By ble on enemy water. Raid by trench mortar by 1st & 10th Gordon Highlanders unsuccessful owing to fire being opened by Hun dull on our left by the right near. Return our trenches covered by 6"-130° bdys shrapnel.	
ditto	27.10.16		Wire cutting continues. Rain. 8" By shells rearm shafts west of 76 By Ster.	
ditto	28.10.16		Wire cutting continued. Rain.	
ditto	29.10.16		Wire cutting continued. Rain.	

WAR DIARY
or
INTELLIGENCE SUMMARY

Army Form C. 2118

40th Bde RFA

(Erase heading not required.)

Place	Date	Hour	Summary of Events and Information	Remarks and references to Appendices
HEBUTERNE	30/12		Mine enemy continues recon	
do.	30/12		Mine enemy continues. Fine. Aeroscope raid by 8" our yorkes at 6.20 pm 23rd Bdy cut the gap for them.	HEBUTERNE 10000

3rd Divisional Artillery.

40TH BRIGADE R.F.A.

NOVEMBER 1 9 1 6.

3rd Divisional Artillery.

Brigade Major
3rd D.A.

Herewith War Diary
for the month of November 1916.

1/XII/16

[signature] Lieut Colonel
O.C. 40th Bde RFA.

WAR DIARY
or
INTELLIGENCE SUMMARY

Army Form C. 2118

40th Bde R.F.A.   HEBUTERNE

Place	Date	Hour	Summary of Events and Information	Remarks and references to Appendices
HEBUTERNE	1-11-16	6.40 am	Wire cutting & trench W. of SERRE. Heavy bombardment for 5 minutes.	Rain. 6" Bty shelled with 6 in A.P. 16/18 pdrs + 4 How in action
ditto	2-11-16	6.40 am	Wire cutting continues W. of SERRE. Heavy bombardment for 5 minutes.	Rain. 14/18 pdrs + 4 How in action
ditto	3-11-16		Wire cutting continues W. of SERRE.	Rain. 15 18/18 Pdrs + 4 How in action
ditto	4-11-16	6.20 am 11.30 pm	H.A. bombardment. All Battery performed shoot for ½ cwt Hy 4.2". W. of SERRE	6.45 am 3rd Bty in operations postponed unsatisfactory. Rain 9th Inf Bde relieve 6" Inf Bde. Rain
ditto	5-11-16	11.30 pm	Wire cutting continues W. of SERRE	16/18 pdrs + How in action
ditto		1 pm		LT BAAS 23rd Bty wounded. 1 gun 23rd Bty knocked out. 8 O.R. wounded at 116 m
ditto	6-11-16		Wire cutting continues W. of SERRE Intense bombardment for 5 minutes.	Rain 13/18 Pdrs + 4 How — action
ditto		1.00 pm	Intense bombardment for 5 minutes. Rain	outrag's W. Bury, afternoon postponed
ditto	7-11-16		Wire cutting continues. Rain 13/18 pdrs + 4 How in action	allotment reduced to 500 rds per battery. 18 pdrs 250 rds for 4.5 How
ditto	8-11-16		Wire cutting continues. Fine Battle reps of Bty ride at K15 at 6.4 commenced.	14-18 pdrs + 4 Hows in action. RA pass visited aerofiles. Visibility poor. 13/18 pdrs + 4 How in action.
ditto	9-11-16		Wire cutting continues. Weather fine 2nd Lt HUNT & 2nd Lt SHIELDS rejoin from hospital	Visibility poor
ditto	10-11-16	12.5 am	W. day. Visibility poor. Weather fine. 23rd Bty shelled with gas shells. 2nd Lt WRIGHT 6th Bty temporarily attached to 4.9" Bty.	allotment of rounds not restricted 14/18 pdrs + 4 How in action
ditto	11-11-16	2.15 am 2.43 am	X day. Visibility poor. Weather fine. Rounds fired in retaliation to enemy shelling of heavy gunning & infantry. Hostile shelling severe.	16/18 pdrs + 4 How in action

WAR DIARY
or
INTELLIGENCE SUMMARY

(Erase heading not required.)

40TH Bde. R.F.A.

Army Form C. 2118

Place	Date	Hour	Summary of Events and Information	Remarks and references to Appendices
HEBUTERNE	13/9/16	7.14p	RA orders are apper per Bde diary. 130th Bde detailed.	HEBUTERNE 10000
		7.40p	RA smoke No of gunners Mess Corps Cadre 35 officers 154 NCO's 1490 men. Previous = all coming in freely.	
		8.50p	Brain officer reports: Party or K29B10 + 100yds N of this point went some back to front some into enemy infantry severely wounded from close up to the german front line in front of the 8th + 76th Bdes 49th, 35th front back to the enemy support line barrage.	
		11.15p	RA order rate of fire to be reduced.	
ditto	14/9/16	6.50a	Bombardment of german lines no chance attack according to prisoner letter.	
		10.05a	130" Bdy reduce rate of fire to Rgft 1/2 minutes. Rest of day intermittent fire observed from O.P's.	
ditto	15/9/16		Intermittent fire observed from O.P's by day + night.	
		3.18p	130" Bdy barraged from K36b40 – L31C45 rate of fire 1 round per gun per 3 minutes.	
ditto	16/9/16		Intermittent fire by day + night.	
ditto	17/9/16		Intermittent fire by day + night.	
ditto	18/9/16	6.10am	Intermittent fire by day + night. 130" Barrage K55 to 9.5 to K36 to D2 + 18 pdrs. trenches between SERRE & CHALK ALLEY to assist the attack by the 33rd Div on MUNICH & FRANKFORT TRENCHES.	

Army Form C. 2118

WAR DIARY or INTELLIGENCE SUMMARY
(Erase heading not required.)

Instructions regarding War Diaries and Intelligence Summaries are contained in F.S. Regs., Part II. and the Staff Manual respectively. Title Pages will be prepared in manuscript.

40" Bde RFA

Place	Date	Hour	Summary of Events and Information	Remarks and references to Appendices
HEBUTERNE	13/11/16	9 am	RA orders rate of fire reduced to 16 +1 a round a gun per minute. Repetition of programme forbidden. Must conserve ammunition.	
		10.35 am	Gordons reported in WALTER TRENCH between K29 b 6.0 + 8.1. 4.1. RA orders damage to be inflicted 16 SERRE TRENCH between no. above park.	
		10.55 am	Liason officer reports as above. "Attack S of the ANCRE and on BEAUMONT HAMEL and also in our left down been successful.	
		12 noon	3rd DA report 1000 prisoners taken in BEAUMONT HAMEL. 3rd Div attack to be renewed shortly.	
		12.25 pm	3rd DA orders damage to be brought back to German front line + machine gun support.	
		1.27 pm	Liason officer reports 2 officers + 20 men holding out in front line opposite Royal Scots.	
		2 pm	Bde major reports men holding out at K 29 B.1.0 + 200 yds to the N of this point. Bde 23rd Brigade defend to support line.	
		2.15 pm	FOO reports garrison appears due to mend must & on the right + centre, the enemy put up a very heavy barrage on our [?] line.	
		3.14 pm	RA orders Battery fire 10 secs, to present line.	
		5.46 pm	RA notify, that Rio-bombardment will probably not take place tonight.	
		6" Bty OP officer reports Rifle barrage very good, shrapnel bursting well.	
		3.47 pm		
		6.50 pm	RA orders night firing in front + support line except from K 29 B.1.0 - 200 yds N of this point. Rate of fire 40 rounds per battery per hour.	

Army Form C. 2118

WAR DIARY
INTELLIGENCE SUMMARY
(Erase heading not required.)

HEBUTERNE
40TH BDE.
R.F.A.

HEBUTERNE
1.
10,000.

Instructions regarding War Diaries and Intelligence Summaries are contained in F.S. Regs., Part II. and the Staff Manual respectively. Title Pages will be prepared in manuscript.

Place	Date	Hour	Summary of Events and Information	Remarks and references to Appendices
HEBUTERNE	12/11/16	12.10am	Tanks reported to be seeing their survey retiring from Y day. HQN moved to dugouts at K.25.d. 6.4. Weather fine. Visibility poor. 16/18 hours - 4 hours in action. Wire cutting continues.	
ditto	13/11/16		Z day for attack on SERRE.	
		5.45am	Bombardment started in misty weather.	
		6.20am	Liaison Officer reports Royal Scots in enemy front line - many be further.	
		6.30am	R.S.F's reported to have gained enemy front line.	
		7.5am	Liaison Officer reports that the 6" Bde (left of 2nd Div) have gained enemy front line + is doubtful whether Royal Scots have taken the enemy front line.	
		7.25am	F.O.O. reports Infantry reports as follows "Infantry state that they were held up by front line more + now back on our original front line, all ranks supporting the Royal Scots have been absorbed by them."	
		7.50am	Wire from 3rd DA orders barrage today on W. edge of SERRE unless fresh orders sent. I round per gun per minute. Liaison Officer reports 6" + 76" Bdy Bdes back on their original front line. That it is not safe to fire on their German 2nd line as our men may still be in it as we reached the 2nd line.	
		7.55am		
		8.20am	3rd DA order barrage to be put on SERRE TRENCH	
		8.17am	3rd DA - - - - - WALTER TRENCH	
		8.36am	Liaison Officer reports "Part of RSF's are digging in the German front line there may be in the 2nd line. They were held up by wire on their right." (This was front afterwards to be in - correct re wire.) This is the only Battn that said they were held up by wire + I think that and + many fine have down might to held us up there were	

1875 Wt. W593/826 1,000,000. 4/15 T.B.C. &A. AD.S.S./Forms/C. 2118.

Army Form C. 2118

WAR DIARY
or
INTELLIGENCE SUMMARY
(Erase heading not required.)

40TH BDE RFA

HEBUTERNE
10,000

Place	Date	Hour	Summary of Events and Information	Remarks and references to Appendices
HEBUTERNE	19/10		No Rain. Very muddy.	
ditto	20/10		Intermittent firing during the day & night. Enemy barrage by 130 Bty evening at 7:30 a.m. in the morning.	
ditto	21/10		Intermittent firing during the day & night. Dumps to be reduced.	
ditto	22/10		Intermittent firing during the day & night. Fine weather. Lt. PERKINS gone on leave.	
ditto	23/10		Intermittent firing during the day & night. Accident 250 rounds for battery per day. Fine weather.	
			124 Bde military Chalkeys moved to quarters formerly occupied by 124 Bde. Winter quarters begun at BUS.	
		3:50 pm	Brigade barrage on MUNICH & FRANKFORT TRENCH. CHALK ALLEY WHITE TRENCH ETC assisting the 32nd Div attack on MUNICH & FRANKFORT TRENCH.	
ditto	24/10		Intermittent firing during the day & night. Fine weather. 23rd Bty moved 1 section back.	
ditto	25/10		Intermittent firing during the day & night. Rain. Lt WHITRIDGE returned from leave.	
			23rd Bty moved 1 gun back.	
ditto	26/10		Intermittent firing during the day & night. COURCELLES. Rain. MAJOR ALLSUP goes on leave.	
ditto	27/10		Intermittent firing during the day & night. HQrs moved to COURCELLES. Fine Front	
ditto	28/10	8:30 am	Intermittent firing during the day & night. Fine today. 1" air bursts on enemy bombarded enemy trenches.	
ditto	29/10		The enemy bombarded our front line on three separate between 5 p.m & 7 p.m apparently for no reason. The Batteries of the Brigade retaliated with the desired effect of silencing the hostile fire and causing Heavy mist throughout the day which rendered observation impossible.	
ditto	30/10		Quiet day practically no hostile arty. 2/Lt Rollins joined 23rd Battery & 2/Lt Shaw joined 130 Battery 2/Lt Brocke posted to D.A.C. Muddy day.	

J.B.C. & A. A.D.S.S./Forms/C. 2118.

3rd Divisional Artillery.

40TH BRIGADE R.F.A.

DECEMBER 1916.

D.O. 444

Brigade Major
3rd D.A.

Herewith war diary
for the month of December 1916.

1/1/17

[signature]
OC 440th Bde RFA.

WAR DIARY or INTELLIGENCE SUMMARY

Army Form C. 2118.

40 B/R.F.A. HÉBUTERNE 10000. Vol 28

40th Bde R.F.A.

1st to 31st Dec 1916.

Place	Date	Hour	Summary of Events and Information	Remarks and references to Appendices
Hébuterne	1-12-16	9 p.m.	Enemy opened heavy fire on our front and support trenches at 1 p.m. from John Copse to Stone Parisian Road. Palestine, Taupin, and north end of Central were also shelled. Shelling ceased at 1.45 p.m. Fine day but very misty. —	
"	2-12-16	9.45 p.m.	No hostile fire. Fine, observation impossible.	
"	3-12-16	9.30 p.m.	The 76th Infantry Brigade whose front the 40th Brigade were covering moved from Battle H[ea]d[quarters] to Courcelles. Enemy shelled 23rd Battery Position with 4.2"s & 5.9"s from 3.15 p.m. to 3.30 p.m. and from 4.10 p.m. to 4.20 p.m. Fine day but misty, observation practically impossible. —	
"	4-12-16	9.40 p.m.	Enemy shelled Heugate Street with 5.9 at 3.15 p.m. From 3.30 p.m. to 3.55 p.m. K27 C was lightly shelled with 77 c.m.s. Weather misty/just. Weather fine. —	
"	5-12-16	9.45 p.m.	Enemy shelled our trenches in K29C and also having fire from 12.15 p.m. to 12.45 p.m. with 105 mm shells. — In area K26 and K27 & 2 shells were scattered. Winter 21 m & 4 p.m. many dropping near 6th Battery Position — A little rain, very mild.	
"	6-12-16	9.55 p.m.	Enemy shelled our trenches in vicinity of Touvent Farm at 11.30 a.m. which ceased at 12 noon. Between 3.9.5 p.m. & 7.5 in vicinity of Basin and Usk-shaven Wood were shelled with 4.2, 9, 5.9's. — Thaw today for Weather fine.	
"	7-12-16	10 p.m.	Hostile fire practically Nil. At 11 a.m. a few gas shells were sent over in vicinity of K20 C9 A. Visibility impossible. Weather fine, very mild. —	
"	8-12-16	9.30 p.m.	Enemy shelled Taupin trench & vicinity with 4.2's & 5.9's. Rained all day — Observation front. — with 4.2's 9.5 9.5. Gellincourt slightly shelled at 1.34 p.m.	
"	9-12-16	9.15 p.m.	Intermittent fire on 2.93 & hill. Rained all day — Observation front. —	
"	10-12-16	10.p.m.	Intermittent fire kept up on 3[?] 9.4 that went Intermittent fire of C.T.'s on K27C throughout the day. Enemy shelled Touvent Farm & Stuff Close also Route at 5.15 p.m. Fine, observation fair. —	

Army Form C. 2118

WAR DIARY
or
INTELLIGENCE SUMMARY
(Erase heading not required.)

HEBUTERNE

40TH BDE
R.F.A.

Place	Date	Hour	Summary of Events and Information	Remarks and references to Appendices
HEBUTERNE	11/7/16	3.57p	Army shelled MAIRNE TRENCH heavily for 3 an hour. Hostile artillery more active today. We shelled Sunken Road L.20.c. intermittently to annoy him.	
ditto	14/7/16	7.pm	SOUTHERN AVENUE & EUSTON DUMP shelled with 4.2". 23rd Bty shelled with 60 4.2:5.9". Harassing fire kept up on areas L.26.a & K.30.b.	
ditto	15/7/16	3:30am	1st Royal Scots trench raid. Sent S.O.S. sig 13" K.4.R. Fire near 7" K.3.b.1.	
ditto	14/7/16	11:35p	Army shelled K.2.7.c. meeting fire K.28.a.b. COLINCAMPS. etc. in retaliation fire kept up on min -	
ditto	15/7/16	6:15pm 7.pm	Report on hostile communication for 3 minutes - K.30.b. 7.3 - K.24 d 95.65 & L.25 c 4.8. into. intermittent fire kept up on enemy's own min - back areas	
ditto	16/7/16	11 am	Army shelled BLENAU TRENCH. Whilst shelling recon. noted. Enemy thought ourselves moving reinfts from upon 8" Howr into near 1st R.S.F.'s. Whilst shelling enemy's back areas kept up - intermittent fire on enemy's back areas kept up.	
ditto	17/7/16		Hostile shelling below normal Harassing fire on enemy's own back areas kept up -	
ditto	18/7/16		S.O. 3 BA signal calls STORA, rain.	

Army Form C. 2118

WAR DIARY
or
INTELLIGENCE SUMMARY

(Erase heading not required.)

Instructions regarding War Diaries and Intelligence Summaries are contained in F.S. Regs., Part II. and the Staff Manual respectively. Title Pages will be prepared in manuscript.

Place	Date	Hour	Summary of Events and Information	Remarks and references to Appendices
HEBUTERNE	19/7/16		40TH BDE R.F.A. HEBUTERNE 1/10,000	
			Shelly Enemy shelled COLINCAMPS, CENTRAL AVENUE & HITTITE. We fired K.29 d & K.30 a. L.20 c, L.16 b. Night firing on K.30 a & L.25.	
	20/7/16	8.10 pm	31st Div Annandale Dump & Sunken Road K.3 d 76.60 & K.3 d 76.81. 2nd KRRC fired on Rute (6.35). 31st Sunken Road K.3 d 78.60 & K.3 d 76.81. German front line not held today. Divisible fire been normal. Enemy shelled COLINCAMPS, BIHENAU & FLAG AVENUE the front on 1st & 3rd Divs lines also K.30 c & d. Night firing on L.25 art. Sent to Wilson admitted to hospital.	
	21/7/16	12.30 pm	Rain. 1st Inf Bde relieved the 76th Inf Bde in the left sector. 7.KSLI relieving the 2nd R.S. Enemy artillery more active today. Enemy working parties at K.30 c & g.9. We fired on K.29 & REGENT ST, SACKVILLE ST & front line from MATHEW to MARK COPSE.	
	22/7/16	5.25 pm	Rain. 8th Inf Bde relieved from front to the night (K.35 & 8.5). Trench boards put up. SLAG AVE, RLY AVE & SAPPER TRENCH shelled by the enemy. SUSSERIE also shelled. We retaliated on their 2nd & 3rd line. 31st Div fired on 31st Div Road but night firing was on K.29 fet.	
	23/7/16		Fine. Enemy shelled COLINCAMPS NORTHERN & CENTRAL AVENUES. K.25 a & K.27 c also EUSTON DUMP. We fired on hostile working party on K.29 & 65.45 also points L.26 c 58. L.26 a 58. Night firing. L.25 a 31st DA fired on the left movement. 3rd DA about to assist.	
	24/7/16	10 pm	Rain. Enemy shelled NAIRNE, PAPIN & ROIS ROY TRENCHES. COLINCAMPS, LA SIGNY FARM. Night firing on K.30 c. 3rd DA Communication Shoot.	
	25/7/16	6 pm	V. Windy. 4" R.F's. retwinted 12"NORD-T's in the right subsector. 15" Kings knapsack reline 12" West Morts in the left subsector. Hostile fire NAIRNE TRENCH, TOUVENT FARM, BASIN WOOD, EUSTON DUMP, LA SIGNY FARM. K.30 c etc. Night firing K.30 a. We fired on	

1875 Wt. W593/826 1,000,000 4/15 T.B.C. & A. A.D.S.S./Forms/C. 2118.

Army Form C. 2118

WAR DIARY
or
INTELLIGENCE SUMMARY
(Erase heading not required.)

Instructions regarding War Diaries and Intelligence Summaries are contained in F.S. Regs., Part II. and the Staff Manual respectively. Title Pages will be prepared in manuscript.

Place	Date	Hour	Summary of Events and Information	Remarks and references to Appendices
HEBUTERNE			40TH Bde RFA. HEBUTERNE 1/10,000	
HEBUTERNE	26/1/16		Rain. Hostile fire below normal. Enemy shelled OBSERVATION WOOD, MAIRNE & PAPIN TRENCH, TOUVENT FARM. We shelled support communication trenches ~ K 30 a.c. Answered fire in back area. Sniper group in L.S.	
"	27/1/16		Rain. LT GRICE 2nd/1st LT WARRY 2nd/1st LT WILSON + 2nd/1st LT WARBURTON 49 Bty 6" Bty 130 Bty 23rd Bty joined us Bde and are attached to 49 Bty respectively. Hostile fire exceedingly silent normal. K25.c.9.0 shelled. We kept up an intermittent fire on back area during the day. During the night we fired on K30 arc.	
"	28/1/16		Hostility. 9 men return from leave. Reports for wounded. 23rd normal. Enemy shelled COLINCAMPS – EUSTON ROAD with 4.1.3. K27.c shelled with 77 mm during the day. We fired intermittently during the day on back areas in L25.a. During the night in front of SERRE. 9th ROBBINS 23rd Bty wounded in the arm on the ammunition point.	
"	29/1/16	1.30 p	Rain. Major ROBINSON 2/Lt WAKELING return from leave. Born in the front of the Sucrerie during the night by the wind. Hostile fire spasmodic than normal. Shelled K27c. PALESTINE, TAUPIN, CENTRAL AVENUE of EUSTON DUMP, SUCRERIE, Suspicious ammunition munition. We fired on K29d K27d K30arc K30arc. During the night we fired no K29 arc.	
"	30/1/16		Rain. Intermittent shots in the morning in this neighbourhood (K27 c + K23 c (H P)). Every rather active normal. Battery position: Observed seven approaches of enemy near & deport 6 + K23 K7 (HP). Every ambushery active normal. EUSTON DUMP - COLINCAMPS ROAD, TAUPIN, RED COTTAGE, K25+ K27 c (49 Bty) Ranking shelled, the fried on L19d. 3.4 L25.a.6.8. K30 + 5.1. L25.a.68. Every hostile fire on L25a K30 arc	
"	31/1/16		This during the day many night trench shelled. CENTRAL & PALESTINE TRENCHES, SOUTHERN AVENUE & E of COLINCAMPS. One fire on OP's BOX WOOD, and slight firing on K30 arc. Major accepts attends off the strength of the Bde.	

Signed,
O.C. 40th Bde RPA

11/17

3RD DIVISION
DIVL ARTILLERY

40TH BRIGADE R.F.A.
AUG - DEC 1914

3rd Divisional Artillery.

40th BRIGADE R. F. A.

AUGUST 1914.

WAR DIARY 40th Bde R.F.A.
Commencing 5th August 1914

1914
5 Aug.

1st Day of Mobilization

5th to 16th successive days of mobilization procedure normal. Brigade ready to move on 6th day. Remaining days, Drill orders & Gun Drill. Considerable confusion was caused by horses arriving independently from the Horse Collecting Parties with the result that there were no head collars for them. An extra supply of head collars would have avoided this.

Weather very wet the first few days, but very hot afterwards.

<u>Note</u> War diary up to 17th Aug. was lost with baggage at Le Cateau (23rd Aug)

2

Aug 17th
7.45am Leave AMESBURY Station as per programme

9.45 am Arrive SOUTHAMPTON

18th
3.0am Leave SOUTHAMPTON DOCKS in S.S. Indore. Horse accommodation bad & made loading very slow

6.0pm Arrive HAVRE. Unloading arrangements bad, dock cranes not powerful enough to lift guns

19th
7.0am Leave docks for REST CAMP

2.30pm Orders to entrain at 10.30pm

10.30pm Commence entraining

20th
3.0am Leave HAVRE

20" Cont.	
5.15 pm	Arrive BUSIGNY
6.15 pm	" AULNOYE & detrain
10.30 pm	Billet at BERLAIMONT. 49" B'de arrive 2 am
21st	
7.0 am	Move: joined by 23rd at AULNOYE from LANDRECIS. Route HARGNIES — LA LONGVILLE
2.30 pm	— GOGNIES. Billet ½ mile S of GOGNIES
12 mn	Amm. Col. arrive at ~~Bettigny~~ BETTIGNY
22nd	
6 am	March in 3 cols northwards. Starting point BONNET (7 am)
3 pm	Arrive MESVIN & billet. Whole Bde present for first time. Positions on HAUT LE BOIS reconnoitred

23rd Aug	
5·0 am	Ready to move. First wet day: Fine later
10-11 am	Take up positions reconnoitred

6" Bty covered on Eastern spur of HAUT LE BOIS
    facing NE.
Targets Bty coming into action on BINCH – MONS
    road Rg 3200˟
    Also a few Inf moving West

23rd Bty Semi covered: top of HAUT LE BOIS
    facing East
Targets Inf moving South Rg 3000˟
    Bty " " " "

49" Bty
A 1 Section at pt. 62 N of N in MONS.
B 2 " On HAUT-LE-BOIS facing NE
A close support of Mdx. Regt.
B.

6 pm	Enemy attacking road MONS – GIVRY

+ Enemy appear in rear of 6" Bty

Guns formed in a circle. Gordon Highlanders
in intervals. No attack by enemy

23rd con't 7:30 pm	Guns withdrawn by hand & hooked in at bottom of hill. Retire to ~~Nouveller~~ NOUVELLES; continuous attacks on MONS-BINCH road repulsed by our Inf
12 mn	Bivouac at NOUVELLES
	<u>Note</u> Maj MAIDLOW missing badly wounded Capt LYSTER left at NOUVELLES hurt Lieut HEPPER RAMC. Left with dressing Sta
24th Aug 5 am	Enemy shell 42nd Bde (?). Positions looked for just N of NOUVELLES. None suitable. Retire
9.0 am	to a position near NORCHAIN. No target
11 am	Further retirement to position NW of QUEVY-LE-PETIT. 6" shell enemy's Bty near FRAMERIES. Enemy's shell burst in

		6
24" Cont	our teams located by aeroplane; 3-4 horses killed	
2pm appr	Retire: route:— BLAREGNIES — BAVAI —	
8pm	AMFROIPRET. Billet there	

<u>Note</u>
  Difficulty in getting supplies. They were dumped near by but no wagons to fetch them. Eventually brought up in motor lorry

25" Aug 5 am	Retire via — WARGNIES — LE QUESNOY —
	ROMERIES — SOLESMES — VIESLY —
4pm	BAUDRY Billets Heavy showers

26" Aug 4.30 am	Move & take up a position behind
	AUDINCOURT. 6 & 23rd to W & 49th E
	No enemy guns definitely located.
	6 Battery shell wood in which enemy were

26" cont'd	massing with great effect in spite of heavy fire on themselves. Rg 2200ˣ
	23" & 49" fire on Inf advancing between 2800ˣ - 3500ˣ
4 pm	Order to retire. Bde gets away except 3 guns of 6"B'y for which there were no horses. Retire via MONTIGNY — ELLINCOURT — BEAUREVOIR (9 pm) Long halt gradually move on at dawn
	<u>Note</u> Bde Cooks Wagon lost
27ᵗʰ Aug	Retire via BELLICOURT — HARGICOURT —
9 am	4 hours halt ordered at COLOGNE positions reconnoitred
11 am	Enemy began to shell BELLICOURT
	Order to retire ~~via~~ VILLERET —

27 cont'd	— LE VERGUIER — VERMAND
	23rd B'ty takes up a position near BOIS DE G'D PRIEL. No target. Return through Le VERGUIER & take up a position on ridge N of VERMAND. Remainder of Bde march'd will 8" Inf'y G road.
6.7 pm	Bde arrives at VERMAND: halt on road; cook meal; & pick up supplies
12 m'n	Start night march via
28 Aug	MARTEVILLE — ETRIELLERS — FLUQUIERS —
5 am	HAM (halt outside. N)
9-11 am	Retired through HAM

28th Aug	23rd take up position in HAM. No target
afternoon	23rd & 6th in action ½ mile E of GUISCARD no target
6-7pm	Billet at GENVRY
29th Aug 11-12am	Bde take up position W of CRISOLLES with 9th Inf Bde as Rear Guard. No targets
6pm	Retire via NOYONS — PONTOISE — CUTS
30th Aug 12.5am	Halt at CUTS from 12mn to 5am
5am	Retire via HAMPCEL — Nu MOULIN — BERNY-RIVIERE — VIC-SUR-AISNE
4pm	COURTIEUX Billets

11

Aug 31st
7am

Retire via MONTIGNY — MORTFONTAINE — VIVIERES — VILLERS COTTERETS — VAUCIENNES — VAUMOISE (4pm) & billet. Railway at Crepy blown up during night; soon repaired.

R.J.J. Elkington Lt. Col.
Comdg. 60th Bde.

Major R.A. Anstruther DSO
late R.F.A.

STATION
KILCONQUHAR

CAIRNIE
COLINSBURGH
FIFE

16.2.23.

Dear Sir

I see you ask in the "Official History of the War" for records of marches of units of the 3rd Division.

I enclose a record for the XL Bde R.F.A. of which I was Adjutant at the time.

I can supply, if required, a record of all moves of this Bde up to 16th January 1915.

Yrs truly
R A Anstruther

Marches of XL Bde. R.F.A. from Aug 20th to Sept 5th

August 1914.
20th   6th & 49th Btys & H.Q. detrained Aulnoye
        billetted Berlaincourt.

21st   Marched 7am. Harguies, la Longueville, Frignies,
(14 miles).   Goegnies (23rd Battery joined during march).

22nd   Marched 6am. Bonnet, Mesvin
(9 miles)   Ammn column joined.

23rd   Into action Haute le Bois 11am. Withdrew to
(4 miles)   Nouvelles after dark.

24th   Marched 5am Genly, Quevy-le-Petit, Blaregnies,
(18 miles).   Bavai, Amfroidpret.

25th   Marched 5.am. Varguies, Le Quesnoy, Romeries,
(21 miles)   Solesmes, Viesely, Caudry.

26th   Into action 4.30am near Audencourt. Retired 4 pm.
(14 miles)   by Montigny, Elincourt, Beaurevoir.

27th   Marched 4.30am. Bellicourt, Cologne, Le Verguier,
(18 miles)   Vermand.

28th   Marched midnight Attilly, Etreillers, Fluquieres,
(22 miles)   Ham, Guiscard, Genvry.

29th   In position near Crisolles, Retired 6pm by Noyon,
(12 miles)   Pontoise, Cuts (halt for 4 hours.)

30th   Marched 5am. Nampeel, Moulin, Berny Riviere,
(12 miles.)   Vic-sur-Aisne, Courtieux.

31st   Marched 7.30am Montigny, Mortefontaine, Vivieres,
(15 miles)   Villers Cotterets, Vaucienne, Vaumoise.

1st Sept.   Marched 3am Gondreville, Levignen, Fresnoy,
(13 miles)   Villers St Genest, Cherreville.

2nd   Marched 4am. Bregy, Forfry, Genres,
(9 miles)   Montyon.

3rd   Marched 7.30am. Penchard, Meaux, Boutigny,
(11 miles)   Vaucourtois.

4th   Marched 4pm. Sancy, la Chapelle, Tigeaux,
(20 miles.)   Neufmontier, Chatres, Liverdy,
        Retal. Arrived 5am on 5th.

5th   Rest.

Total Miles 212.

3rd Divisional Artillery.

40th BRIGADE R. F. A.

SEPTEMBER 1914.

XL Brigade R.F.A.

Date 1914	Miles	
6th Sept.	15	Marched 5.30 a.m. Chatres, Neufmontier, La Houssaye, Crevecoeur, Hautefeuille 10. p.m.
7th "	13	Marched 10 a.m. Faremoutiers, Les Charmes, Les Parichets, Coulommiers, La Bretonniere, Chauffry. 7 p.m.
8th "	8	Marched 5 a.m. Le Plessier, St Denis, Rebais, Gibraltar (in action) Orly 8 p.m.
9th "	6	Marched 6.45 a.m. Bussieres, Nanteuil, Croutles 7.30 p.m.
10th "	13	" 5 a.m. Besu le Guery, Ventelet F^me, Platriere, Marigny, Veuilly la Poterie, Chezy. 6.30 p.m. (Rain)
11th "	9	Marched 7.30 a.m. Dammard, Neuilly St Front, Vichel, Oulchy la Ville (Rain)
12th "	12	Marched 6 a.m. La Grand Rozoy, Launoy, Les Croutles, Maast, Braine 5 p.m. (Rain)
13th "	4	Marched for Chassemy 6 a.m. Shelled. Retired 1 mile at dusk
14th "	17	" 3 a.m. Crossed to Vailly after long wait. No positions available. Retired by Soupir, Pont Arcy, Canal Bridge (badly shelled) Vieil Arcy, 1 mile S of Brenelle.
15th & 16th		In reserve.
17th & 18th		2 Batteries in action near Brenelle.
19th		Reserve in Braine. Came in after dark 18th
20th		Relieved 42nd Bde E of Chassemy after dark.
25th – 28th		In reserve. Braine & on 28th Chateau Belleue.
29th		Into action near caves further East opp. Soupir.
1st Oct.	17½	Marched 9 pm Braine, Augy, Curie Housse, Arcy, Bengneux, Oulchy le Chateau 2.30 am (2nd).
2nd "	10½	Marched 7.30 pm. Oulchy-la-Ville, Rozet St Albin, Vichel, Chouy, Noroy, - Troesnes, 2 am (3rd).
3rd "	18½	Marched 6 pm. La Ferté Milon, Fort de Domaniel, Coyolles, Vaumoise, Crepy en Valois 1 am.
4th "	13	Marched 6 pm. Duvy, Rully, Raray, Villeneuve, Roberval 11.30 pm.
5th "	7½	Marched 3 pm. Rhuis, Verberie, Le Mieux. Entrained
6th "	6.	Arrived Abbeville 8 am. Detrained. Marched to Le Titre.
7th & 8th		Halt.

9th Oct	13	Marched 2 am La Motte Buleux, Crecy, Dompierre, Rayz 7.30 am. Started again 5.15 pm.
10th "		Rachinette, Guigny, Le Quesnoy, St George, Fresnoy,
	25	Incourt, Eclimeux, Humeroeuille, Bermicourt, Fleury, Le Marais, Hestrus, Taugry, Sains les Pernes. 5 am.
11th "	14	Marched 8 am. Taugry, Pernes, Floringhem, Auchel, Allouauge, Pont de Rerillon, Choques, Hinges 6 pm.
12th "	5	Marched 8 am Cornet Malo, La Croix Marmuse. Sections in action
13th "		Marched 5 am. Vielle Chappelle. Sections in action over canal.
14th – 16th		All guns in action E of canal.
17th		Advanced Croix Barbee, Rouge Croix, Fauquissart.
18th – 21st		Batteries in action near Aubers.
22nd ✱		Withdrew to Fauquissart, & later to positions near La Flinque & Fauquissart.
4th & 5th Nov.		Reserve 1 mile E of Vielle Chappelle.
6th to 9th "		In action near Neuve Chappelle.
10th to 14th "		Reserve at Fosse.
15th "		Marched 8.45 am. Lestrem, Estaires, Trou Bayard, Doulieu, Noot Boom, Vieux Berquin 6.30 pm.
16th "		Marched 6 am. Neuve Eglise, Dranoutre, Locre. Relieved French in action near Kemmel Farm.
29th to 3rd Dec.		In reserve near Berthen
4th to 11th		In action near Kemmel.
12 & 13		Reserve near Berthen
14th & 15th		In readiness during attack on Petit Bois etc
17th to 26th		In action near Kemmel.
26th to 1st Jan.		In reserve near Berthen
1st to 11th		In action near Kemmel
11th to 16th		In reserve St Jans Cappel.

September 1914

1st Sept	
5 am	Ready to Move
8 am	Retire via GRONDVILLE — LEVIGNEN
	Bde later up a position facing NW
	just N of V in LEVIGNEN in case of attack
	5th Divn on left appears to be engaged
	from sound of firing
4 pm	Continue retirement via FRESNOYE —
	VILLIERS ST GENEST — CHEVREVILLE —
8 pm	& billet
2nd Sept	
4 am	Retire via BREGY — FORFRY — GESVRES —
12 noon	MONTHYON & billet
2 pm	Reconnoitre positions near MARCHE

3rd Sept	
7.30am	Retire via PENCHARD — MEAUX — Reconnoitring patrol sent to high ground S of FUBLANE. Bridges at MEAUX blown up. Continue retirement via BOUTIGNY. Bde takes up position
2pm	reconnoitred to cover retirement
7pm	Billet at VAUCOURTOIS
4 Sept	
	Remain in billets till 4pm. Reconnoitre positions near LA BRETAGNE
4pm	Retire via SANCY — LA CHAPELLE — TIGEAUX — Obelisque 1½ miles W of MORTCERF — NEUFMONTIERS. March all night

		14
5ᵗʰ Sept	Night March	JM
4am	CHARTRES — LIVERDY — RETAL	
7am	Billet & Rest	
6ᵗʰ Sept		
5:30am	Advance started again via LIVERDY — CHARTRES — NEUFMOUTIER — Halt till 1·0pm move will	
1pm	8 Inf Bde as Reserve à LA HOUSSAY Short Halt — CREVECOEUR	
10pm	— HAUTFEUILLE & bivouack	
7ᵗʰ Sept		
10·0 am	March via FAREMOUTIERS — LES CHARMES — LE PONCET — LES PARICHETS ST PIERRE — COULOMMIERS —	

7 Sept cont	— LES CAPUCINS — LA BRETONNIERE — LES CORVILLES — CHAUFFRY
7pm	& billet
8 Sept	
5·0 am	Move as **Advanced** Guard via LE PLESSIER — ST DENIS — REBAIS —
10 am	GIBRALTAR. 23rd & 49th just E of road
	Targets 23rd Bn Inf in wood just W of BUSSIERES & retiring from it: Range 3700 – 5000
	49th Bn Battery in concealed position very near HERMETIERE exact position not certain Range 4000ˣ aprox
	2nd Position CHAMALION. Target Inf retiring over sky line due N Range 5300
	and Flashes of battery in same direction Range 5300ˣ

		16
8" cont	6 took up a position ¾ mile SW of GIBRALTAR did not shoot.	
	1 gun later gg run down into wood in front of GIBRALTAR fired one round as gun retired	
	Enemy retire from ORLY between 5 & 6	
8 pm	Billet in ORLY	
Sept 9th		
6.45 am	Move with 8" Inf Bde in Reserve via BUSSIERES — VILARÉ — NANTEUIL	
9 am	Halt at bridge from 9 am till 6.30 pm. Move into billets at ~~CHARTERS~~ CROUTTES.	

Note. Henry Farman 352 fired at by Enemy lands safely 5.15 pm.

17

Sept 10th 5·0 am	Move via BEZU-LE-GUERY — VENTELET
	Fm — PLATRIERE — MARIGNY —
6·30 pm	VEUILLY-LA-POTERIE — CHEZY & billet
Note	& day Wet night, Many signs of hasty retreat of En. Divn take 500–600 prisoners

Sept 11th	
7·30 am	Move via DAMMARD — NEUILLY —
3 pm	VICHET — & OULCHY-LA-VILLE & billet
Note	Wet day & night

Sept 12th	
6 am	Move via ~~Nepan~~ LE GRAND-ROZOY —
	LAUNOY — CROUTTES — MAAST —
5 pm	S of CUIRY HOUSSE — BRAINE & Billet
Note	Very wet day & night

13 Sept	
5:0 am	Move as A.G. with 8 Inf Bde via road to CHASSEMY. Shelled on emerging from wood ½ mile from CHASSEMY.
	6" & 23rd form up under cover of woods
	49th come into action in front of wood. Shelled by En. Heavy How. all day especially 49th Bty who withdraw detachments to Wagon line
	49th lose 2 guns & 1 wagon & several men. Lieut Owen killed Lieut. Bateman Wounded.
7 pm	Batteries withdraw at dusk & bivouack in rear of woods.

		19
14th Sept		

3am	Move to VAILLY & wait for pontoon bridge to be completed
5.30am	Cross AISNE into VAILLY & move into valley immediately E of St PIERRE up to Chateau. No Arty. position Enemy's Inf begin to attack hills above Retire to N edge of VAILLY & reconnoitre positions S of ROUGE MAISON. No suitable position.
1-2pm	En begin to get round left of 8th Inf Bde, 40th Bde retires along SOUPIR road shelled very slightly with shrapnell Bridge at CHAVONNE broken; go on to PONT ARCY. Heavily shelled

14th Sept Cont'd | with High explosive crossing canal
| bridge Lieut. Armstrong RAMC killed
| Lieut. Archibald wounded
|
| 6-8 men killed
| 20-30 horses killed
|
| Retire via VIEIL ARCY & report to
| C.R.A. ordered to come into action
| (2 & 3 & 6) near 3rd E of BRENELLE
| En positions out of Range
8 am | Bivouac ½ S of BRENELLE

15 Sept
4:30 am | Move & take up a position in Reserve
| just NE of BRENELLE
6 pm | Return to same bivouac

16th Sept		21
4 am	In Reserve in same place as on 15th	
3 pm	Relieve 23rd Bde 23rd & 6th on N slope of embank West of BRENELLE 49th In Reserve	
6 pm	Move to billets at Chateau BELLEME	

17th Sept	
5 am	In action in same positions Various targets Infy & Guns West of FOLEMPRISE Fm. Guns very hard to locate. Return to billets at dusk. Ranges between 5000ˣ – 5500ˣ Guns left in position with gunners Horses to billets

18 Sept	
5.30 am	In action. Targets same as 17" except one Bty located ½ mile SW of FOLEMPRISE Fm behind wood. Our Observing Sta shelled a 8.30 am
4.30 pm	Bde relieved by by 23rd Bde, & moves into billets in BRAINE
19" Sept	Rest
	1 complete section joins Bde 1 Sub to 49th 1 " " 6 Making 49" & 6" 4 gun Btys 23rd

20th Sept		Rest till 6pm
6pm		Bde moves to relieve 42nd Bde ½ mile W of pt 164: not in position till 9pm. Horses & men in caves
	Note.	Weather wet on & off since 12" Oct
21st Sept		Same positions. Targets. Entrenches & guns between ROUGEMAISON & FOLEMPRISE Fm. Heavy How's shell position & vicinity at odd intervals no damage done Weather Fine

22nd Sept	Same positions & targets as 21st. Fine
23rd Sept	Same positions & targets as 22nd. Fine
24th	Same. 1 Section 23rd sent to a position 600x S of Bde position in order to shoot up OSTEL VALLEY does not fire
25th Sept 6.30pm	Same. Bde withdraws to billets in BRAINE
26th Sept	Rest

27" Sept 5 am	Alarm Message. "En reported crossing CONDE' BRIDGE in large numbers" False all quiet by 6.30 am Rest.
28" Sept 2 pm 5 pm	Bde Cmdr & BC's to RA HQ by 2pm Bde clear of Billet 4pm BC's examine previous position taken up by 42nd Bde R.F.A. Billet at Chateau BELLEME
29" Sept	Bde Moves to position. 49th 1.30am 8" 4.0 am 23rd in Res at Chateau

29" Cont'd	Bde HQ at LA GRANDE CARRIERE
	49th 2 Sections 600ˣ ~~on either side~~ E & W of HQ
	6th 1 Section 600ˣ to S of HQ
	Remain Section in Res NE of BRENELLE.
	Lt X 49th wld be exposed if it fired.
	All Horses with Reserve section.
	Target ~~gun~~ En trenches opposite the guards & En guns in vicinity. Not much firing
30th Sept	Same very little firing

R.G.F. Elkington
Lt. Col. R.F.A.
Comdg 45th Bde R.F.A.

3rd Divisional Artillery.

40th BRIGADE R.F.A.

OCTOBER 1914.

WAR DIARY, 40th Bde RFA
October 1914

1st Oct	Same positions as 30th Sept. Very little firing on either side
6.30 pm	Bde receives order to move at 7.30 pm leaving 2 Section in action. *Note* not enough notice given; result Bde did not leave BRAINE till 9 pm
9 pm	Night march via AUGY — CUIRY HOUSSE — ARCY — BEUGNEUX — OULCHY-LE-
2:30 am	CHATEAU going into billets; all vehicles & horses & men to be under cover from aeroplanes. *Note.* Very cold night

Oct 2nd	In billets all day
7.30pm	Move via OULCHY-LA-VILLE — [ROZET-ST-ALBIN — VICHEL — CHOUY — NOROY] to
2.0 am	TROENES — billet under as before
2.	

3 Oct	Misty day
6 pm	Move via LA-FERTÉ-MILON — [D of FORET DOMANIALE — F in FORET] — COYELLES — VAUMOISE — CREPY-EN-VALOIS arrive 1 am & billet

4th Oct	Move 6pm HQ: 23rd Bde: ½ am bn with 8 Inf Bde via DUVY — [RULLY — RARAY — VILLENEUVE] ROBERVAL arrive 11.30 pm

4 Oct cont	Billet.
6 pm	6ᵗʰ - 49ᵗʰ - ⅔ Amm col. move [via
	BETHANCOURT — Cr de VAUDRAMPONT]
	BREVIERE & billet 10 pm
5 Oct	Billet (HQ: 23: ⅓ Amm Col)
3 pm	Move [via RHUIS — VERBERET] —
7 pm	LE MEUX HALTE entrain at 7 pm
11 pm	Leave 11 pm. [Left 3 Amm Wgs at LE MEUX owing to insufficient accommodation]
1 pm	6ʰ: 49ʰ: ⅔ Amm Col. move to COMPEIGNE arrive 4 pm entrain at COMPEIGNE 7 pm Leave 10 pm

Bde less 49th

6th Oct 8.0 am	By train [via CREIL — AMIENS] ABBEVILLE [wait till 2pm] & detrain move to billets [via HAUTVILLERS] to LE TITRE 49th go on to ETAPLES but come back & detrain at NOYELLES billet at NOUVION
7th Oct	Rest. 5 Remounts arrive 3 Wgns 23rd turn up 49th join Bde again
8th Oct 9th 2 am	2pm Orders for billeting parties to move at 4pm Bde move 2 am
9th Oct	Night march [via LA MOTTE BULEUX — CRECY — DOMPIERRE] RAYE & billet at 7.30 am

Oct 9th Cont.	Move at 5.15 p.m. ~~main~~ (8th F. Amb. RE 40th Bde)
	Via 1 in ROCHINETTE — GUIGNY —
	LEQUESNOY — ST GEORGES — FRESNOY
	— INCOURT — ECLIMEUX — HUMEROEILLE
	— BERMICOURT
10th Oct	— FLEURY — LE MARAIS — HESTRUS
	— TANGRY — SAINS-LEZ-PERNES &
	billet 5 a.m.
	Note 8th Inf Bde move in Motor Lorries
	Bde joins divisional Arty near GUIGNY
	Rest
Oct 11th 8 a.m.	Move 8 a.m via TANGRY — PERNES —
	FLORINGHAM — AUCHEL — ALLOUANGE
	— PONT-DE-REVEILLON — CHOQUES
6 p.m	HINGES & billet 6 p.m

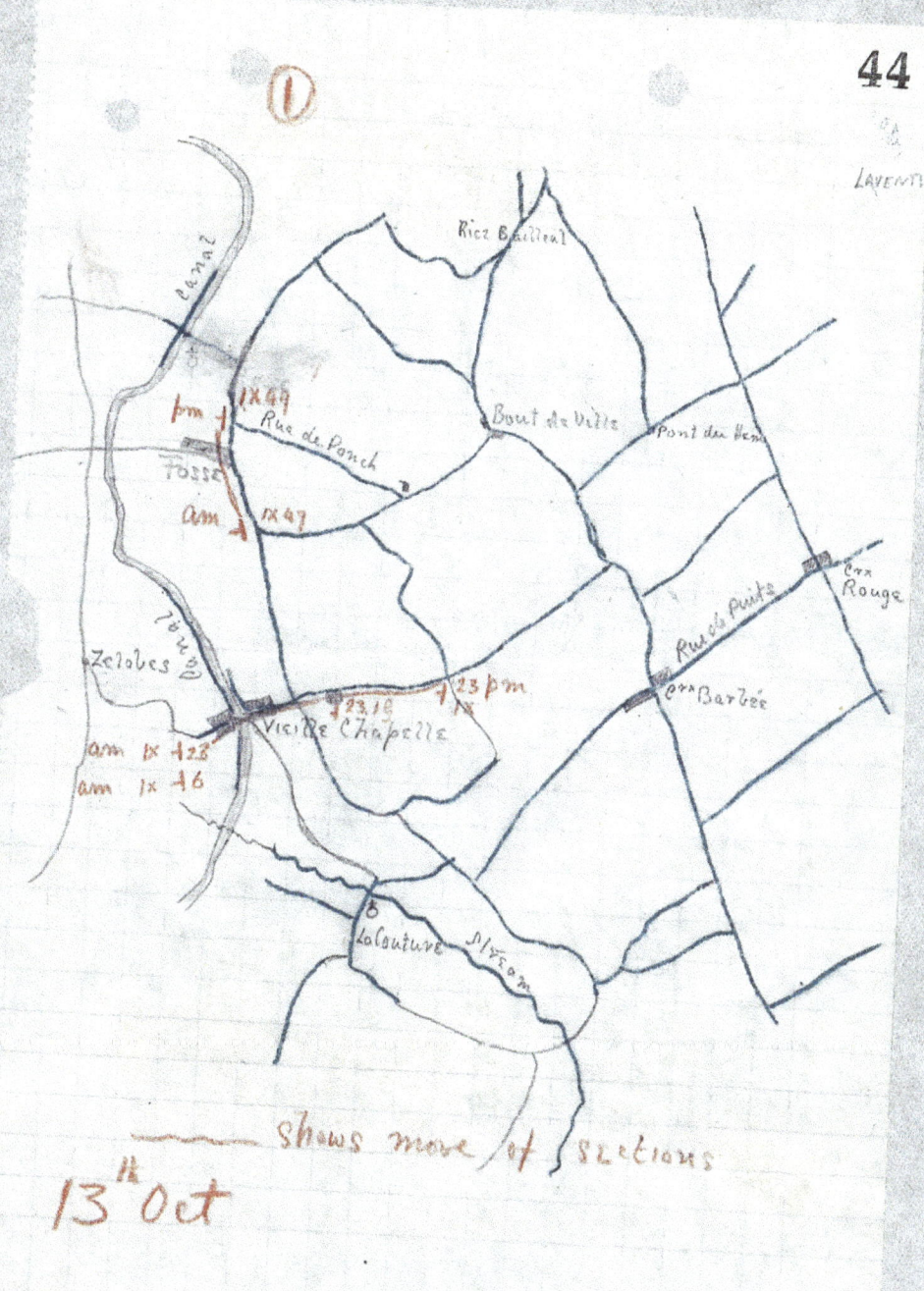

12"0	Move 8 am 23rd A.G. via CORNET MALO
afternoon	LA C?? MARMUSE.
	1 Sect Lig in action MARMUSE
	1 " 6th " " just N of V & VIEILLE CHAPELLE
	also 1 Sect How? on Rt of 6th
	Inf hold canal & cross later.
	Go into billets at 6pm 500x S of LA u
	LA MARMUSE in 3 Fms

13th Oct

5am	Move at 5am into same positions +
	23rd bring 1 Section on Rt of 6th Section
	49th ————— E of LA MARMUSE
9am	49th & 23rd push section across canal
	49th LA FOSSE
	23rd 11 in VIEILLE CHAPELLE & forward
6pm	Billet at VIELLE CHAPELLE 6pm
	See map attached ①

45

②

Rue Bailleul

Rue de Ponch.
1×49 Pont de Ville
TOSSS1×49   1×49   Pont du Hem
How1
How 1×
1×
49
23 H₃W 23 1×   Crx Barbré
+15 +1×   6 1×
Vieille Chapelle   1 1×   How
Crx Rouge
Rue du Puits

La Couture Stream

— 14ᵗʰ
• 15ᵗʰ   ⁓ moves of Section

14th O^t 4.10am	Move 4 am for position see attached sketch ②
Note	very difficult country for artillery. Guns & sections were pushed up almost into the firing line with observing officers actually in the firing line connected by telephones. Lot of shooting done <u>entirely</u> by map
15 Oct	Gen situation Same as 14th position marked in green on map ②
16 Oct	Same as 15th. ~~Other~~ Inf take line on main road at night

17th Oct	
9 am	Advd with 8 Inf Bde as Reserve via CROIX BARBÉE — ROUGE CROIX — CHAPIGNY — FAUQUISSART
	49th in action to assist French Cav dismounted attack on FROMELLES
	Fire from 1pm to 2pm
	Billet at ~~Barrosa~~ LES MOTTES Fm ½ mile W of AUBERS
18th Oct	
7.30 am	Ready to move
10 am	Move to "position of readiness" just W of Ht POMMERAU Fm
11 am	49th in action at LE PLOUICH Fm firing at FOURNES

35

18th Oct 1pm	23rd in action ¼ mile W of Ht POMMERAU Fm Observing Officer with Wilts at INVENTURE Fm. Target: En trenches road between Illies & Chateau 6" in action near 49th Targets Fournes 3200x supporting French Cav attack (dismounted)
19th Oct 5am	Move at 5am 23rd in action as on 18th remainder in Reserve on road ½ SW of POMMERAU Fm
11am	49th in action at this place [Target FOURNES & PILLY] 6" in — just N of AUBERS Target Fournes & Pilly

(sketch map: Fromelles, Le Plouich Fm, AUBERS, 6")

20th Oct 5.30am	6th in action 5.30 am
	Forward Officer at Le RIEZ connected by telephone. very satisfactory
	directs fire on ground E of PILLY
	& also on to En Battery & silences it
12 noon	49 & 23rd in action on left of 6th
	Shell BAS FLANDRES & ROSEMBOIS
	& materially repulse German attack
6pm	Retire to billets 1 Section 23rd left in action.

21st Oct 6.30am	In action same positions & targets as 20th.
	Billet 49th Section left in action

22ⁿᵈ Oct	
3 am	Alarm. En broken through: 49 Sectⁿ withdrawn. False Alarm.
6.30	Bde in Action as before & fire at RIEZ & vicinity. (less 6ᵗʰ) Trench leave FROMELLES. Our Left flank rather exposed. 49ᵗʰ Bty withdrawn to X Rds FAUQUISSART 6ᵗʰ in Reserve at FAUQUISSART
6 pm	All Batteries withdrawn to FAUQUISSART Billet Here
10 pm	Orders to Limbers up & take up position W of FLEURBAIS — NEUVE CHAPELLE Road, reconnoitred previously.

23rd Ut Positions

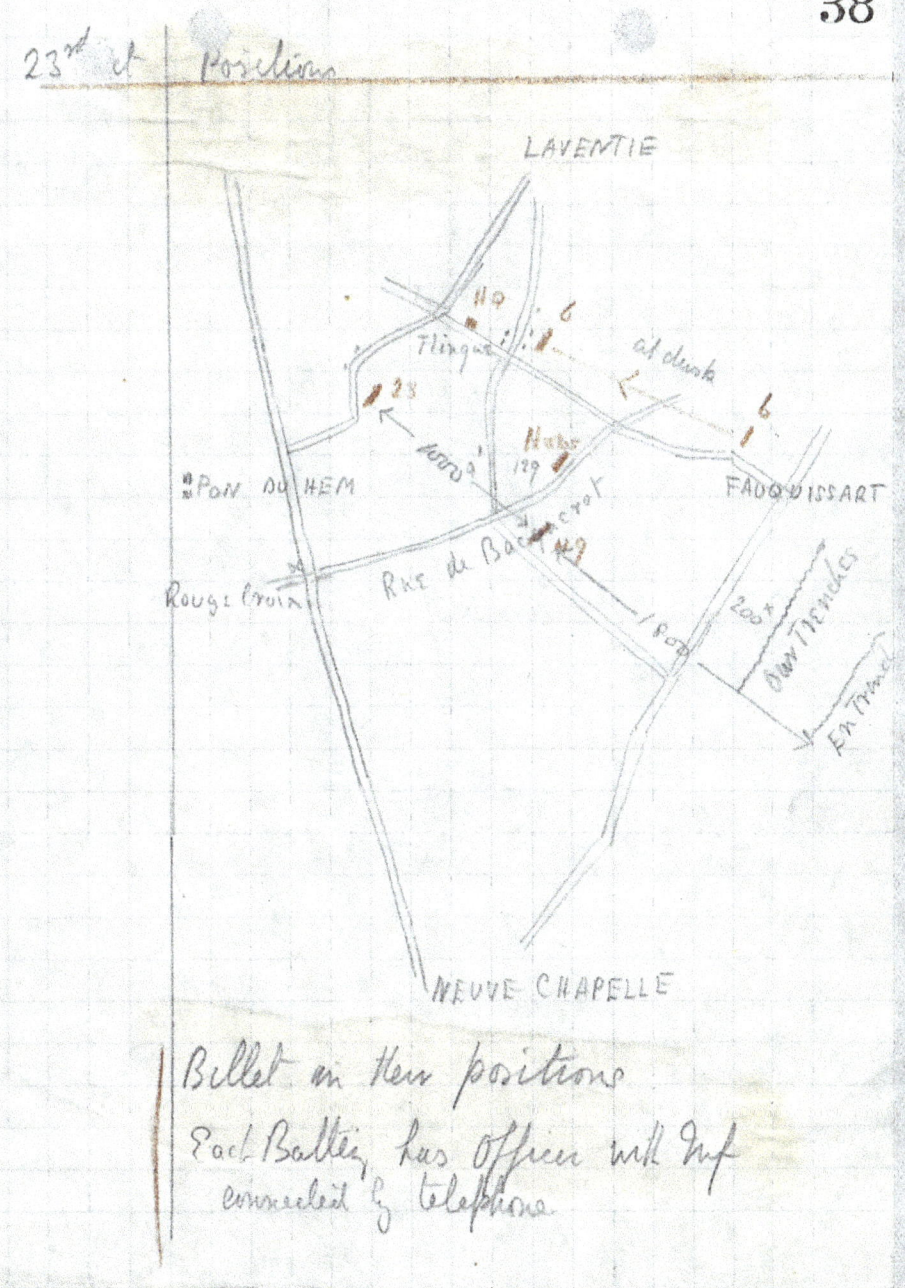

Billet in their positions
Each Battery has Officer with Inf
connected by telephone

24th Oct	Same positions. 1 Section each battery at its post each night. Several attacks during night. All orders to Batteries to fire at En trenches & heavy firing heard in their zone during night
25th Oct I.	Same as 24th occasional attacks
26th Oct	Same as 25th
27th Oct	Same as 26th 1 or 2 casualties men & horses from ours. None of the Batteries have apparently been located by En

28th Oct	No change. Frequent firing at night. No very serious attacks
29th Oct	No change
30th Oct	Rumour of being relieved. Finally 1 Bde to be relieved at a time for reserve
31st Oct	II Corps are relieved except 8th Inf Bde of Indian Corps

1/11/14

R. J. Welken ? Lt. Col. R.F.A.
Comdg 40th Bde. R.F.A.

40

40th Bde. R.A.

Date	Killed	Officers Wounded	Missing	Killed	Other Ranks Wounded	Missing
14.10.14					1	
15.10.14					2	
28.10.14		2/Lt Gow Renwick			1	
2.11.14						

3rd Divisional Artillery.

40th BRIGADE R. F. A.

NOVEMBER 1914.

War Diary. 40 Bde RFA Nov. 191[ ]

NOVEMBER

1st Nov.	Position & situation same as on 31st October
2nd Nov. 1pm	23" & 6" turn their fire onto ground in front of 9th Ghurka trenches N of Y in PONT LOGY
	8" Inf Bde HQ. heavily shelled from 12 till 4pm
3rd Nov.	No change

4" Nov. 4.30 am	Move to billets at 4.30 am 1 Mile East of VIEILLE CHAPELLE & Rest
5" Nov	Rest. 3pm reconnoitre 42"d Bde positions
6" Nov 4.30 am	Move into 42nd Bde positions see attached sketch (Z). Very misty
7" Nov.	No change still misty

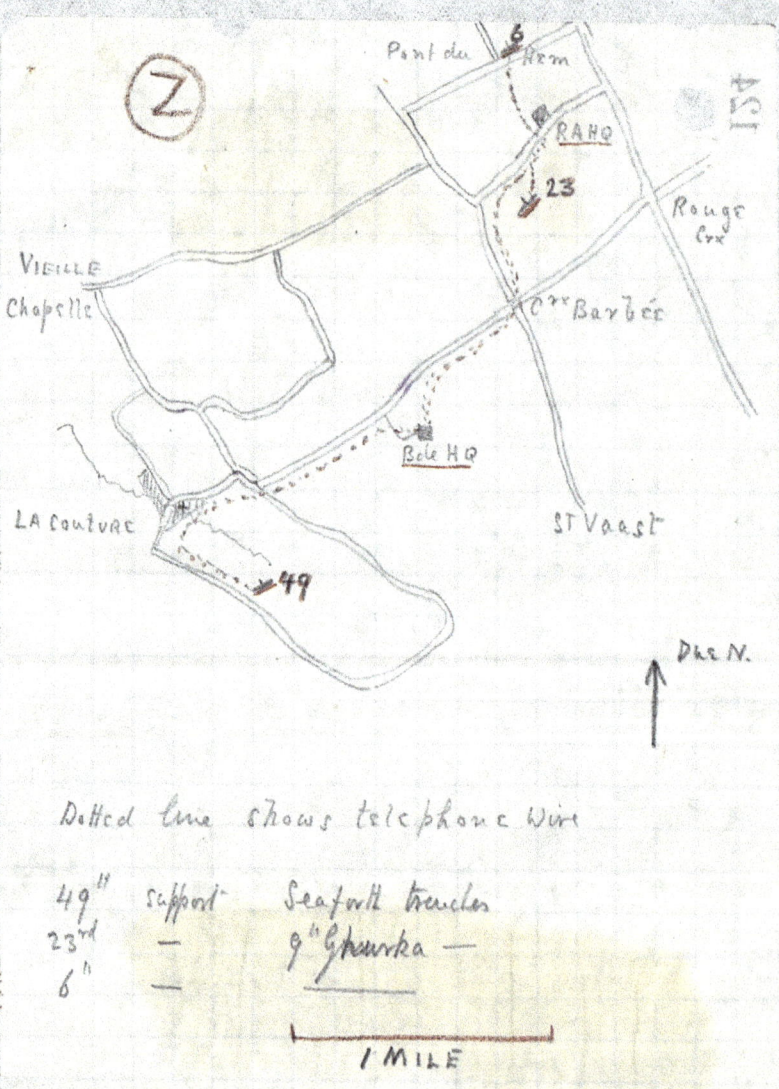

44

8" Nov.	No change; clearer. All batteries remain in action at night. No attack.
	Note: in these positions all batteries had forward observing officers
9" Nov	
Nov 9"	No change.
10" Nov 6 am	Move to billets at Chateau ½ mile N of canal bridge in FOSSE 8 E of canal. Rest.

11th Nov.	Rest Wet & Windy
12th Nov.	Rest except 49th relieve N Battery at 7 am ¼ mile S of 6th Bty last position.
13th Nov	Rest
14th Nov.	Rest N Bty relieve 49th. orders to move next morning

15th Nov.

8.45 am	Bde moves via LESTREM — ESTAIRES — TROU BAYARD — DOULIEUX
12 noon	billet at NOOTE BOOME
3 pm	Turned out by 2nd Cav Divn; wrong area having been allotted to Bde Move to billets in VIEUX BERQUIN arrive 6.30 pm

Note
Rain & wind all day

16th Nov.

6.30 am	Move via road S of NOOTE BOOME — LA LEUTH — NEUVE EGLISE — DRANOUTRE — LOCRE & come into action N Slopes of Mt KEMMEL see sketch Y

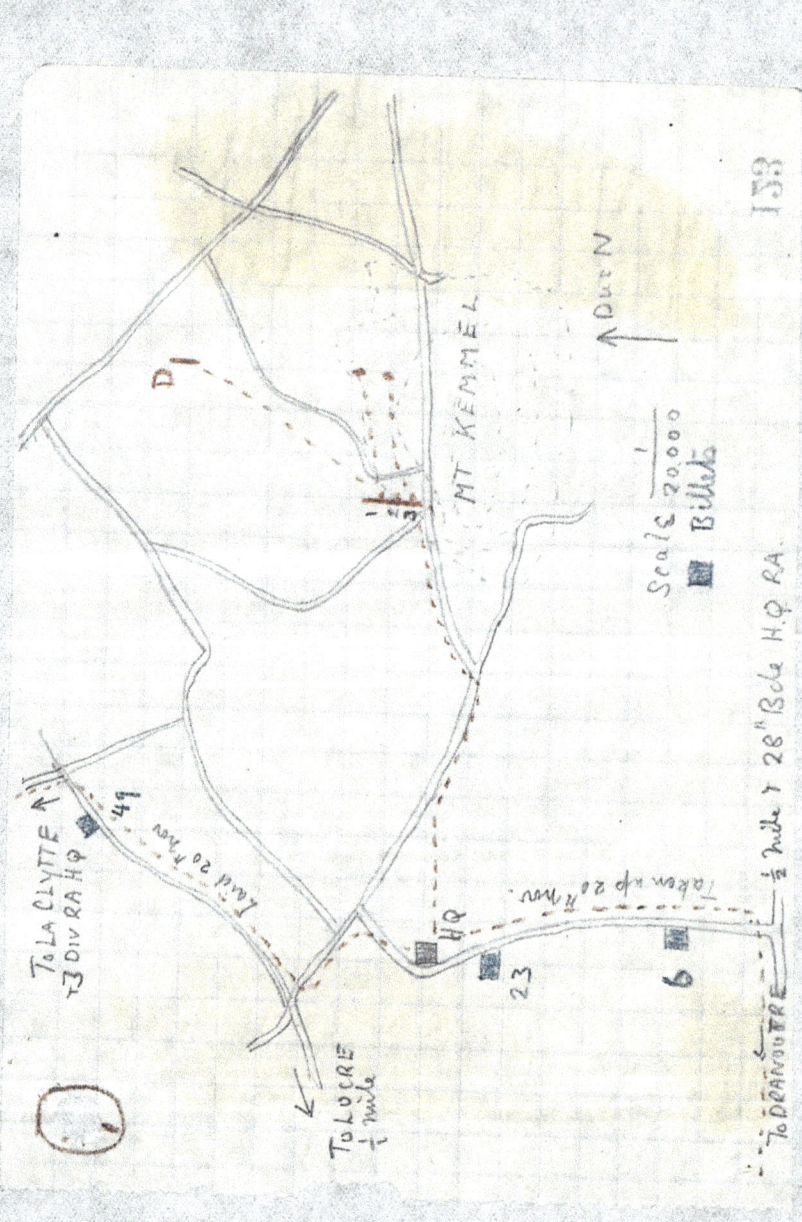

16th Nov. cont.	under 5 Div CRA position occupied see sketch (Y) 1 position French Battery 2 — 23rd " 3 — 6" " Very Wet.
17th Nov.	D Battery & 130th How Battery attached to us. D Battery rest 130 relieve 6" Battery Targets. Ridge running from KEMMEL to WYTSCHAETE & pt 75 D Battery reconnoitres position N's of KEMMEL. Very Wet

Nov 18th	No change. Batteries fire very few rounds. One battery in action at night. One battery always in Reserve. <u>Note</u> Very cold
19th Nov.	How 130 Battery goes away <u>Note</u> Very cold ½ inch of snow. Fine
20th Nov. 10 am	D Battery in action see sketch (Y) French battery leaves Come under CRA 3rd Div. D Battery orders to ~~move~~ join 2nd Cav Div. 1 Section each battery in action at night.

Nov 21st 6.30 am	49th comes into position.
Nov 22nd	No change
Nov 23rd	No change. R.A.H.Q. shelled
Nov 24th	30th Battery (How) come under Bde in action on Left of Bde. R.A.H.Q. at our H.Q Farm
Nov 25th	No change. Misty. Note Re Receive 11 miles of telephone wire. Have been short since Le Cateau

Nov. 26th	No change
Nov 27th	No Change
Nov 28	No change
Nov 29th	From 6.0 – 7.0 am relieved by 42nd Bde – Move to rest billets round Mt KOKEREELE
Nov 30th	Rest. Receive Wire Telephone 4 miles

End of November

<u>Note</u> Very little firing done by our batteries or enemy on the Mt KEMMEL position.

3rd Divisional Artillery.

40th BRIGADE R. F. A.

DECEMBER 1914.

WAR DIARY 40" Bde RFA 63

December 1914

1st Dec. | Rest near Mt KOKEREELE

2nd | Rest. Reconnoitre 23rd Bde positions

3rd
4.30 am | Move into 23rd Bde position
6.30 am | In action. For position see sketch map. (X)

Major INGHAM (OC 23rd Bde) slightly wounded

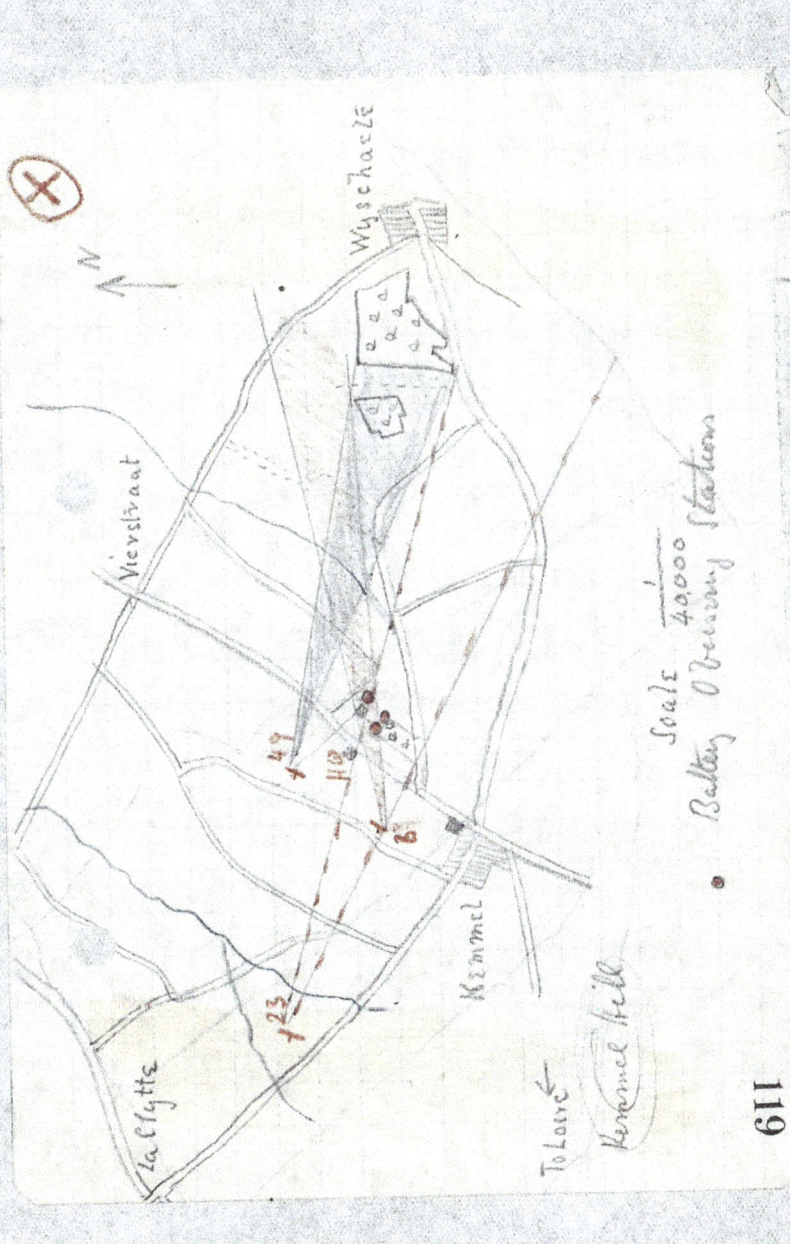

		64
4th Dec	no change	
5th "	no change	
6th "	no change	
7th "	no change	
8th "	no change. 49th Observing Sta shelled OC has to move to Fm 200x North.	

Note. Observing Sta given away by Inf wandering about in front

9th Dec	No Change
10th "	No change
11th 6.30am	Relieved by 42nd Bde go into Rest round Mt Kokerelle again
12th "	Rest
13th "	Rest: orders to move billets on 14th

14th Dec 6.0 am	Bde moves to new billets HQ & 49th In farms on East of LOCRE — DRANOUTRE road.
23rd	Farm ½ mile S of WESTOUTRE
6th	Old billet

Bde remains harnessed up till 4.0 am.

noon
3rd Div'n & 2 French Corps on left attack MESSINES — WYTSCHAETE ridge, supported by R.A. 5th & 4th Div'n.
40th Bde in Reserve.
Some Progress made i.e. Advance in front of PETIT BOIS about 50x

15th D.	Further bombardment no further progress
16th	Operation of last 2 days over Bde takes over from 23rd Bde see sketch map. Ⓦ HQ, 6th & 23rd by 4pm 49th 6.30 am next morning
17th	No change.

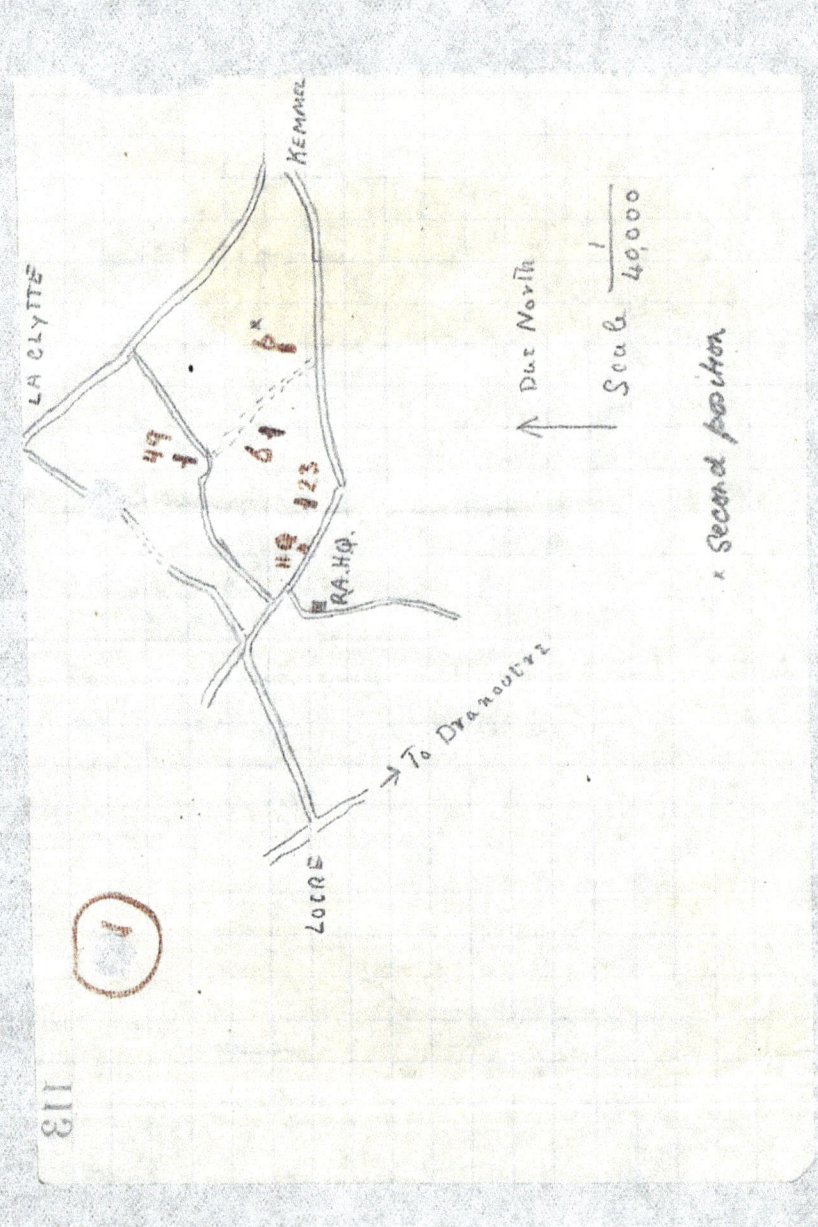

18th | Bombardments under orders of
CRA.
1). 10:0 am to 10:2 am
    10:12   —   10:15 "

2). 1:0 pm to 1:2 pm
    1:12 "   1:15 pm

3). 3:0 pm to 3:2 pm
    3:12 "   3:15 "

Targets
  6"   pound. 74
  23rd   "   73
  49   Petit Bois

15 Rounds per gun at each bombardment.

19th Dec | Same targets: slow rate of fire
40th Bde 12 to 1.0 pm
          & 3.15 pm to 3.45 pm

Bombardment
          3.0 pm to 3.3 pm
          3.12 pm to 3.15 pm

10 rounds per gun

20th | Bombardment
          2.0 pm to 2.3 pm
          2.17 — 2.20 pm

10 rounds a gun

21st Dec	No Change
22nd	No Change
23rd	No Change
24th	During night 24-25 III Div extend their front 500x Southward to point 60. 6" Battery move up to cover new front See sketch (W)

25th Dec	No Change
26th 4.30pm	Relieved by 42nd Bde. Moved into rest billets N.E of Berthern
27th	No Change. Rest.
28th	No Change Rest
29th	No change. Reconnoitre for new positions. Rest

30th Dec.	No change. Reconnoitred 28th Brigade positions. Rest.
31st	No change. Rest.

End of December.

R.G. Elkington
Lt. Col.
Cmdg. 40th Bde. R.F.A.

STATION:
KILCONQUHAR

CAIRNIE
COLINSBURGH
FIFE

10. 4. 23.

I enclose a record of the moves of the XL Brigade R.F.A. from 6th Sept 1914 to 16th Jan 1915 which you asked for in a letter dated 20th February.

I have been away from home ever since then, hence my delay in sending it.

R A Anstruther
Maj. late R.F.A.

Index.

SUBJECT.

3rd DIV.

No.	Contents.	Date.
	R.F.A. 40th BRIGADE. WAR DIARY, JAN - DEC, 1915	

$\frac{121}{4210}$

3rd Division

40th Bde. R.F.A.

Vol VI. 1—31.1.15.

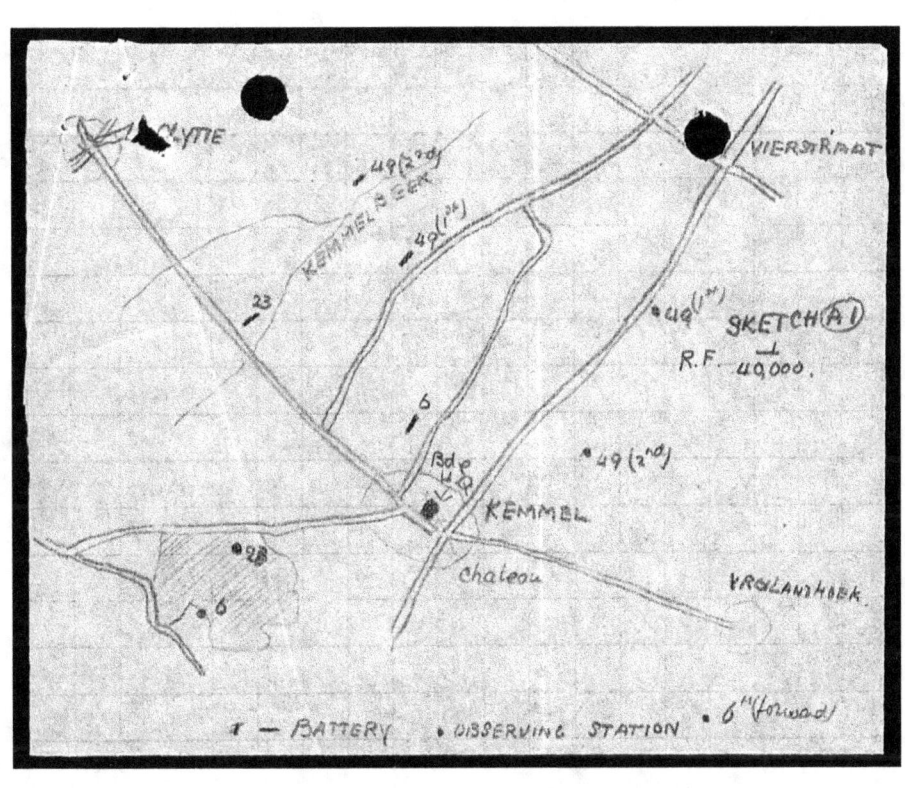

WAR DIARY 40th BRIGADE R.F.A.

January 1915.

Jan: 1st 4.30 am	Move into 23rd Brigade positions.
7.30 am	In action. For positions see sketch map (A.1)
2nd	No change
3rd	No change. 49th Battery observing station shelled. O.C. moves to new one see map (A.1). 49th Battery in line of German guns. O.C. decides to take up new position. Two casualties in 49th Battery.

Jan 4th 7:30am	No change, except that 119th Battery took up new position before 7:30 am
5th	Brigade H.Q. shelled between 1pm and 2pm. No casualties. No change. 7th Inf Bde shares billetts
6th	No change =
7th	No change =
8th	No change. 7th Inf Bde H.Q moved out 9th Inf Bde H.Q moved in.

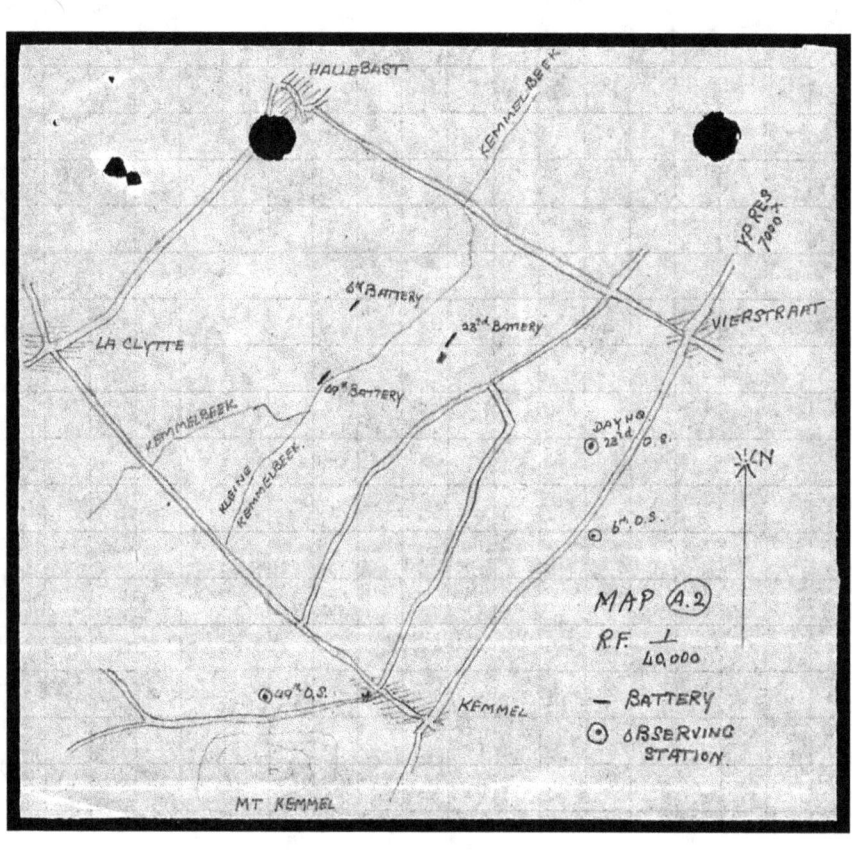

Jan 9th	No change
10th	No change
11th 7.30	Brigade relieved by 23rd Brigade move into rest at St Jean Cappel.
12th	Rest No change
13th	Rest No change
14th	Rest No change. Reconnoitred 42nd Brigade positions.

Jan 15th 7.15am 4.30pm	relieved 42nd Brigade R.F.A in action. see Map. (A.2)	
16th	No change	
17th	No change	
18th	No change	
19th	No change	
20th	No change. Stray shell wounds one man in 119th Battery waggon line	

Jan 21st	no change
Jan 22nd	no change
23rd	no change
24th	no change
25th	no change
26th 5 pm.	relieved by 42nd Brigade R.F.A. moved into rest at St Jean Cappel. Same billetts as last time.

Jan 27th	Rest.	No change
28th	Rest.	No change
29th	Rest.	No change
30th	Rest.	No change
31st	Rest.	No change

R.J.B. Elkington
Lt. Col. R.F.A.
Comdg. 40th Bde. R.F.A.

1/2/15

3rd Division

40th Bde. R.F.A.

Vol VII   1 – 28. 2 .15

121/4610

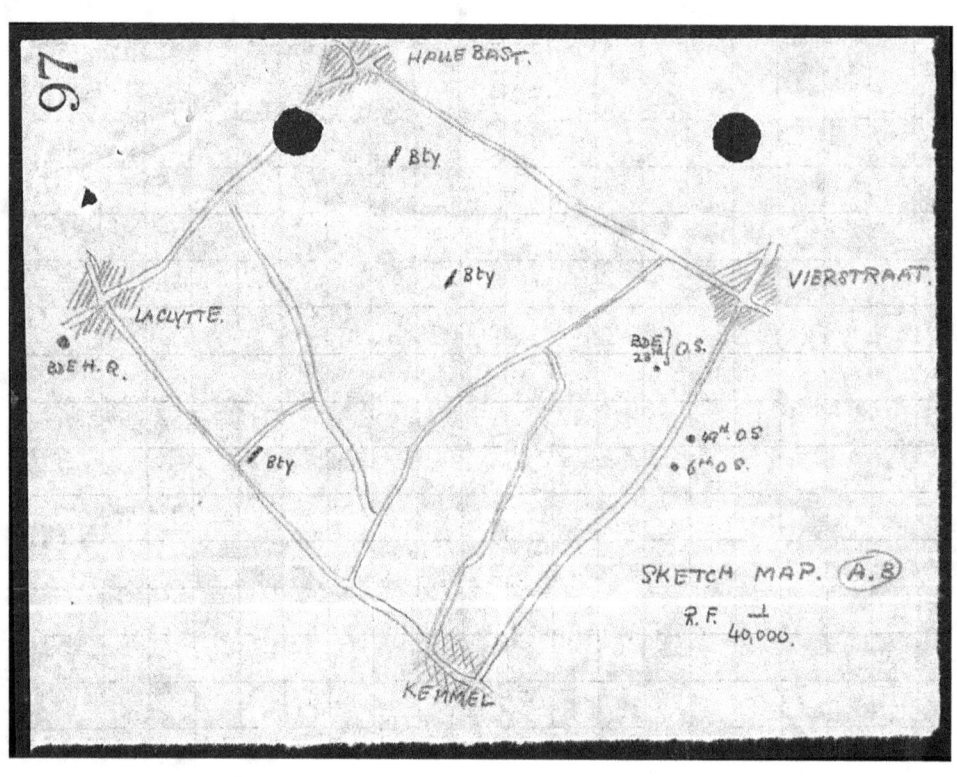

WAR DIARY

40th Bde R.F.A.

Febuary 1915

Feb 1st	Rest.	No change
2nd	Rest	No change
3rd 5 p.m		relieved 42nd Brigade in action. For position see sketch map (A.3). Affiliated to the 8th Inf. Bde. Two batteries in action, one in reserve.
4th		No change
5th		No change
6th		No change
7th		No change. Misty weather

Feb 8	No change =
9	No change =
10	No change =
11	No change =
12	No change weather very misty for last few days. =
13th	no change =
14th	no change =
15th	no change =
16th	no change =

Feb 17th	no change
18th	no change
19th	no change
20th	no change
21st	no change
22nd	no change
23rd	no change
24th	no change
25th	no change

Feb 26th	No Change
27th	No Change
28th	No Change

END OF

FEBRUARY

B.J. Elkington
Lt. Col.
Comdg. 40th Bde. R.F.A.

2/3/15

121/4672

3rd Division

40th Bde: R+H.

Vol VIII 1—31.3.15

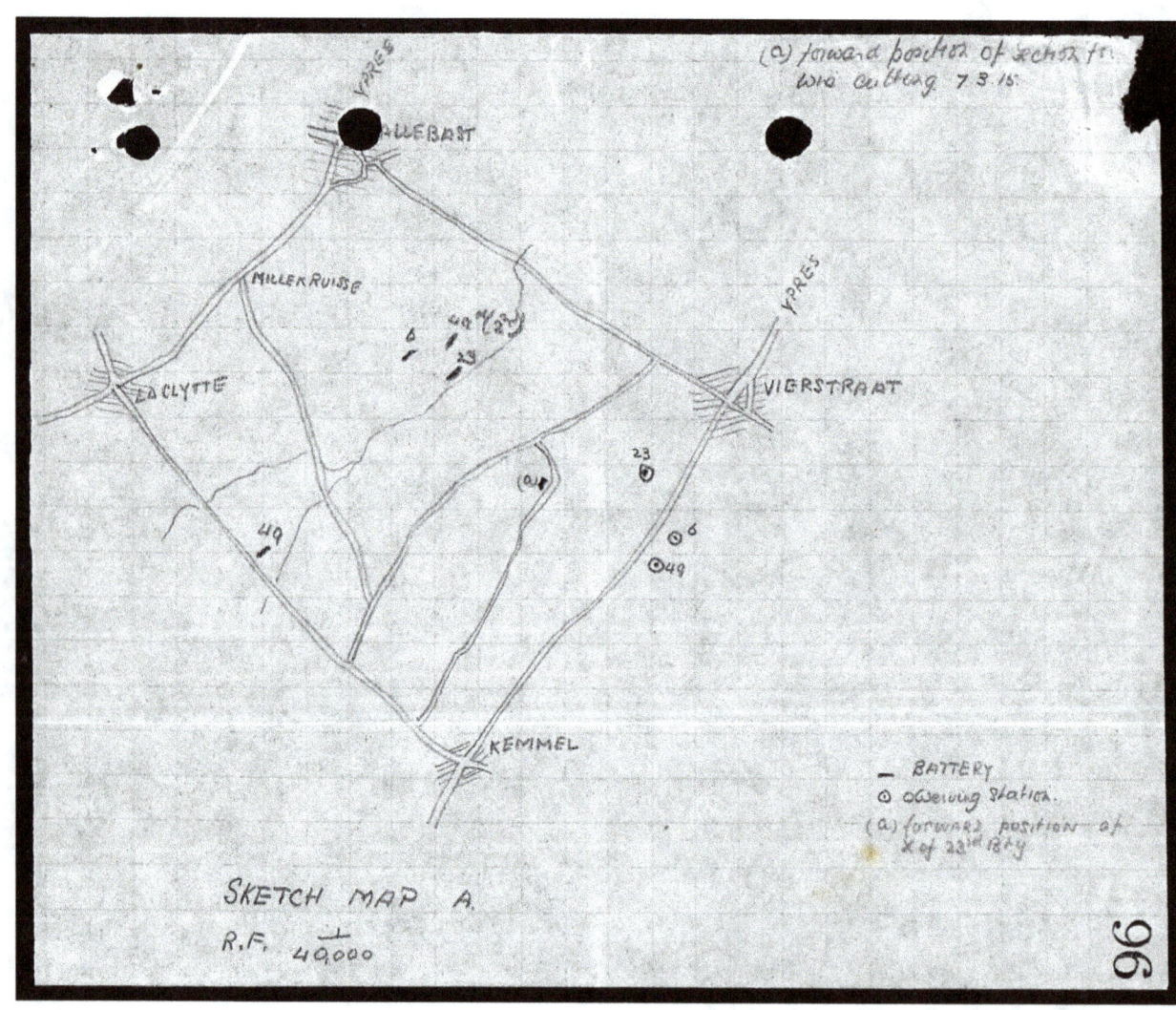

WAR DIARY

40th Bde R.F.A.

MARCH

March 1	No change Inpochoisser(A)
2nd	No change. 6" Battery observing station shelled OC observers from 23rd Bty O.S. ~~given~~ R.g.n. Captain Gedy and one NCO wounded
3rd	No change
4th	No change
5th	No change
6th	No change

March 7	23rd Battery carried out a wire cutting scheme in front of HOLLANDSCHES SHUUR FME Section of 6th Bty (then in rest) borrowed and taken to a forward position (See Map A)
8th	
4pm	**Bombardment** 6th and 49th Batteries N and W sides of PETIT BOIS 23rd Battery to watch HOLLANDSCHES FARM and to take opportunities
9th	Bde carried out programme as ordered by III Div Artillery.
10th	Bde carried out programme as ordered by II Army Corps
11th	Bde carried out programme as ordered by II Army Corps

12th	Bde carried out programme as ordered by IInd Corps Army
13th	Bde carried out programme as ordered by II Army Corps
14th	Bde reverts to its old dispositions
15th	No change
16th	No change
17th	No change
18th	No change
19th	No change
20th	No change
21st	No change

22nd	no change
23rd	no change
24th	no change
25th	no change
26th	no change
27th	49th Battery moves to new position see map
28th	no change
29th	no change

30th	no change
31st	no change

END OF

MARCH

R.G. Elkin[?]
Lt. Col. R.F.A.
Comdg. 40th Bde. R.F.A.

2/4/15

121/5108

3rd Division

40th Bde R.F.A.

Vol IX 1 — 30.4.15

WAR DIARY
40th B.D.F. R.F.A.

APRIL

1st	No change (for position see sketch map)
2nd	No change
3rd	No change
4th	No change 49th Bty moves back to old position
5th	No change
6th	No change
7th	No change
8th	No change
9th	No change
10th	No change
11th	No change
12th	No change

13th	No change
14th	No change
15th	No change
16th	No change. V Div attacked & took HILL 60 N o/ ST. ELOI
17th	No change
18th	No change
19th	No change
20th	No change
21st	No change
22nd	No change
23rd	No change
24th to 30th	No change

30.iv.15.

R.J.G. Elkington
Lt. Col. R.F.A.
Cmdg 40th Bde R.F.A.

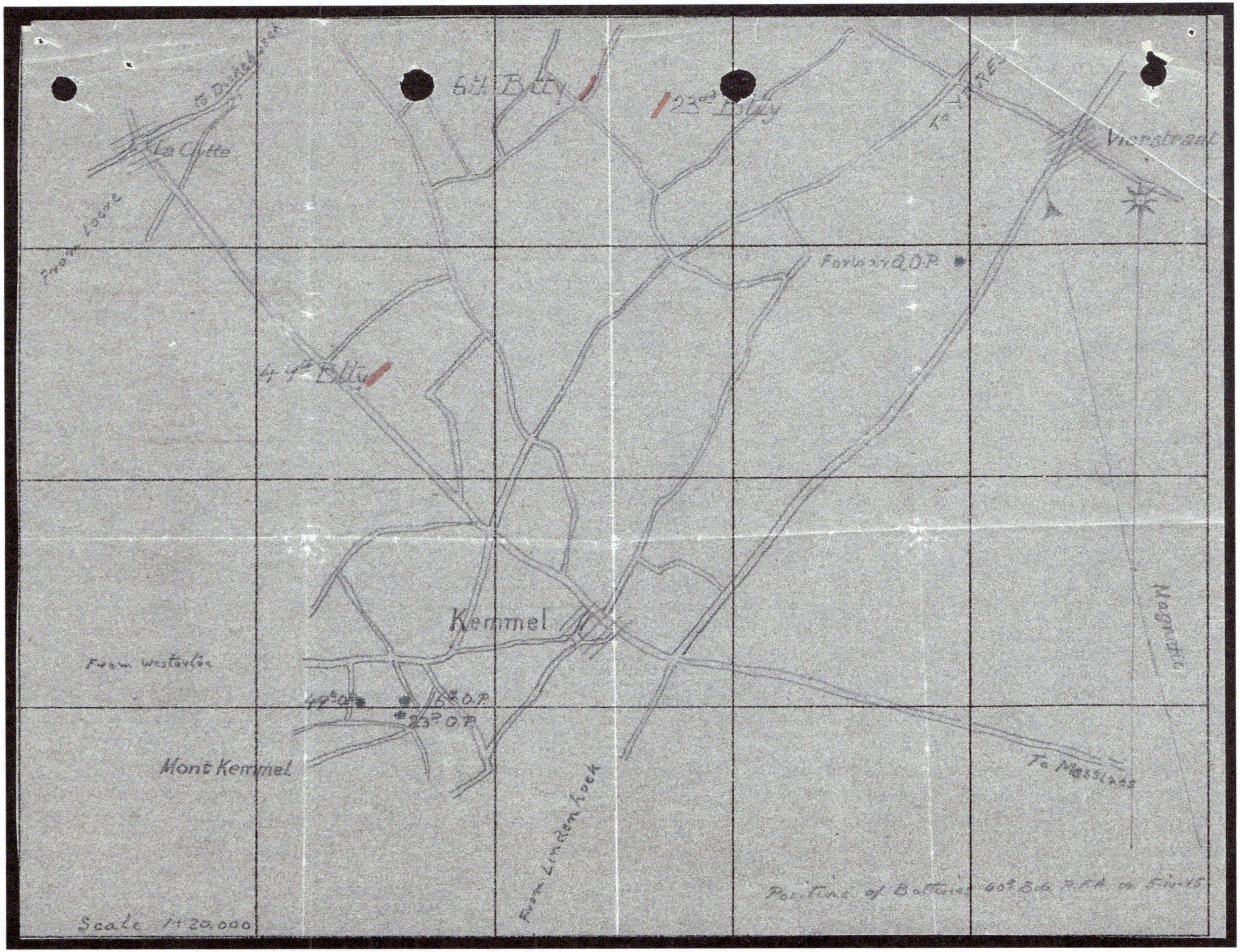

La Clytte
From Locre
6th Btty
23rd Btty
Vierstraat
Forward O.P.
44th Btty
Kemmel
From Westoutre
6th O.P.
23rd O.P.
Mont Kemmel
From Lindenhoek
Magnetic
To Messines
Positions of Batteries 40th Bde. R.F.A. on 5-iv-15
Scale 1:20,000

121/5481

3rd Division

40th Bde R.F.A.

Vol X 1. — 31.5.15

War Diary

40th Brigade R.F.A.   Month of May '15

1st   No change

2nd   "

3rd   "

4th   "

5th   "

6th   "

7th   "

8th   "

9th   6th Battery attached to 42nd Bde R.F.A. for tactical
      purposes and affiliated to 9th Inf Bde
      23rd and 49th affiliated to Notts and Derby Bde
      of N. M. Div. but still kept under orders of 3rd Div Arty

10th No change

11th   "

12th   "

13th, No change

14th No change

15th No change

16th No change

17th No change

18th No change

19th No change

20th No change

21st Lieut H.S. Browne to command Am Col pending promotion.

22nd No change

23rd No change. Maj. H.O.O. Ward ptd to command a brigade in 2nd Div pending promotion
Capt E.S. Allsop to command 49th Bty pending promotion.

24th No change

25th   No change

26th   No change

27th   No change

28th One section of each battery withdrawn and replaced by one section each of three batteries of 46th Bde R.F.A.

29th Sections of batteries withdrawn last night went into action just E. of YPRES, relieving corresponding number of guns of 1st Bde R.F.A. Remainder of Bde withdrawn from positions at LA CLYTTE being replaced by the 46th Bde R.F.A.

30th Rest of Brigade came into action - as shewn on map - relieving remainder of 1st Bde R.F.A. at about 9.30 p.m.

31st No change.

R. M°Ilwaine   Lieut Col R.F.A.
Comdg 40th Bde R.F.A.

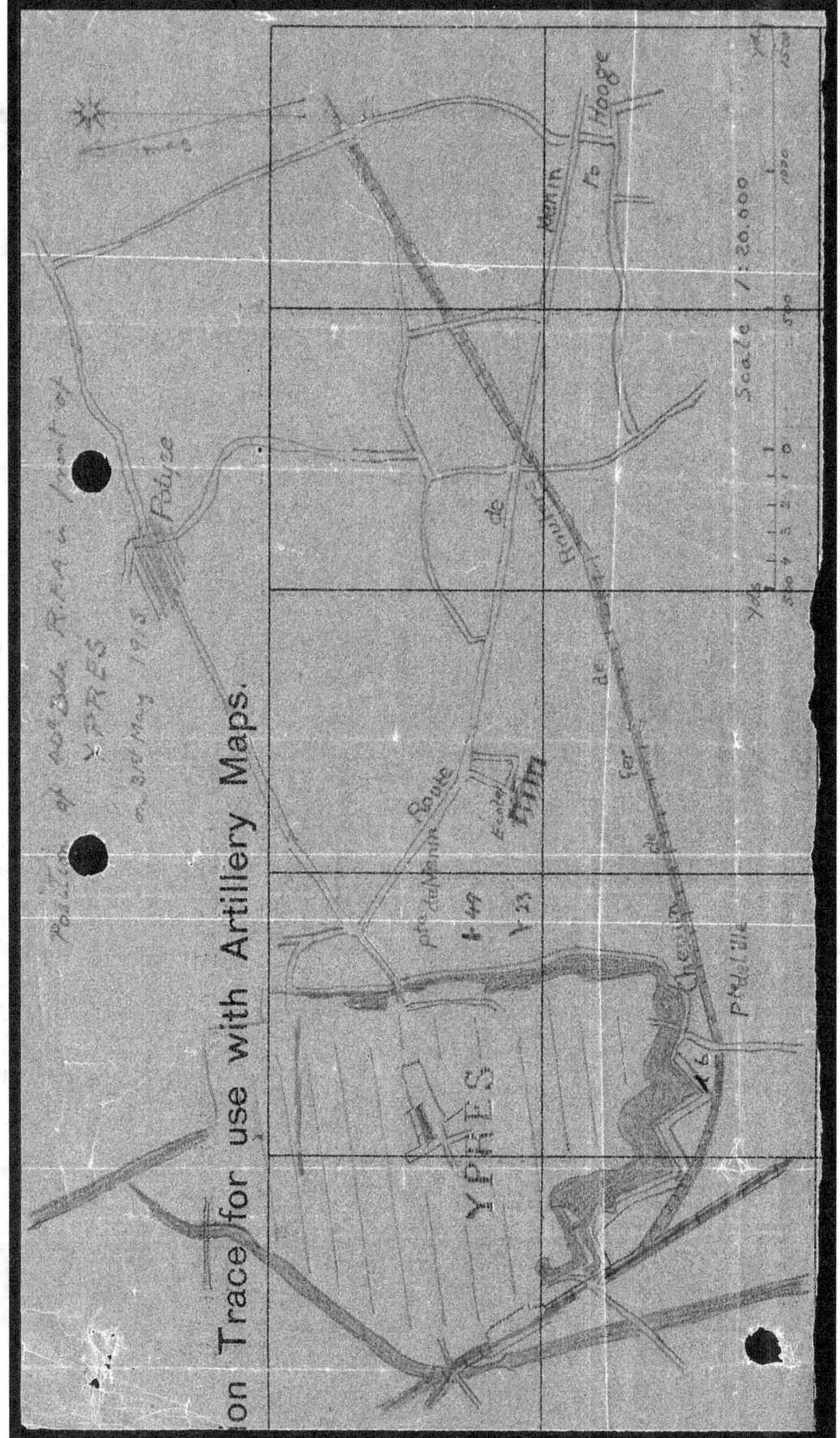

3rd Division

40th Bde R.F.A.

Vol XI   1 — 30.6.15.

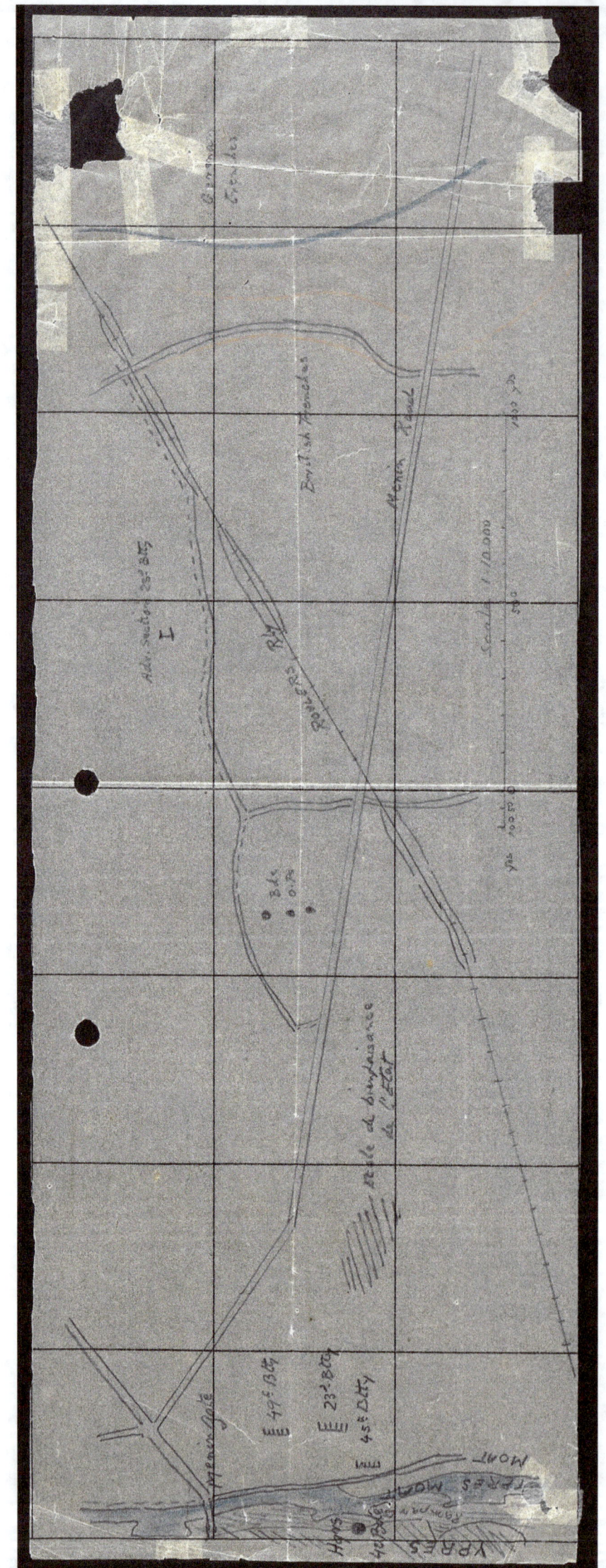

War Diary of the
40th Brigade R.F.A.

1st No change.

2nd Very heavy shelling by Germans especially between 1 pm. and 5 pm.

3rd No change. Quieter day.

4th   "

5th   "

6th   "

7th   "

8th   "

9th   "

10th   "

11th   "

12th   "

13th   No change

14th 6th Battery grouped with 42nd Bde and 45th Battery grouped with 40th Bde for tactical purposes from 5 a.m. onwards. One section of 6th Btty grouped with 23rd Btty, and called A group.

15th One section 6th Btty manned by 23rd Btty went into action as shewn on sketch.

16th At 2:50 a.m. A group opened fire according to a programme ordered by C.R.A. III Div. The advanced section engaged the advanced German parapet at a range of 975 yards. They got repeated hits with H.E. percussion on both front line and that 40 yds in rear. The position was much exposed and though shelled during the day was not given away.

    The batteries were in action all day – first through the various phases of the attack and later in covering infantry advance, they also got into parties of enemy in DEAD MAN'S BOTTOM and elsewhere.

    2nd Lieut R.A. Jennings Bramley of 23rd Battery RFA. and 2nd Lieut Watson of 45th Btty were both wounded while performing the duties of Forward Observing officers in the trenches.

    German front line trenches on a front of about 1000" were captured.

17th   No change

18th   Forward section withdrawn, and leaves A group.

19th   No change

20th   No change. Tactically at disposal of 14th Div.

21st   C/49 How. Bty put under command of O.C 40 Bde. from 12 midnight.

22nd   Re-Registration of zones in morning. At 7.30 began bombardment of strong point near BELLEVARDE FARM, and was carried out according to programme arranged by 14th Div Arty.

23rd & 24th   No change

25th   One section of A group batteries relieved by sections of 46th Bde R.F.A. One section of 6th Bty relieved by 1 sec. 45th Battery. Sections relieved — to rest

26th   Remainder of Brigade relieved by 46th Bde and 40th Bde went into rest near POPERINGHE

27th
28th
29th   } In rest.
30th

2nd July 1915

R.J.G. Elkington
Lieut Col R.F.A.
Comdg 40th Bde R.F.A.

18/6/49

3rd Division

40th Bde R.F.A.

Vol XII   1 — 31.7.15.

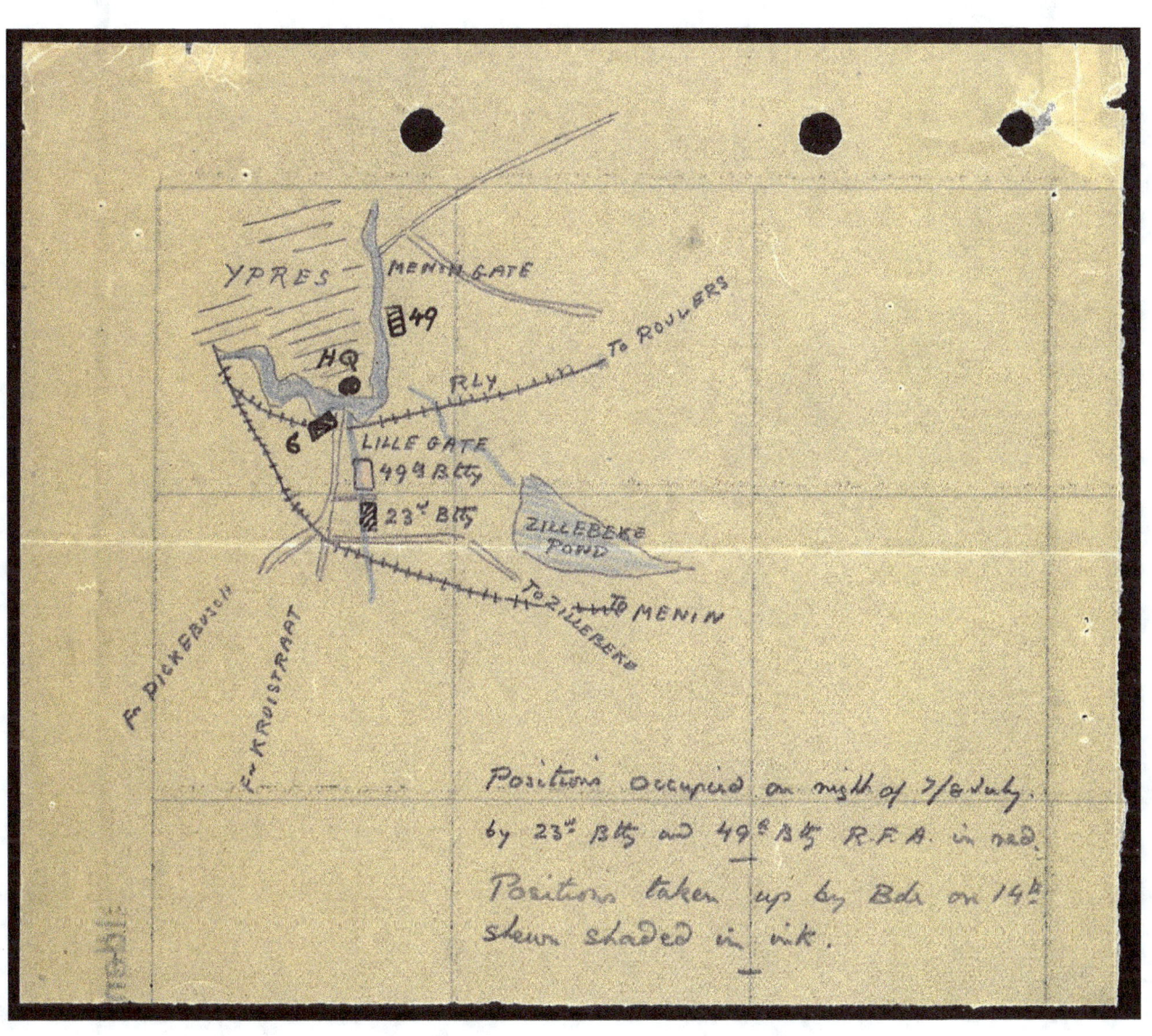

Positions occupied on night of 7/8 July
by 23rd Btty and 49th Btty R.F.A. in red.
Positions taken up by Bde on 14th
shewn shaded in ink.

War Diary July 1915.

40th Bde   R.F.A.

1st ⎫
2nd ⎪
3rd ⎪
4th ⎬   In rest near POPERINGHE
5th ⎪
6th ⎭

7th ⎫ On night of 7th went into action as shewn on
8th ⎬ the attached sketch. Three batteries registered the
    ⎭ neighbourhood of HOOGE, left guard on guns and
       detachments back to rest.

9th ⎫
10th ⎪
11th ⎬   In rest.
12th ⎪
13th ⎭

14th   Bde moved into action as under.
       6th Btty took over from 45th Bty 42nd Bde
       49th Bty   — . —   41st   "   "
       28th Bty remained in same position as it
       occupied on night of 7/8.
       HQrs at Lille Gate. These positions
       are shewn shaded on attached plan.

15th   Quiet day

16th	No change
17th	No change
18th	No change
19th	At 7p.m. mine exploded under german redoubt near HOOGE. 40th Bde fired in accordance with programme arranged by 3 Div. Considerable activity during the night.
20th	Considerable activity during day and night
21st	Very quiet day. One section per battery relieved by section 48th Bde - XIVth Div.
22nd	Relief completed. Brigade went into rest near POPERINGHE
23rd to 31st	No change

31-7-15   R.J.G. Elkington
                         Lieut Col RFA.
                         Cmdg 40th Bde RFA.

699/21

3rd Division

40th Bde R.F.A.
Vol XLV
Sept 15

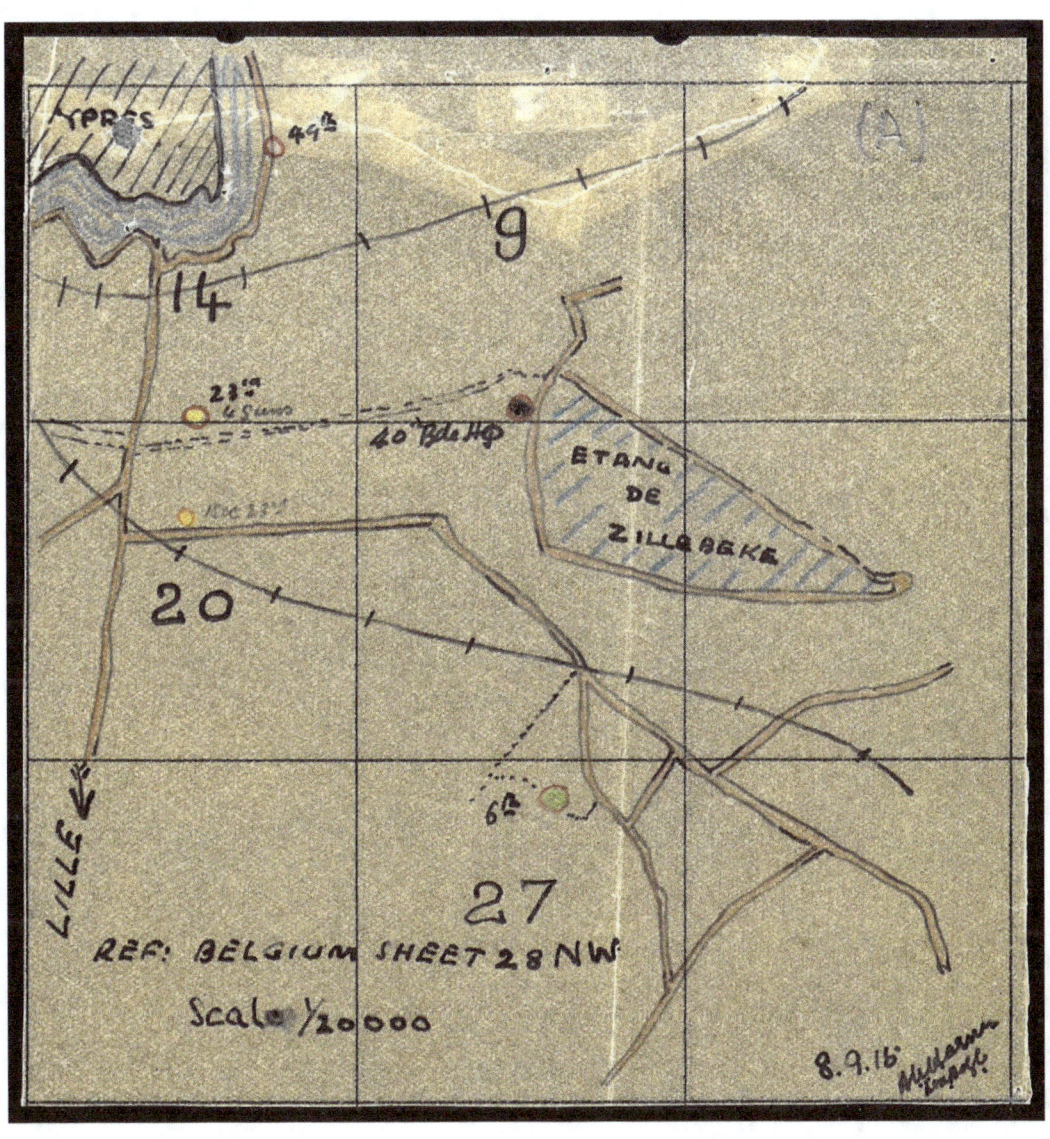

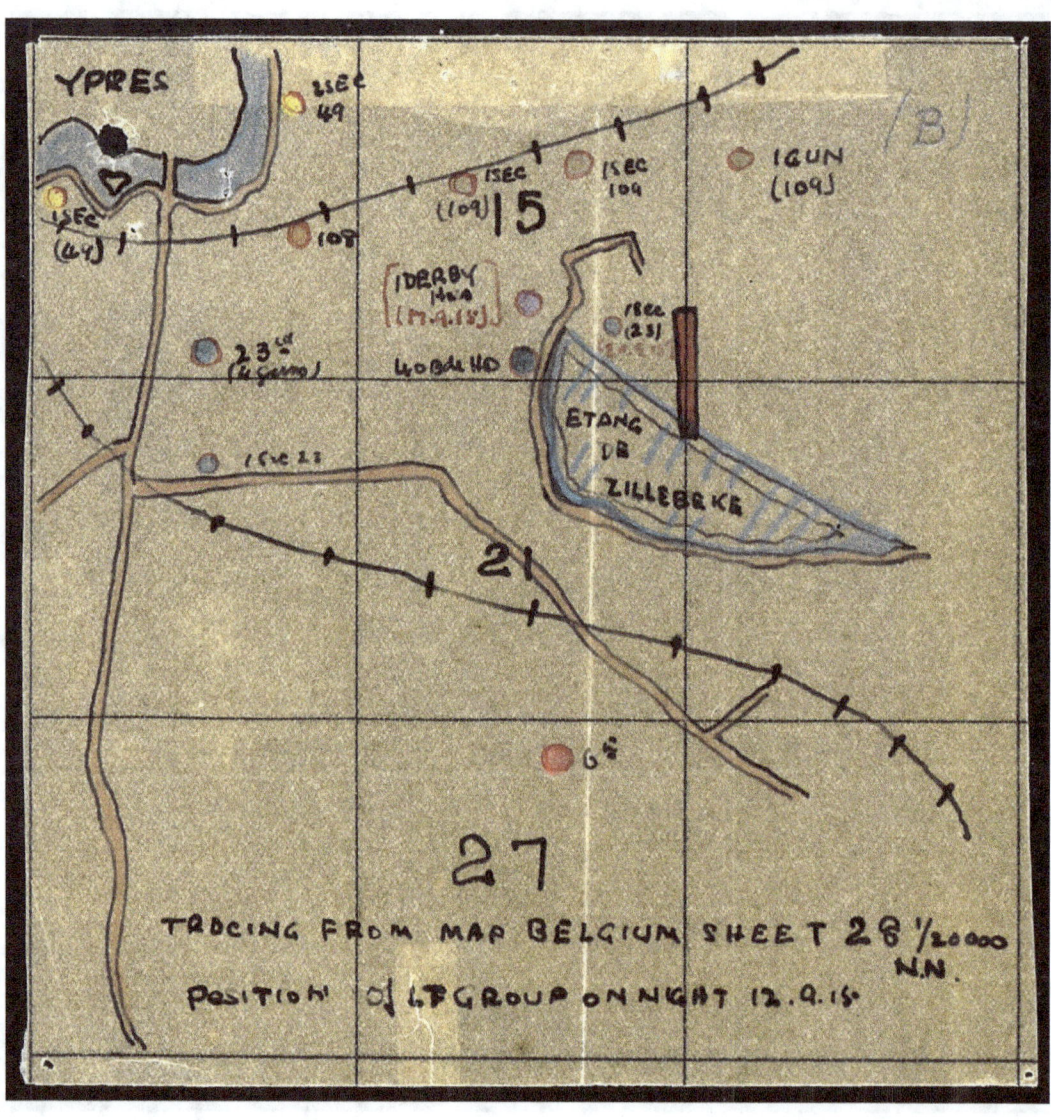

War Diary Sept 1915

40th Bde R.F.A.

1st 4 AM. Bombardment of trenches near HOOGE

2nd 5.15 AM Bombardment of trenches near HOOGE

3rd Bombardment of line close near HOOGE 4.40 AM. 23rd Battery shelled with crumps

4th Bombardment of trenches near HOOGE 10.30 AM. 23rd & 49th Batteries shelled with Crumps & Cumplets

5th Bombardment of trenches near HOOGE 4.40 AM & 12.5 PM. 23rd & 49th Batteries shelled with Crumps

6th No change

7th In evening 23rd & 49th Batteries change their positions. fresh positions shown on attached sketch map.(A)

8th No change

9th No change

10th Registered 4 targets by aeroplane (6th & 49th Also)

11th No change.

12th In Evening at 11.45 pm. 8th Inf Bde Relieves 7th Inf Bde. OC. 40 Bde assumes command of LEFT GROUP (6th 23rd 49th 108th & 109th Batteries) See Map (B)

13th firing with Experimental H.E. Carried out- 2 prematures in 23rd Bty which seriously damaged 2 guns.

14th firing with Experimental H.E. 1 Gun of 6th and 1 Gun of 49th put seriously out of Action

September 1915 (Cont.) 13

14th Cont. by 2 prematures. Damaged guns replaced by loan of guns from 42nd Bde.
15th - Nothing fresh -
16th - No Change -
17th 12 noon 1st DERBY HOW Bty comes under command of O.C. Left Group.
18th Bombardmt of German position 2 pm by field guns & heavies. 7th & 9th Inf Bdes relieve 8th Bde. 108 & 109 Btys transferred to RIGHT GROUP at 12 nn.
19th Bombardmt of trenches near HOOGE CHATEAU by field guns & heavies at 9.50 AM.
20th Bombardmt of trenches near HOOGE by field guns & heavies at 4.5 p.m.
21st Bombardmt of trenches near Hooge 5 AM
22nd do   do   do   do   do 9.20 AM
23rd do   do   do   do   do 12.5 PM
24th do   do   do   do   do 4.20 AM
25th ~~~~~~~~~~~~~~~~~~~~~~~~~~~~~~~~~~
25th Brigade participated in an attack against German trenches near HOOGE. Bombardmnt 3.50 AM Mine Exploded 4.19 AM Assault 4.20 AM. Brigade covered front of 7th Inf Bde. First and second line German trenches were taken in places but had to be abandoned owing to heavy hostile cross fire. Brigade fired 4860 rnds,

September 1915 (Cont).

25th Cont. rounds during the day. Temporary
2/Lt R.T. COBBOLD was killed in action while performing the duties of forward observing officer for the 6th Battery R.F.A.

26th A very quiet day. At about 10 P.M. Brigade received S.O.S call from the infantry and fired about 1200 rounds. The operation consisted of a minor Bombing fight. All quiet by 11.15 P.M.

27th   No Change

28th   No Change

29th At 12 noon 1st Derby Bty ceases to be under O.C. Left Group. At about 4.30 P.M. Enemy explode a mine near HOOGE and occupy 150 yards of trench each side.

30th Participated in an attack by 8th Lf. Bde with two batteries.

Added On Evenings of 20th and 21st 23rd Bty
21st} Moved 1 gun of Right Section each evening to
22nd} a position N of Zillebeke Lake as on sketch map 'B'

1.10.15.   R.J. Elkington Lieut-Col R.F.A.
                Commanding 45th Bde R.F.A.

12/7431

an a/6

3w/5 wain

Loria Bsa R.i. A.

Dec 15

Vol XVI   Vol XV

August 1915

15th No change
16th — —
17 — —
18 — —
19 — —
20 — —
21st Withdrew guns from DICKEBUSH
22 No change in rest
23 — —
24 — —
25th In Evening 1 section per battery moves into action relieving 3 Section of 2nd Bde R.H.A.
26th In Evening Remainder of Bde moves into action W of ZILLEBEKE relieving 2nd Bde R.H.A. and covering front of 7th Inf Bde in front of HOOGE. Positions as on attached tracing.
27th Lt. A.L. HARMAN took Adjt. 4 B Bde R.H.A. vice Capt R.M. RENDEL to England.

28th – 31st No Change

1.9.15.
Sd. R.J.G. Elkington
Lt Col R.A.
Commanding 4. Bde R.H.A.

Copy

War Diary August 1915.

40th Bde RFA.

1st   In Rest
2nd   — —
3rd   — —
4th   In Evening Brigade moved into action to perform duties of Counter battery. Position occupied as shown on attached sketch map.

5th   No Change
6th   — —
7th   — —
8th   Registered 5 targets by aeroplane for counter battery work tomorrow
9th   Opened fire at 2.65 AM. according to prearranged programe. fired a lot during day. Trenches & Chateau at HOOGE retaken. Quiet night.
10th   No Change
11th   — —
12   — —
13   — —
14   Detachments withdrawn to rest at Poperinghe POPERINGHE guard left on guns in position

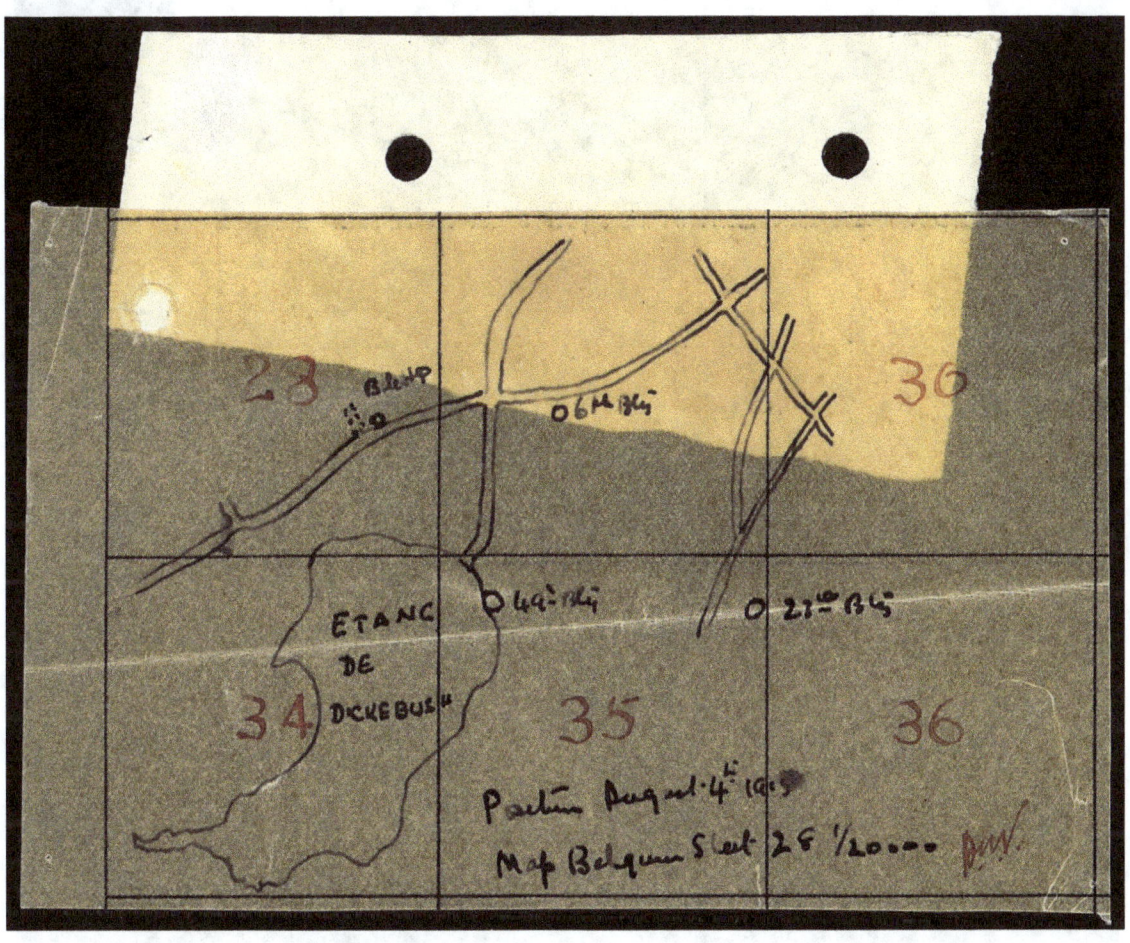

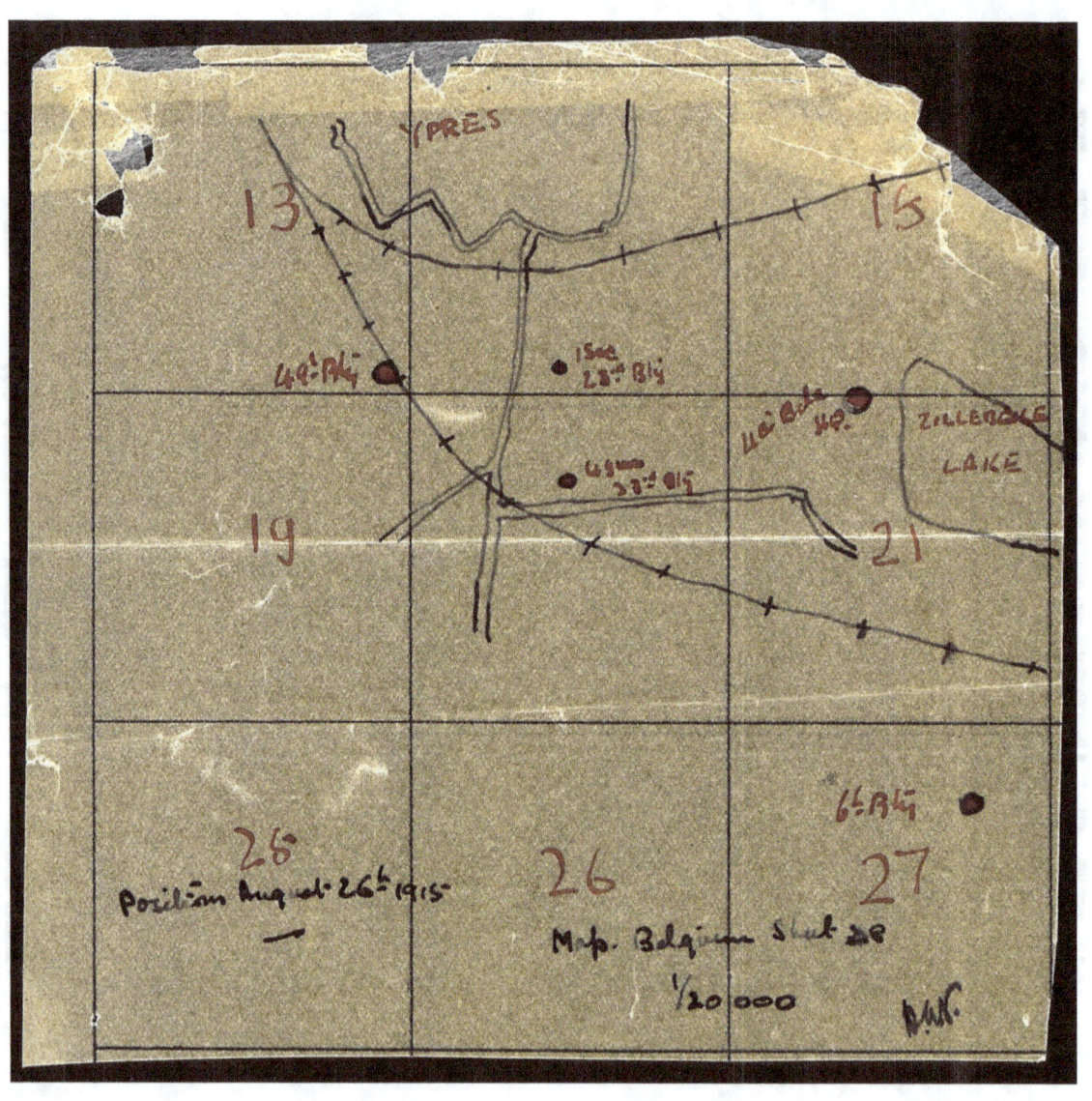

3rd Division

40th Bde R.F.A.
4 DEC. 1915
XV
Corps
Sent ?

121/7655

War Diary of 45th Bde RFA

Month of October 1915

1st	No change
2nd	No change
3rd	No change
4th	No change
5th	No change
6th	No change
7th	Lt Col R.J.G. Elkington CMG. to be Brig Gen and to Command Div Artillery of 36th ULSTER Division. Major T.M. Archdale D.S.O. to Command 45th Bde pending promotion
8	No change
9	do
10	do
11	do
12	do
13	do
14	do
15	do
16	do
17	do
18	do
19	do
20	do
21	do

October 1915.   45 Bde RFA   16

22nd   No Change = 9th Inf Bde relieved by
           50th Inf Bde, 17th Divn
23rd   Artillery relief of III Divn by 17th Divn Arty commenced
           1 Sec 23rd Btty relieved ⎫
           2 Sec 49   "   "   ⎬ By 80th Bde RFA.
           1 Sec 6th "   "   ⎭
24th   In Evening Remaining Section 45 Bde
           and Bde HQ relieved by Section & HQ
           80th Bde RFA. 45 Bde proceeded
           to go into Reserve in neighbourhood
           of ST. SYLVESTER CAPPEL
25th   IN Rest
26   do
27   do
28   do
29   do
30   do
31   do

                                T. M. Archdale
                                    Major RFA
                            Commanding 45 Bde RFA

40ᵗʰ Bde R.F.A.
Month of November 1915:
(Cont)

24ᵗʰ Advance Sections of Batteries 3rd Divisional Artillery move up into Action to relieve Batteries of 24ᵗʰ Divisional Artillery.

25ᵗʰ Remainder of Batteries 3rd Div Artillery move up to take over from 24ᵗʰ Divisional Artillery — Guns Exchanged. 40ᵗʰ Bde (less 1 sec per Battery) relieves 106 Bde R.F.A. in Action near DICKEBUSH and covers Right half of front of 9ᵗʰ Inf Bde. Positions on attached sketch map.

26ᵗʰ No change
27ᵗʰ No change
28ᵗʰ In Evening 8ᵗʰ Inf Bde relieves 9ᵗʰ Inf Bde in Action
29ᵗʰ No change
30ᵗʰ No change

Added. Nov 3ʳᵈ Capt A.W. Pursur taken over command of 23ʳᵈ Battery

2.12.15.

T. M. Archdale
Lt Col R.F.A.
Commanding 40ᵗʰ Bde R.F.A.

War Diary   November 1915. 17

45th Bde R.F.A.

1st	In Rest near ST SYLVESTER CAPPEL
2nd	do
3rd	Major G.S. Tovey 23rd Battery R.F.A. posted to 15th Division to command 88th Bde R.F.A. pending promotion.
4	No Change
5	do
6	do
7	do
8	do
9	do
10	do
11	45th Bde inspected by Army Commander
12	No change
13	do
14	do
15	3rd Divl Arty inspected by Army Commander
16	No Change
17	do
18	do
19	do
20	do
21	do
22	do
23	do

Army Form C. 2118.

WAR DIARY
or
INTELLIGENCE SUMMARY
(Erase heading not required.)

Map References Belgium Sheet 28 /20000

Place	Date	Hour	Summary of Events and Information	Remarks and references to Appendices
DICKEBUSCH	DECEMBER 1915			
	1st		No change	
	2nd		6" Battery were firing 2 guns into action on Dickebusch Lake at H35a 3.8	
	3rd		No Change	
	4th		6" Battery firing 2 more guns alongside 2 on Dickebusch Lake	
	5th		No change	
	6th		No change	
	7th		No change	
	8th		No change	
	9th		No change	
	10th		No change	
	11th		No change	
	12th		No change	
	13th		No change	
	14th		No change	
	15th		No change	

40 Brigade RFA.

WAR DIARY or INTELLIGENCE SUMMARY

Army Form C. 2118.

Map Reference BELGIUM Sheet 28 $\frac{1}{20000}$ unless otherwise stated.

Place	Date	Hour	Summary of Events and Information	Remarks and references to Appendices
DICKEBUSCH			DECEMBER 1915 (continued).	
	16.		No change.	
	17.		Major G.S. ALLSUP Commanding 41st Battery R.F.A. wounded. To Hospital.	
	18.		No change.	
	19.	5AM.	Enemy gas attack on 6th Corps Front N. of MENIN ROAD. Everywhere repulsed. Gas felt at DICKEBUSCH necessitating gas helmets which proved effective.	
	20.		No change	
	21.		No change	
	22.		No change	
	23.		Lt Col T.M. ARCHDALE sick to Hosp. Major H.A.C. Rose to command Brigade during absence.	
	24.		No change. Capt. C.A. O'DRISCOLL RAMC to Hosp.	
	25.		No change	
	26.		1 Section of each Battery selected by section of 28th Brigade R.F.A. Remaining section of 40 Brigade relieved by section of 2 & 3 Bde R.F.A. Command of Right group passes from 40 Bde to 28th Bde R.F.A. Brigade moved reserve Billets near BOESCHEPE.	
BOESCHEPE	28. 29. 30. 31.		IN RESERVE	

1.1.16.

N. Newman

Lt. A. Adjt.

for O.C. 40 Bde R.F.A.

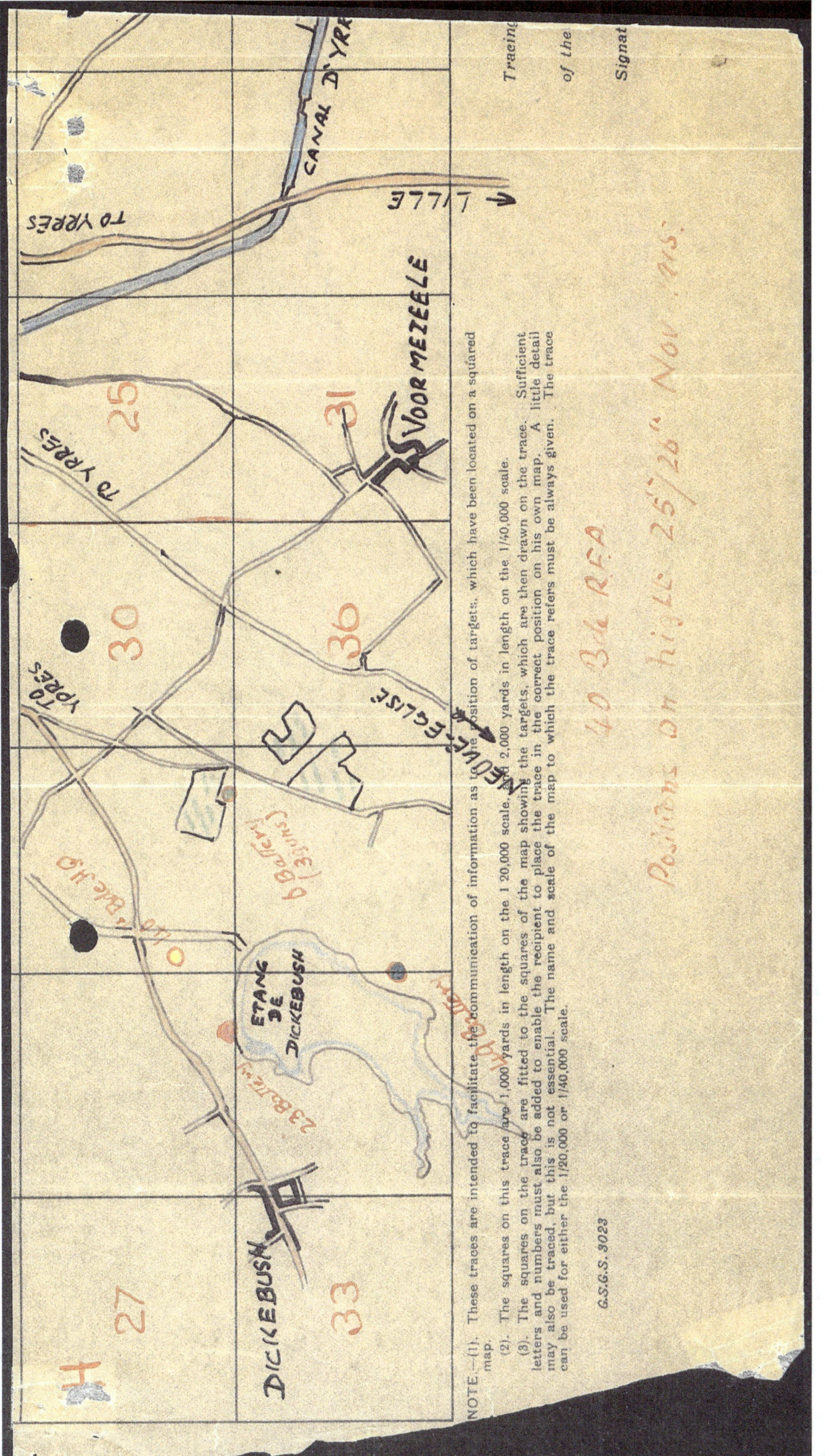

Index..................

SUBJECT.

3RD DIV

No.	Contents.	Date.
	R.F.A., 6TH BATTERY WAR DIARY OCT - DEC, 1915	

6" Batty R.F.A. 40 Bde
Oct + Nov. 15
Vol. I

121/2957

WAR DIARY

DATE	SUMMARY OF EVENTS	REMARKS
1st Oct.	Fired 32 Mixed at CORNER HOUSE & GLENCOURSE WOOD for neutralization of attacked Iny Offices also 8 rounds at J13 c 4.3 during night.	
2nd "	Fired 8 rounds at cross rds J13 c 4.3 during night.	
3rd "	Did not fire.	
4th "	Fired 21 Shot & 4 HE at Mortar near WALL Iny report a drive R.it. Also 3 rounds at 8PM at Standpoint on MENIN Rd. Also 8 rounds near WALL during night.	
5th "	Fired 8 Shot & 1 HE at mortar near WALL also 8 rounds at J13 a 6.3.	6th Capt. T.C. FOX posted to 40 Batt. A.C.
6th "	Fired 2 Lot rounds & 8 rounds at standpoint at J13 a 6.3 at dawn place.	7th Capt A.W. PURSER from 23rd Bde A.C.
7th "	8 rounds during night at J13 a 6.3.	Strems following received
8th "	Fired 8 rounds & round C3 retaliation, 7 rounds at working party opposite C2. 8 rounds at road J13 a 6.3.	on the 9th. "7Pdr C.O. Royal Fusiliers
9th "	Fired 14 rounds in slow salvous during day at Battery Johns & 34 rounds at GLENCOURSE WOOD, 12 rounds over C3L retaliation & 8 over C2 also 8 rounds at transport.	given to rank the Battery for the way my fired over C2 tonight"
10th "	Fired 2 Lot rounds at at a working party & 20 in retaliation.	12th.
11th "	Fired 1 Lot round 139 opposite C3 retaliation. also 10 rounds at working party.	No 62537 L. TAYLOR. H
12th "	Fired 80 rounds opposite C2 & 3 retaliation & 8 rounds at CLAPHAM JUNCTION.	wounded.

WAR DIARY

DATE	SUMMARY of EVENTS	REMARKS
13th	Did not fire.	14/9/15 2nd Lt. H. LAVI-BROMET joined from Base.
14th	Fired 72 rounds over C2 & C3 in retaliation on hostile normal & 8 rounds at CLAPHAM JUNCTION during the night	
15th	Fired 114 rounds opposite C2 & C3 called for by S.O.S.	
16th	Fired one lest round & 12 at working party opposite C2 & C3	
17th	Fired 118 Shrap & 3 HE at trench mortar & in retaliation on C2 & C3 also 8 rounds during evening at J13 C.4.4.	
18th	30 rounds during registration	
19th	Fired 46 rounds	
20th, 21st & 22nd	Did not fire. Centre & right sections pulled out & move to rest billets at ST SYLVESTRE CAPPEL	
23rd	Left section pulls out & goes to ST SYLVESTRE CAPPEL	
24th	In Rest till end of month.	

Mw Capt
Comdg 6th L. B.y R.F.A

WAR DIARY

DATE	SUMMARY OF EVENTS	REMARKS
Nov. 1st	In rest at St SYLVESTRE CAPPEL	2/Lt J.F. BLIGH posted to 50th Bty RFA
2nd	—	2Lt H.E. LEFROY joined from Base
3rd	Under instruction marched to wagon line near RENINGHELST & manned up & took a section of B/106 at DICKEBUSCH during night of 24th/25th	3rd Capt A.W. PURSER posted to command 33rd Bty RFA Lt D. St G. MORRISON posted from 130th Bty RFA as Captain
25th	The right section came into action with our guns at DICKEBUSCH	
26th	& the other at VERBRANDEN MOLEN	
27th	Fired 13 rounds registering	
28th	Fired 38 rounds registering, on hostile MG emplacement & a sniper's post on MOUND fired 59 rounds at hos MG emplacement on MOUND with Lt EMPSON as F.O.O. both MG emplacements were hit on being destroyed	See 3rd Div Summary
29th	Fired our last round	" " "
30th	Fired 3 last rounds & 11 checking normal zone 6" crumps about 200x in front of Bty.	" " "

3rd DIVISION

SUMMARY OF INTELLIGENCE.   No: 40.

Enemy's transport was heard last night between 8 and 9 pm. It was probably near cross roads I.34d 7.1.

At 1-30 am this morning there was continuous firing from about 8 rifles in the German line. Firing ceased about 4-30 am, at which hour the Germans sounded a gong.

R.W.Fusiliers snipers claim 2 Germans. One was watching an aeroplane. He was wearing a brown cap - uniform blue, with white piping on the collar. When he fell, a whistle was sounded. This whistle signal is now generally believed to mean "stretcher be bearers wanted". The 2nd German killed only exposed his head. He was seen to throw up his rifle. He had just previously killed one of our men.

R.S.Fusiliers snipers claim 4 Germans. Three of these were exposed and shot, when one of our shells knocked down their parapet.

N.Fusiliers reports as follows "Our guns shelled a hut in the German lines situated at O.4b 9.1 - the results were satisfactory".

Sniping officer 1/R.Scots reports:- Hostile aeroplane flew over our line yesterday at 2-30 pm. It was driven back by one of our aeroplanes, but evidently not before it had seen our t trench railway, as at 3 pm our "dump" was shelled with 7.7 cm shrapnel.

2/LT. Spencer R.S.F. reconnoitered the ground in front of P.4a and P.4b last night. He reports that his patrol reached a disused trench when they were 75 yards out towards the enemy and were unable to go further than this, as they were fired on. The enemy were working hard all along their front, and also seemed to be putting out wire. The patrol returned and the artillery were turned on to the working parties. Report ends.

Sniping on both sides in the St ELOI sector was active yesterday.

Enemy were showing themselves more than usual at their T2 crater posts, the relief of these posts has been carefully listened for at night, but so far the times named in a recent summary cannot be verified.

N.Fusiliers snipers claim 2 Germans working on wire opposite 34 trench.

One of our shells striking the enemy's trench near the mound and west of it; caused an explosion yesterday. A large column of black smoke going up.

Enemy M.G. and snipers post located at O.3d 2.8.

A red light was sent up on right front of 3.2 at 4-50 pm

Intelligence officer 1/C.H. reports :-

From 2 pm to 3 pm white puffs of smoke or steam were seen at regular intervals coming out from a point O.4a 9.8 on the edge of the Canal bank.

From the BLUFF a party was seen near O.4b 6.7 walking along a path near C.T. Our snipers fired and the whole lot immediately jumped into the trench; no certain casualties could be claimed. One German was however hit in the front trench opposite trench 30.

3 German aeroplanes were observed at 5-15 pm apparently over HOLLEBEKE CHATEAU. 2 of them dropped white lights which broke into several stars. No result of this was observed.

The German front on which was thought to be a "MOUND"

at I.34d 2.5 was carefully observed. It appears to be strongly fortified, and the neighbouring trenches are well loopholed, but the work itself presents more the appearance of a strong dug-out than of a M.G. emplacement or fort.

The sniping Officer 8th King's Own reports as follows:-

The enemy's front line opposite 32 to 35 trenches appears to have an unusual number of loopholes and dug-outs in it. (NOTE Brigade Major 76th Brigade confirms this report and adds that smoke is continually rising from these dug-outs and it is thought that the enemy lives more in his front than his support trenches at this point, probably owing to the fact that unless our own trenches are cleared our Artillery cannot shoot at them owing to their proximity to our own front.)

The enemy wire is strong all along his front.

There is a large dug-out 110° magnetic from extreme left of trench 35.

At 10-30 a.m. 2 German aeroplanes were seen flying over their own lines. At 10-32 a.m. when opposite the left of trench 35 one machine dropped a white light. At 10-32 a.m. enemy 4.1" Light Howitzer Battery opened fire with universal shell. These burst directly behind left of trench 35. Exact bearing of Battery from left of trench 35 was 160° Magnetic.

(NOTE. True bearings should always be given).

The R.A. report, with reference to the suspected railway mounted gun mentioned in the last 2 Summaries, gun is thought to be on the railway. It was firing last night on a line from H.24c 1.1 to 0.12d 8.9. Shots were fired every 7 minutes exactly.

A strong point either a M.G. or an O.P. is reported at 0.4b 2.7.

Position of the Mound at 0.2d 2.7 is confirmed, no work appears to be going on at it.

Germans still bailing opposite P.4.

28th November, 1915.   W. La. T. CONGREVE, Captain,
General Staff, 3rd Division.

3rd DIVISION INTELLIGENCE SUMMARY No: 41.

From 10-30.am. to 12-15.pm. 35 support trench was shelled by 4.1" H.E. Fifteen shells were fired. True bearing of battery from left of trench 31 was 158 degrees true.

The enemy were active with machine guns from opposite trenches 28, &, 30, 31. These guns were firing from several different emplacements.

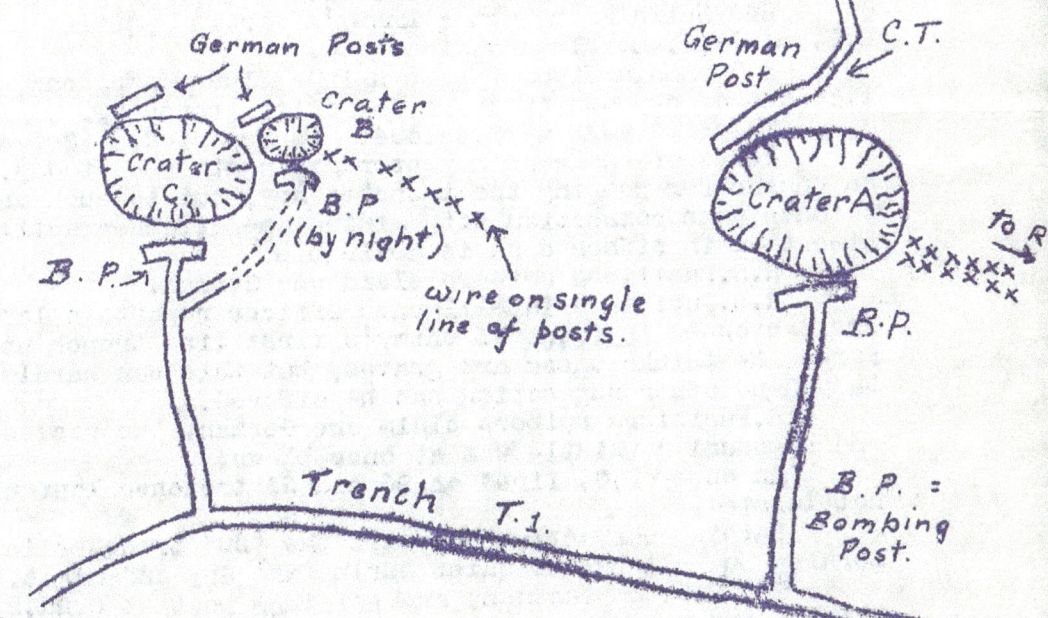

Reconnaissance of craters in front of T.1 by 2nd Lieut Hill on evening 27/11/1.15.

Patrol went out at 7.p.m.

<u>Route</u> From bombing post in front of Crater A. round lip of crater to edge of of German Post. Returned same way. From post in front of Crater B. round our barbed wire on to ground between Craters A and B. German Post at A appeared to be held by at least 6 men, probably 10. A communication trench runs back from this post towards the German trenches. Work could be heard going on in the communication trench.

Crater B and C appear weakly held probably 5 men in all. There is no sign of a communication trench between posts A and B, nor any signs of one leading back to the German lines from B and C.

Ground between A and B very broken and difficult to move over.

Fairly good wire entanglement runs from A to trench R.

Single row of posts with wire run from B about a third of the distance to A.

German in C Post sent up 5 flares while patrol was out.

The mound reported yesterday at 0.2d2.7 was thought to contain a machine gun. It was destroyed by the fire of the 3th Battery.

Belgians report that the enemy's trenches in their sector appear in fairly good condition. The right of the 2nd line trench opposite 32 seems to be slightly damaged. No new work has been noticed.

Favourite places for the enemy's artillery to shell appear to be :-

C.T. at I.34d.8.8.
C.T. at I.34a.7.4.
Square Wood behind 53 and 54 trenches about I.34b.3.8.

P.T.O.

The enemy have repaired the parapet and wire entanglements of their front trench opposite 53.

Kings Own snipers claim one German – he was repairing a dug-out in the front trench. Another German was then seen pulling him in and was fired at, result uncertain.

Intelligence Officer 4/G.H. reports :-

New work was seen at O.4a.4.4. It appears to be a new trench to join up two old ones. A M.G. emplacement has been located here. Our artillery fired 10 rounds at this work but the shells hit principally at O.4a.5.2.

2nd Suffolks report - Enemy's working parties seen at O.4D O.7. at 7-15.am. It was dispersed.

A German officer was seen in a blue peaked cap, exactly like one of our own in shape, opposite trench 28.

The same work at O.4a.4.4. is reported. (See 4th G.H.report).

Puffs of smoke seen yesterday, again seen today. It may be an engine for pumping the trenches dry, but is much more likely to have some connection with mining operations - artillery attention in either case is desirable.

R.S.Fusiliers snipers claim one German.

R.S.Fusiliers Intelligence Officer reports a large number of small crosses <u>in front</u> of enemy's first line trench under Piccadilly Farm. He thinks these are graves, but this can hardly be the case, though no other suggestion can be offered.

R.Fusiliers snipers claim one German. He was seen to fall and as usual a whistle was at once blown.

An enemy M.G. fired on 25 and 26 trenches last night - it was not located.

Sniping was active opposite the "20" trenches in the early morning but all became quiet during the day and night.

The M.G. emplacement and sniping post at O.2d.2.8. was shelled today by our artillery. The emplacement was destroyed and the sniping post has not been used again.

Enemy had working parties at dawn yesterday on their wire S.W. of T.2. and due S. of T.3. Our rifle fire dispersed them.

Two enemy loopholes in front of 24 trench was smashed yesterday with the new steel point 303 ammunition.

An enemy trench mortar near Piccadilly Farm fired on P.4R last night at 7.pm. Our artillery stopped its activity.

20/11/1915.

W.LeT.CONGREVE, Captain,
General Staff, 3rd Division.

WAR DIARY

DATE	SUMMARY OF EVENTS	REMARKS
1st DEC	fired 24 rounds over R, retaliation, at 1.30PM wood shelled & got men off guns clear returned about 3.30PM.	
2nd "	fired 22 shrap & 20 HE, left sec came into action in a new position on bund.	
3rd "	fired 29 rounds at DERRICK & hosts.	
4th "	fired 36 rounds registering left sec & 6 at DERRICK centre sec moved to new position on bund.	
5th "	fired 60 rounds registering & 18 L retaliation.	
6th "	fired 33 rounds in retaliation. A gun withdraws to wagon line.	
7th "	fired 46 rounds at request of Inf & 30 at O.P at Q.D	8.5-
8th "	fired 30 rounds at support trenches behind MOUND 30 rounds in retaliation D, 8 rounds a sunken Road.	
9th "	fired 4 rounds at support trenches & 6 rounds at transport.	
10th "	fired 109 rounds at EIKOFF FARM & trenches.	

WAR DIARY

DATE	SUMMARY OF EVENTS	REMARKS
11th Dec	fired 69 rounds in retaliation	12th
12th "	fired 10 rounds in retaliation & tests also 100 cutting wire opposite Q2 & 5 at dugouts opposite Q1. & 23 rounds in retaliation	Lt MORRISON posted to 30th Bde RFA
13th "	fired 7 rounds at OB a 9.0 45 in retaliation over R bracket. 30 retaliation D & 19 in retaliation over RS	
14th "	fired 16 rounds at HOLLEBEKE CH²⁰ in conjunction with 8" Hows, 16 rounds at hty 09 c 8.5, also 6 rounds during evening at 08 b 9.0	
15th "	fired 3 test rounds & 17 at EIKOFF FARM	
16th "	did not fire	
17th "	fired 3 tests & 20 in retaliation over Q2 also 23 at working party at 11.30 PM near MOUND	
18th "	fired 141 rounds at trenches round MOUND	
19th "	stood to with gas helmets on at 6.30 AM but did not fire. Fired 52 rounds checking lines & trying giant periscope	

WAR DIARY

DATE	SUMMARY OF EVENTS	REMARKS
20th Dec	fired 174 rounds at wire & new trench opposite R3 also 3 test rounds	
21st "	fired 1 test round.	
22nd "	fired 72 rounds at 05 b 5.8 for transport 3 tests & 8 at 08 d 9.8 to 08 A 9.0	
23rd "	fired 46 rounds at front trenches 4 HE at 09 d 7.8 & 2 tests.	Major Rose Temp to comd 40th Bde
24th "		
25th "	did not fire	Capt LUCAS from 23rd temp. to comd 6th Bty.
26th "	leading sec relieved by 107th Bty & withdrew to wagon line	
27th "	remainder of bty relieved by 107th Bty. marched to rest billets at BOESCHEPE	27th Lt PERCIVAL posted as Capt from 29th Bty. 30th Capt H.C. Smith posted in place of Lt Percival

T. Rose Major
Comdg 6th Bty RFA

WAR DIARY

DATE	SUMMARY OF EVENTS	REMARKS
1st to 19th Jan	In rest billets at BOESCHEPE	7. Major Rose rejoins Bty.
19th Jan	One section goes into action in relief of a section of 3rd Bty 7th Regt Belgian Artillery	Capt LUCAS rejoins 23rd Bty.
20th "	a section relieves the remaining sec of Belgian Bty & 6th Bty comes under DESHESNE'S group	
21st "	complete registration.	
23rd "	fired 50 rounds registering & 17 HE in retaliation	
24th "	fired 35 rounds in retaliation over 29	
25th "	fired 32 rounds registering over 29	
26th "	fired 63 over 29 retaliation & 30 at 05 c 4.3 retaliation H	
27th "	lent wires to a 8" & 9.2 Bty fired 67 HE & 17 shrap at 04 a 8.7 to 134 d 0.1	
28th "	fired 4 rounds at two working parties	
29th "	did not fire.	
30th "	Fired 14 rounds at working parties.	
31st "	Fired 2 rounds at working party & 16 at	

WAR DIARY

DATE	SUMMARY OF EVENTS	REMARKS
31st Jan	hostile front line trenches in retaliation. Right section came into action in relief of 2nd Belgian Battery. Right Section under Lt Murray under Centre Group	

J Rose Major
Condg 6th By RFA

3 DIVISION. TROOPS.

40 BRIGADE ROYAL FIELD ARTILLERY.
1914 AUG TO 1919 FEB.

1400

3 DIVISION. TROOPS.

40 BRIGADE ROYAL FIELD
ARTILLERY.
1914 AUG TO 1919 FEB.

1400

BEF

3 DIV TROOPS

40 BDE RFA

1917 JAN — 1917 DEC

WO 95 / 1400

WAR DIARY.

40th. Brigade R. F. A.

3rd. DIVISION.

JANUARY.1917.

WAR DIARY or INTELLIGENCE SUMMARY

Army Form C. 2118

40 Bde R[FA] Vol 29

Place	Date	Hour	Summary of Events and Information	Remarks and references to Appendices
HEBUTERNE	1/7		40TH Bde RFA. ASBUTERNE 10.000 Lt MORRISON attached to 3rd SAC [Trench?] communication with Wilson intercepted. Bde Bump at COLINCAMPS opened. Hostile fire much below normal. RED COTTAGE + SACKVILLE ST + K27a shelled in the evening. We shelled L.25, K30 and intermittent shelling on back areas. Our night firing on K30a, at 6 rounds per hour. 8" KO(RL) relief 10 RWF's in right subsector by 8" KO(RL)	Bde Bump at Red Cottage [illegible]
ditto	2/7		RED COTTAGE, LA SIGNY FARM, 8 TOUVENT FARM, STAFF COPSE, EUSTON — COLINCAMPS ROAD, BAILLEUL RING POSTS K29c + K30c + K33c + 6 rounds per hour — HEBUTERNE. We shelled SERRE & our anything moving on SOUTHERN RAILWAY & TAUPIN TRENCHES the Bivouac shelled per hour. Heavy enemy shelling at night. L29 Battery rifts + gaps & R [illegible] in woods sent forward.	
ditto	3/7	1am	Enemy fire much below normal. A few MG's on RED COTTAGE + 4.2's on K32 a 37. But our fire SQaII K30a 2c + prints on and E of SERRE. Our night firing on front trenches K29 − 30. 6 rounds per hour. 10th RWF's relieve in right subsector. 8" KOH relieve 8" KO RL	
ditto	4/7		Enemy fire above normal. EUSTON — COLINCAMPS ROAD, K26B, LA SIGNY FARM, MINT TRENCH, SOUTHERN TAUPIN — K27c all shelled. We fired on K29 & K30b enemy hard seen. 8/37 aeroplanes our night firing on K29c + d + K30 a c at 6 rounds per hour.	
ditto	5/7	5.30pm 11pm	Enemy fire below normal. Enemy shelled K27c, K26 + K27 + SOUTHERN AVENUE. Our fire on K35 [illegible] 91.4 — K36 871) at 6 rounds per hour. 8" KORL relieved MG HQ Cellar mess under 2nd RWF [illegible] under 10th RWF on the night 4/5 [illegible]. Gas alert K35 d 1.7. SOS fire reported opposite us at 11.50 pm. Our response immediate. 200 [illegible] up on Divisional front	
ditto	6/7		Enemy fire RED COTTAGE, NORTHERN & TOUVENT FARM, L22 a 4.7, L17 a 4.7, LA SIGNY FARM, SOUTHERN T. TAUPIN, FAGNYEVET + VADADE and fire L29 + 2, L19 b, L30.f, J19.b. TEN TREE AVE + K35 d. Our night firing K.35 b 4.2, S.1 − K36 a 0.55 + 6 rds per hour. Relief of 3rd Div commenced gun by 14" d'b9b96 76.85 9] "	
ditto	7/7	6.30am [illegible]	Enemy fire on front line + L298 ROY. Enemy fire on front line + L298 ROY. Other batteries fire aggressive — our fire no response to them heavy enemy fire and night firing on K.35 & 41 s t, SOS — K36 a 0.55. SOS sent to our infantry front	

Army Form C. 2118

WAR DIARY
or
INTELLIGENCE SUMMARY

40TH Bde R.F.A.

(Erase heading not required.)

Instructions regarding War Diaries and Intelligence Summaries are contained in F.S. Regs., Part II. and the Staff Manual respectively. Title Pages will be prepared in manuscript.

Place	Date	Hour	Summary of Events and Information	Remarks and references to Appendices
HEBUTERNE	8/7		Recce of infantry composited with heavy enemy shelling on K21c ROB ROY SOUTHERN TAUPIN NEWGATE, K21c K20 & EUSTON DUMP etc. The 40th Bde have all day were shelled in K15 & TEN TREE ALLEY our night firing K31b 41.5b - K36c 0.52.	10000
	9/7		Wet. Artie in normal. MOYES trench, JOHN/COPSE, MALLARDS & TAUPIN registry shelled our firing incl. FRA programme on night firing on K29 & 57 - K32 & 42. K30 c 15.95 - K30 a 37 21" 49' +130 Return as before.	
	10/7		Fine. Enemy firing normal SACKVILLE & MATHEW COPSE FLAG AVENUE, TAUPIN TRENCH, NEWGATE ST. JOHN COPSE shelled. Artn. Our firing in answer by RA our night firing on K29 & K2c K30 a 2c. K36 a - K36 B.	
	11/7		Fine. Enemy fire LOSINCAMPS EUSTON DUMP K26 & K27 etc our firing incoming to Raiders. night firing the same on land night.	
			Wet	
	12/7	2pm	130 Railway Shell with 4.2's	
			Enemy shelling concentrated on K23 etc. QT's K29. K28 etc + TAUPIN, SOUTHERN EUSTON DUMP & K7c ROB ROY & neighbourhood. No firing in answer by RA. EUSTON DUMP — gunner Battn. 1206 Ammunition Lorries.	
	13/7		Camp. Ourselves think night action. Enemy shelled our front line again & must quit.	
		3.40pm	We retaliated 3 hours on his front trenches. No night firing	
	14/7		97th Inf Bde relieved by 76 etc. Fine. Enemy again shelled our front line & again on 5am on outskirts on K30 a 2c. Shrunn lorries fire been moved on enemy Bde CENTRAL RAILWAY, SOUTHERN AVENUE EUSTON - LOSINCAMP ROAD out from L 25a + L26a. might firing on enemy batteries & supply lines	
		4.30pm	5/87 withdrew from the group.	

Army Form C. 2118

WAR DIARY
or
INTELLIGENCE SUMMARY
(Erase heading not required.)

Instructions regarding War Diaries and Intelligence Summaries are contained in F. S. Regs., Part II. and the Staff Manual respectively. Title Pages will be prepared in manuscript.

FRANCE 100,000/15000 HEBUTERNE 40TH BDE. R.F.A.

Place	Date	Hour	Summary of Events and Information	Remarks and references to Appendices
HEBUTERNE	15/7/17		Hostile fire below normal. On MONK TRENCH & NEWGATE ST. and line behind SERRE + L.25 our night firing on enemy communication trenches. 2nd Lt WRIGHT transferred to R.F.C.	
"	16/7/17		Slow bombardment all day on K.29.c.7.d. Enemy fire below normal. Night firing 4F39 L.25.at. 1 section for battery behind 165 Bde.	
"	17/7/17		On previous day 9th Battery ammunition transport lorries at B.D.S. LES AUTOS YERT GALAND.	
"	18/7/17		The Bde marched to ST OUEN from B.43 via LOUVENCOURT BEAUQUESNE.	
ST OUEN			FARM HAVERNAS HALLOY &c.	
ditto	19/7/17		Training at ST OUEN	
ditto	20/7/17		Training at ST OUEN	
ditto	21/7/17		Training at ST OUEN	
ditto	22/7/17		Training at ST OUEN	
ditto	23/7/17		Training at ST OUEN	
ditto	24/7/17		Training at ST OUEN Col MAIR to C.C.S.	
ditto	25/7/17		Training at ST OUEN	
ditto	26/7/17		Training at ST OUEN	2/Capt HARPER + W. term forsch (in tanks) (130TH BTY)
ditto	27/7/17		Training at ST OUEN 2nd Lt EMPSON return from leave. Lt/Capt WARBURTON to C.C.S.	
ditto	28/7/17		Training at ST OUEN	
SARTON	29/7/17		Bde move to SARTON via BERTAUCOURT CANAPLES HAVERNAS NAOURS BEAUQUESNE MARIEUX &c.	
AUBROMETZ	30/7/17		Bde move to AUBROMETZ via ORVILLE DOULLENS BOUQUEMAISON PREVENT BOUBERS NEULETTE	
ditto	31/7/17			

B.1845 Wt. W593/826 1,000,000 4/15 J.B.C.&A. AUBROMETZ A.D.S.S./Forms/C. 2118.

WAR DIARY.

40th. Brigade R. F. A.

3rd. DIVISION.

FEBRUARY.1917.

WAR DIARY or INTELLIGENCE SUMMARY

Army Form C. 2118

40 Bde R.F.A.

1st - 28th FEB 1918

Place	Date	Hour	Summary of Events and Information	Remarks and references to Appendices
LA COMTE	1/2/17		The Bde marched to LA COMTE via BOUBERS. PREVENT. SERICOURT. BUNEVILLE. TERNAS. MARMCOURT EN COMTE. Owing to state of road(ic) the Bde did not arrive till 5.30pm. 8 hrs on the march. Weather bitterly cold & wet. Sleet. Training continues. W.330pm 8 hrs out ans 3 hrs late up.	
"	2/2/17		ditto	
"	3/2/17		ditto	
"	4/2/17		ditto	
"	5/2/17		ditto	
"	6/2/17		ditto	
"	7/2/17		ditto	
ETREE WAMIN	8/2/17		The Bde is transferred to the VI Corps & marches to ETREE WAMIN via BAILLEUL SUR CORNAILLES. AVERDOIGNT. MAZIERES. MAGNICOURT SUR CANCHE. Training continues.	
" ditto	9/2/17		ditto	
ditto	10/2/17		ditto	
ditto	11/2/17		ditto	
ditto	12/2/17		ditto	
ditto	13/2/17		ditto	
ditto	14/2/17		2nd Lt WARBURTON reformed 49/135 from hospital	
ditto	15/2/17		Bde Comdr. BC's & their officers reconnoitring positions at ARRAS. Major EMPSON BAIRD CPT FORMAN. MTR THOMSON. LT HARKER – LT WILSON all wounded. CAPT FORMAN & LT HARKER TO HOSPITAL 49TH BTY move out into action at G 26 d 00.75, under WEST GROUP wagon lines at WANQUETIN. Rem of Bde continue training. 30 men per battery working party to ARRAS. They left ...	
ditto	16/2/17		- ditto -	
ditto	17/2/17		- ditto -	

Army Form C. 2118

WAR DIARY
or
INTELLIGENCE SUMMARY
(Erase heading not required.)

LENS 1/100000
ST B NW 3. 1/10000

Instructions regarding War Diaries and Intelligence Summaries are contained in F.S. Regs., Part II. and the Staff Manual respectively. Title Pages will be prepared in manuscript.

Place	Date	Hour	Summary of Events and Information	Remarks and references to Appendices
ETREE WAMIN	18/3/17		Bde less 49" Bty continue training. Working party digging position at ARRAS	
ditto	19/3/17		ditto. ditto ditto	
ditto	20/3/17		49" + 23" Bty continue training. 23rd Bty march to WANQUETIN. BDE H.QRS. moved to WANQUETIN	
			Working party continues	
WANQUETIN	21/3/17		at ETREE WAMIN 9am 23rd Bty 3/70 into action at ARRAS at	
			Working party continues digging	
ditto	22/3/17		G 2 & b 7. 8. invited WEST GROUP ditto	
ditto	23/3/17		6" Bty moved to repair lines at WANQUETIN. 1.30 pm Bty continues training. Working party at ARRAS	
ditto	23/3/17		6"Bty + 130. Bty continue training. Working party at ARRAS	
ditto	24/3/17		ditto ditto	
ditto	25/3/17		ditto ditto	
ditto	26/3/17		ditto ditto	
ditto	27/3/17		ditto ditto	
ditto	28/3/17		ditto ditto	

WAR DIARY.

40th. Brigade. R. F. A.

3rd. DIVISION.

MARCH. 1917.

WAR DIARY or INTELLIGENCE SUMMARY

Army Form C. 2118

40TH BDE. RFA

1st to 31st March 1917.

FRANCE '51 & NW 3 LENS 11

Place	Date	Hour	Summary of Events and Information	Remarks and references to Appendices
WANQUETIN	1/3/7		2nd Lt 49th Bty watching the line under O.C. 42nd Bde.	
ditto	2/3/7		Unusually quiet. Bad weather. SE of ROLLINCOURT.	
			130 – 6" Btys remain at WANQUETIN	
ditto	3/3/7		23rd 49 Btys under 42nd Bde on the line	
			6" + 130 Btys remain at WANQUETIN	
ditto	4/3/7		23rd 49 – ditto	
			6" + 130 Btys – ditto	
ARRAS ditto	5/3/7		Bde Hqrs moved to 96 RUE ST AUBERT ARRAS. 1 section 130 Bty move into ARRAS. G33a 7.7.	
	6/3/7	6.50am	2nd Lt SHAW posted to K gallery A.A. Unicorpse nest on Nauaye muchin E of ARRAS. G36c 50. 8.5- Arty	
			Pete hunghi 6" Bty move to ARRAS. G33c 4.6. With 1 Gordon Highlanders. 40th Bde to operate.	
			1 gun 23rd 49 Btys under 42nd Bde. 6" + 2 sects 130 remain at WANQUETIN.	
ditto	7/3/7		23rd 49 – Btys under 42nd Bde. 6" + 1 sect 130 remain at WANQUETIN.	
ARRAS	8/3/7		Bde Hqrs move to 96 RUE ST AUBERT. ARRAS. Major Snijoon granted 3 days leave. True	
			23rd 49" + 1 sect 130 at ARRAS Remains at WANQUETIN	
ditto	9/3/7		ditto	
ditto	10/3/7		6" Bty regist 2 guns on H25d S.1. by aeroplane. Ammunition expenditure 104. rds.	
ditto	11/3/7		23rd Bty moved into new position. G27 d 8.0. 1 section. Tres. Amm expended 63. rds.	
ditto	12/3/7		4 O.P's selected, Tank, Bde 20a Brewery Road (a) 6B at 60E Goda helm (130 r 23) 21. Rue	
			Jeanne d'Arc. (49). Pontoon Call Woronet JH 63. R. Amm expended nil.	
ditto	13/3/7		6 lorde remr returns from CAP MARTIN. CAPT BODY posted to BDE.	1500 yds SW of WANQUETIN CHURCH on the WANQUETIN – FOSSEUX ROAD
			British Inf 185 yrds. sent to R.A. Amm expended nil. Bde HQ. WAGON LINES. 23rd Bty	1500 yds on the WANQUETIN – FOLLEW ROAD
ditto	14/3/7		Major Robinson ditto Ltur 130 + 135 Btys Amm received 1948.	6" Bty
			changer. Amm expended nil.	23rd. 1500 yds SW of WANQUETIN HAUTEVILLE ROAD
ditto	15/3/7		Tres Amm expended nil. Ammer received 2679.2.	49. 1300 yds SW of church on WANQUETIN – FOSSEUX ROAD
				130. WANQUETIN to the WANQUETIN – FOSSEUX ROAD

WAR DIARY
or
INTELLIGENCE SUMMARY

Army Form C. 2118

(Erase heading not required.)

LENS. II 1/100,000
40TH Bde R.F.A.
FRANCE 51 B N.W. 3. 1/10,000

Place	Date	Hour	Summary of Events and Information	Remarks and references to Appendices
ARRAS.	16/7/17	6.30pm	Ammn expended 30. Bde Hy mortars & 33 Rue Jean D'Arc ARRAS. Fire	
do	17/7/17		Ammn expended 72. Reservoir 12430	
do	18/7/17	7am	35 Bde Inf Bde raid on 9.30 to 21 minutes. Bde's co-operated. Fire Ammn expended. 9" Hy Bde relieved the 8" Bde in the Line. Fire	
do	19/7/17		Ammn expended. 76. Reservoir 2292. + 2436. 23rd Bty reverted WEST GROUP for S.O.S. West	
do	20/7/17		Ammn expended. 27. Reservoir 840. 23rd Bty retained a reserve gun at 9.36.B.64½	
do	21/7/17	6pm	Bde Cdrs conference with B C.B. No fire	
do	22/7/17 22/7/17	9pm	Expended Ammn. 4 + 6. Reservoir. 40" Bde co-operated 1 st R.F.A.'s and Austrian 9.36.B.1.8. machineguns & aeroplanes on 1st 31st Bde 9.36.B.9.1.9. Fire Ammn expended. 1826. 130 18 lb rounds by aeroplane on 1st 31st Bde 9.36.B.9.1.9. Fire Reservoir. 1540	
do	23/7/17		From this date onwards 6" Bty's captured Martin trenches northern by firing 3 rounds every 5 minutes during night German trench exchange were cutting at 9.36.B 6.7. Fire 35 Bde Inf Bde raid on enemy W.20. W.21. 49t & 11th Bde co-operated & for preventing relief Ammn Expended 397 enemy short shrapnel & the Evening Station on ACHICOURT Rd	
do	24/7/17	6.45am	6" Bty served 3 rd Div French trench mortars Shoots for Lettony onwards. The 6" Bty's again co-operated Ammn expended. unknown adopted with R. F.M.S.	
do	25/7/17	11 pm	Lt 2nd/Lt BALSTON posted to Bde attached 6" Bty	
			Ammn Expended 379 Retd to ARD 45	
do	26/7/17		23rd Bty organize a 4 Bde shoot in front of DEVOY. Enemy mine cutting on 2nd Brigade & back. Ammn more cutting by 15 pdrs on 3 enemy lines in front of TILLOY. Ammn Expended. 995 Reservoir 1680.	

WAR DIARY
or
INTELLIGENCE SUMMARY

Army Form C. 2118

48TH BDE R.F.A.

LENS II 1/100,000
FRANCE 57.13. NW 3. 1/10,000

Place	Date	Hour	Summary of Events and Information	Remarks and references to Appendices
ARRAS.	27/7/17	7. am	Enemy retaliation 2nd & Love patrol to the Bde ⁓ to the 23rd Bdy wet. Enemy bombardment on G.36.b. G.30.d. Our guns retaliated by Batterie. Minor shelling continues.	
		3 pm	Barrage practised. G.30.d. G.36.b. H.31.a etc. CRA Bde Comr ⁓ B.C.s observe upper. Bdy up of 8 Gunners arrived. Minor shelling continues. ⁓ 10 Gunners arrived.	
do	28/7/17	6.30 pm	Neighbourhood of 13th Bde Hy Howitzers. Minor shelling continues fine. 6" Bdy cooperated with TM's during the day.	
		4.30 pm	130 Rgt shelled. 568 2 set 3 sets of wire now cut by Batterie. Minor cutting continues. Ammunition expended 99.3. Fine.	
do	29/7/17		Bde Hy now to N°1 Rue de TROIS POMMETTES. Ammunition expended 79.3. Reserve. Fine.	
do	30/7/17		6" Bdy cooperate with TM's. Front kept now cutting rest of Batteries continue minor cutting on 2nd & 3rd rows. Ammunition expended 178. Drawn 1925. Wet.	
do	31/7/17	1 pm	This most of the day made main in the effort. Enemy retaliated by a general shelling of front line. Brigade cooperate with TM's trench mortars. Minor cutting continues. No. 11. G.20 & G.6.	
			A/49 Battery attached to the Brigade in position No. 11. G.20 & G.6. At the end of the month the whole of the guns are up at ARRAS on forward wagon lines. 200 yds S.E. of road junction 3 RUE DE TROIS POMMETTES. WANQUETIN - FOSSEUX - HAUTEVILLE Churches on the WANQUETIN - FOSSEUX road. ARRAS.	
			HQ. 3 RUE DE TROIS POMMETTES.	
			6 G.13.c.4.6. 1500 yds SW of WANQUETIN CHURCH - HAUTEVILLE ROAD.	
			23 G.27.d.9.1. 1650 yds SW of " - "	
			49 G.26.d.75.00. 1500 yds SW of " - "	
			130. G.33.a.7.7. 1500 yds SW of " - FOSSEUX ROAD.	
			Amm Expended 680 Res. nil.	

Brian Grant Colonel
O/C 48 F. Bde RFA

WAR DIARY.

40th. Brigade. R. F. A.

3rd. DIVISION.

APRIL. 1917.

WAR DIARY
40TH Bde R.F.A. INTELLIGENCE SUMMARY

Army Form C. 2118

40 Bde RFA
LENS 1" 100000
FRANCE 57B NW3 1/20000

Place	Date	Hour	Summary of Events and Information	Remarks and references to Appendices
ARRAS.	1/5	11.5pm	Fine but cool. Enemy shelling rather more than normal A/159 reported a shelter (trestles) at ARRAS necessitating forward wagon lines. Wire cutting continued by see Capt Bosley moved out of forward position at G.29.a.58. to old position. Battries. 6th Bty moved out of forward position by Group P. 707 Ammunition expended G.36.c.4.6.	
ARRAS.	2/5	5.30pm	Fine in the morning, rain towards evening. Two sets of Ruining Out storing drawn from DUISANS + 4 Maps boards from R.A. dump Refilled the 22 wagons. Not enough from BOULOGNE had 31st Decentralised 23rd 8 49.3 130.11. Battries Regt replenish to bring up 6 wagons of ammunition for Battries over the selected dump Nos. 2 DAC loan 15 GS wagons to front. 130 Batt to try up ammunition at night. BC's and Colonels confirmed reconnaissance for Brigade registration. authority received to draw 50 extra main bands of gaps on the mine N of the CAMBRAI during the day. The 6" Bty kept up intermittent fire on the gaps in the wire. N of the CAMBRAI ROAD. The 23 in Bty on the 2nd & 3rd line wire. Wire cutting continued but greatly hindered by bad visibility. Retaliation on German support line on the Bry shelling incline (by instruction of WEST GROUP) by 49 arrived. Amm expended 849. Amm expended Luzer's 6" 34. 23rd 33. 49" 33. 130" 11.	
ARRAS.	3/5	4-5pm	R.S.M. Mara 10D 18 fds Amm. Ammo from Ordnance. Luzer's 6" 10. 23" 11. 49" 12. 130" 11. Enemy movements distributed at wagon tin, 6" 10. 23" 11. 49" 12. 130" 11. 11.9 S Wagons SAA available for 130" Bt4 y. The enemy during the day were quite subdued at 130" at H.31a.90. the remainder in H.31a/B.h. wire cutting. During the night the 49 and 130th Bty, registered by salvoes. Hardly any fire out during the day.	
ARRAS.	4/5	6.30am 6.36AM	V. hazy. fine 8.30am Phase A 18 pdrs on front System. G.30.d.15.10 - G.36.15.70. night firing on gaps. 40 Bde take over the defence of the line from G.30.d.32.50. to G.36 & 35.05. 8.69 Recd from Corps 1024 Amm expended for wire cutting returned to 900 per Bty.	

1875 Wt. W593/826 1,000,000 4/15 T.R.C. & A. A.D.S.S./Forms/C. 2118.
Gun Reports 18pdrs Abd. Stove. 6. Amm asked for wire cutting returned to 900 per Bty.

WAR DIARY or INTELLIGENCE SUMMARY

Army Form C. 2118

40TH BDE R.F.A.

LENS 1/100000
FRANCE 57B NW 3 1/10.000

Place	Date	Hour	Summary of Events and Information	Remarks and references to Appendices
ARRAS	4/9		Enemy enemy trench bombardment only slight. Wire cutting carried out all day.	
		11:50pm	2nd Lt. PRICE & PREEBLE to take 4th Bde SOS rockets to 42nd Bde.	
dito	5/9		W. day. Wire cutting continued. Enemies quiet.	
		2:10am	Enemy No 9 6/4 of 130th By. completely destroyed by big shell. Lgh of 4/2 shell. Major ROBINSON severely wounded, 2 2/L FAUSSET gassed. Lgh of 4/2 shell. Major ROBINSON severely wounded by being blown out of gun pit by an explosion. In trying to recognise position he was wounded in hip. Gun pit was now no. 1 gun reported totally unworkable. Shell so he gun pit were men gas shells. There was very little enemy fire but enemy shells to moon by group 5/89	
			Enemy repeated to moon by group firing from ammunition difficulty	
			at 6.15am & 7.0 am artillery from a hostile remains in the wagon lines.	
		11:55pm	2/Lt. MOYO & 2/Lt LAMBERT were attacked to the Brigade continue in the afternoon. Some gas alarm in ARRAS.	
ARRAS	6/9		Fine 2 day deployed 24 hour time in the morning warmth. Paired behind our line.	
			The group continue wire cutting. Some wagons (ammunition) hostile. On Bde 18th Inf Div.	
			2nd position have a very tough time, appreciated 12 of new approx	
			and 2/3 no in no ammunition & men of equipment. The horses opposite 2 rounds, were in our S. Bn. received a direct hit. 3 officers wounded & groups 7 & 7	
			Lt. Pratt Jas. Briar visited this H.Q. Ammunition expended by groups 747	
		12:5pm	GOCRA 7th Div visited this H.Q.	
		6:0pm	Practise barrage, difficult to observe be monitoring	
		6:30pm	appeared good	
		8:20pm	during enemy bombardment. Enemy active during the day.	
		5:50pm		
		8:40pm	Keep nothing in particular apart from N.T.B. Enemy artillery very good. Ammunition expended this was exceed 8 day, it was a fine day, visibility very good. Nos & in CAMBRAI ROAD.	
ARRAS	7/9		4390 ammunition on hand to group 38904. Enemy a quiet night with to 12 noon particularly no fire before 11am, be continued intermittent from RSF: as G.36 & 2.9	
		9pm	Raid by 1st W.RSF's at G.36 & 2.9 after a failure.	
		11:05am		

Army Form C. 2118

WAR DIARY
or
INTELLIGENCE SUMMARY
(Erase heading not required.)

40TH Bde RFA   FRANCE 51 B NW3 10,000

Place	Date	Hour	Summary of Events and Information	Remarks and references to Appendices
ARRAS	8/4/17		Y day, and a fine day. Ammunition reported SPQQ on the preliminary bombardment & wire cutting, which continued all day.	
		8.30 am	Practise Barrage today timed but appeared good.	
		3.15 pm	Practise barrage appeared vivid & corrected good.	
		5.30 pm	Conference of B.C.'s when the Colonel explained the situation & orders for the attack.	
		8 pm	2nd Lt's CARBUTT & PAGE, the F.O.O's for tomorrow came to dinner with the Colonel & received their orders given them.	
ARRAS	9/4/17	5.29 am	Z day. Zero hour. Opened the bombardment for the battle.	
		5.30 am	18 pdrs open up.	
		6.30 am	1st gunners reported to have taken 3rd line.	
		7 am	Capt TREVENEN reports GLASGOW TRENCH.	
		7.10 am	Barrage opens 77 mm barrage on our front line, very light.	
		7.30 am	42nd Bde report all objectives opposite to taken.	
		7.50 am	Capt TREVENEN reports our troops in NOMENY TRENCH in N1a.	
		8.26 am	Western edge of the HARP occupied, reported by FOO A/59.	
		8.30 am	Report from 42nd Bde. Our men in TILLOY and attacking the STRING.	
		8.50 am	Report from 2nd Lt PAGE. Seven men at N.13.1.6. all taken appear clearly samt	
		9.20 am	Report from 2nd Lt PAGE. Enemy again on the move S. of TILLOY.	
		9.40 pm	3rd Bn orders 40" Bde for tomorrow. We the permanent position in advance. A/59 returns to its own billets.	
			6" 9.24 c 95.	
			49th 9.29 c 94.	
			29 9.29 c 91.	
			130 9.28 c 93.	

WAR DIARY or INTELLIGENCE SUMMARY

Army Form C. 2118

Place	Date Hour	Summary of Events and Information	Remarks and references to Appendices
ARRAS.	9/4/17 9.45am	The Genl. moved forward his new HQ in the German Dugout in the old German front line at G.36.c.9. FIB NW3 TOWER LEWIS II [Longpré?]	
	12.20am	All Batteries ready to open fire on zero hour.	
	1.15pm	Batteries ordered to open fire on German Dugout.	
	1.45pm	Adjutant moves up to new German Dugout.	
	2pm	42nd Bde ordered to advance by R.A.	
	6.59pm	Fire opened on the Brown Line (FEUCHY CHAPEL LINE) until 7pm.	
	7pm	Barrage lifts, support line behind Brown line still continues barrage.	
	7.57pm	Barrage lifts on to protective barrage ordered as follows: N10 c.8.2 to N10 central.	
	8.45pm	Night firing 60 rounds per battery for the evening moved up into the valley behind the HARP. 42nd Bde could not open fire until 7pm because the cavalry were in the way. Col WEST 42nd Bde takes over the line from Col MAIR 40th BDE at 7.10pm. This front amounts ate nights up to 10.15am.	
ARRAS.	10/4/17 12 noon	Again heavy fire attack on the Brown line. 40th Bde from N10 c.06 to N10 a.05.1.5. N10 c.8.2 to N10 central. lift 100 yds in 3 minutes. 40th Bde still to reconnoitre new positions. Gun teams and limbers for guns allotted.	
	1pm 2pm	Went up to gun position.	
	4.30pm 7.30pm	No 2 section C/40 attached to this Bde for ammunition supplying. Hq moves to GIRLS SCHOOL. Batteries move into action at N2d.	

WAR DIARY or INTELLIGENCE SUMMARY

Army Form C. 2118

(Erase heading not required.)

LENS II 50000
S13 NW3 10000

Place	Date	Hour	Summary of Events and Information	Remarks and references to Appendices
ARRAS	10/7	11.45pm	40TH Bde RFA — The Colonel received orders by 5o B Feuchy Chapel & the 76 Bde were to attack at 5 a.m. The day has been most cold.	
	11/7	7 pm	The attack on QUEMAPPE had taken place at 9 a.m. The infantry taken satisfactorily. This attack was carried up and not any advance in reaching the trenches ahead on the east of the village.	
		2.30 pm	The attack on QUEMAPPE was renewed by the 76th Inf Bde. Much artillery movements in advance gave day at 7 am. Majority of Posts were reported taken on the left. The Royals 4 Coys of 7 men out of 30 Coys of the Tilloy Wancourt Road at M36.17. [illegible] with cement of [illegible] 4 artillery brigades 40 + 50, 53-59 artillery that [illegible] the Colonel with [illegible] Quemappe.	
TILLOY	11/7	7.15 am	This day cold. The artillery protected 130 Bty to fire on machine guns in N14 & T19.	
		10.30 pm	Brigade [illegible] right infantry attack in WANCOURT Bde preparing to like the high ground in N25. 40.000 comparis and R advanced ahead.	
			The 6R Barrs from N16A12 to N12L00 mark 1 metre per battery for Bombardment by the 3rd BA	
WANCOURT	13/7	7 pm	During the day the 9" Inf Bde prepared for the attack on QUEMAPPE which was delivered at 7 pm. The Brigade went up. 16 Inf Bde formed HQ on M10 & 4.6. The 3rd Bde Artillery from the enemy barrage to the 151 Inf Bde. 50 Div 130x129 HQ of 50 Div to Garage in Railway + QUEMAPPE. The attack was a failure. During the night the 3rd Divisional Infantry were relieved by the 29th Div + the 3rd Div Arty came under the command of the CRA 29 Div. This day cold	

WAR DIARY or INTELLIGENCE SUMMARY

(Erase heading not required.)

Army Form C. 2118

Instructions regarding War Diaries and Intelligence Summaries are contained in F.S. Regs., Part II. and the Staff Manual respectively. Title Pages will be prepared in manuscript.

40TH BDE RFA   57 BMW 3 GUEMAPPE

Place	Date	Hour	Summary of Events and Information	Remarks and references to Appendices
WANCOURT	14/7		In the morning with the object of determining new positions in N6c up the road in the corner of the high ground E of Minory Avery Fatm, the movement of the persons was observed which we cc 12a's surrounded by big guns. SOS lines for the majors O8c.64 - O6c.13, O11c ∞ GAMBRAI ROAD O7a - O13b	
WANCOURT	15/7	5.30am	The 29" Div attacked the high ground O2c, immediately for an hour was The 78th & 79 Bdns along the morning & standing barrage respectively. The 40th Bde dealing on enemy ready to move at one hours notice after 7am. The attack did not succeed, two battalions did not move, the remains & 2 rec. the attack & little was done on ADRAS, the four other movement to keep the ground referred to. Wagon lines at ADRAS. SOS lines on F.35 [illegible] N18 central. SOS here 5.30-13 O7d - O13.6 (GAMBRAI ROAD) all day. Slight move to the prevailed stop. Nothing poor throughout the day.	
WANCOURT	16/7	10am 11am	87 by Bde Hq. moves 15 N9d.49 Lewis on Officer and MO Wilkinson gun with return. During the night the 87th & 88 Bde relieved in brigade front at N18 A53 reported SOS Lewis from N18.11 to N18.67 to O7c06, when established new from a weight 8 nanny. The day kept up an reported new. Reps to O19 the young hands of gum lifts up on B13/4 and any staff movement in O19 B. 130 hrs. Attacked GUEMAPPE the whole 0.19 to O10b - O15A to the 23rd Reg. TMB S.S. no at present 130. TMB.49 SOS lines N18.11 - N18.67 - M18.55. Pillow 8276 gun 127 dischinic gun 164	

WAR DIARY
or
INTELLIGENCE SUMMARY

(Erase heading not required.)

Army Form C. 2118

Place	Date	Hour	Summary of Events and Information	Remarks and references to Appendices
WANCOURT	17/5		40TH Bde RFA 57BNW3 1/10,000 GUEMAPPE	
			During during the day. The Bde fired bursts of fire on any observed movement of the enemy which was very small, in O.19. On the enemy rear of GUEMAPPE. S.O.S. lines for the night N18 & 11 - 18 & 26 - N17 & 55. Ammunition expended 296.	
	18/5/17		During the night the enemy shelled the Bty Hqrs/neighbourhood pretty severely also enemy any cavalcade in the Bde later staff without Result. Ammunition expended 3440 rounds. The Hqrs Bty drove over enemy near FEUCHY FREYENT & 6" Bty guns No 2207 continued firing the following targets were engaged during the day. Battery in action at O.14 & 11.5 and observed shots on enemy ammunition an aniple fire. The enemy shelled the North of Wancourt sectors position. shin valleys during the day was poor.	
	19.5.17	5pm	During the first part of the day the Group VBC's ammunition suspension in the morning. COLONEL MAIR later met command at night. Bde Group operating at 40 + 42 Sec RFA & the Bde Hqrs moved to "the dug-out eatery occupied by CRA 3rd Div at N2 & 83. At 1pm stored that the batteries near the pavilion. 6"N15 d 87 21"N16 a 94 44"N15 d 56 136" N15 d 94 Ammunition expended 105 rounds. The smoke I hope for gun ammunition way to HARP. During the day the ministry was poor & any settlement was observed. The enemy shelled the North of Mt Guard pavilion heavily. The SOS line both night M18d 24 15 Y18 & 10 down to No 8 for GUEMAPPE. 9.O.C. KA. 15 Bde Ammn command at N Bde 29 Sir.	
		6pm	The 15" gun relieve No 57 Bde.	
		10.30pm	2nd LT GRIES reported wounded by shell, dying in the morning 2 OR were killed + 4 wounded.	
	20.5.17	1pm	A fine day. Ammunition expended 12 still in noon. Registration carried out on the front from M19d 52.4 RONANT FACTORY Entrance in N14c Enemy Dugouts FEUCHY CHAPEL. The Batteries here fired bursts on the West of MONCHY. AMMY CORNER. N6c N18c.	

WAR DIARY or INTELLIGENCE SUMMARY

Army Form C. 2118

(Erase heading not required.)

Place	Date	Hour	Summary of Events and Information	Remarks and references to Appendices
WANCOURT	20/9	6.45pm	SOS sent given on N.18 d.29 to N.18 b.65.7/2. MAJOR C.E. NEARY DSO. RFA posted to the Brigade.	
WANCOURT	21/9		This day Major NEARY joined the Bde, attached to 6" Bty. A forward dump of ammunition was started 2nd Lt JOHNSON joined the Bde, attached to 6" Bty. A forward dump of ammunition was started at N.9.a.1.3. The heavy enemy shrapnel by No 2 section DAC, wagons dispersed to 12 noon. SOS. No enemy shells were engaged, mainly by 12 noon. Our firing the day was spread about with the ammunition expended. Our firing the day was spread about with the being very poor all morning, no by the enemy & also in every observed enemy within of patrolling any digging in by the enemy & also in every observed enemy movement.	
	22/9	7am–6pm	This day was well ammunition expended 16.1.9. One broken - wagon sample W of the HARP was also in HQ wagon ambulance was night. The water for the horses BC's enemy at 14.9. The Colonel reports the details up the orders for the horses During the day the front over the guns in front of our line and no observed movement N.4.C. was heavily shelled, LES FOSSES FARM – LA BERGERE, WANCOURT also was shelled. Shells also were nearly active, also 2 hostile balloons up behind VIS EN ARTOIS watched movement for the shew.	
		10pm		
	23/9	4.45am	The 1st Infantry made 0.20 a.07. Across the stream to trench before in 0.7 a 9.1. 0.21 central Division the attack up the spur to 0.9 & 0.7.1. battalion in new front line. Which of manifest moved up at a much of the column being made more men not during H.W. extreme in at Z known in front 12 minute decline the attack dawned the enemy outcome near 3 minute 4 minutes 150 to 200 enemy 3 mins, after had from 150 to 200 yards. The first objective except CAVALRY FARM the infantry succeeded in gaining the whole of the first objective, were on all day & night in 0.14 a. and around this spur to along the attack were on all day & night.	

Army Form C. 2118

WAR DIARY
or
INTELLIGENCE SUMMARY
(Erase heading not required.)

Instructions regarding War Diaries and Intelligence Summaries are contained in F.S. Regs., Part II. and the Staff Manual respectively. Title Pages will be prepared in manuscript.

Place	Date	Hour	Summary of Events and Information	Remarks and references to Appendices
WANCOURT	23/7		Contradictory reports were arriving the whole of the day as to the advance suffered in the morning.	
		6 p.m.	The guns (under heavy shelling) wagons were very busy bringing up ammunition. the whole day and at 6 p.m. an 18 pdr barrage was formed on 013.c.85 to 07.d.47, the 46th Inf Bde formed thro' Mr 44 + 45 Inf Bdes + captured the first objective. the barrage manifest on the rate of 100 yds per 4 minutes, rested 300 yds beyond the 1st objective which had become the final objective for the day. The Stun Bty fired on the N flank of the COJEUL RIVER 100 yds in front of the 18 pdr barrage.	
		13:45 p.m.	At midnight the following SOS lines were given L/C. 0.14.d.7½.4.2 to 0.14.6.7½.0. Mr 130 Bty fired on ROBART FACTORY. 16 pdrs 86 lbs per hour 24 rds per hour. CAPT MUNT LIAISON OFFICER	
			Ammunition expended up to 12 noon 5112 rounds. 2nd LT STAGG in Bn FOD	
WANCOURT	24/7		The guns began to open new ground during the morning, during the day 015c. 015d LANYARD Battery. The day was first warm, pumping 300 yds above + 100 yds N + S. TRENCH. 0.14.d. 015a. Remaining enemy ... on the 1st objective advance was already keen	
		4 p.m.	At 4 pm guns stood for the final attack. 2nd LT SHIELDS an Bde F.O.O. to-day.	
		6.5 p.m.	LT WILSON Liaison Officer — 2nd LT FISHER	
			Ammunition expended to 12 noon 10101.	
		12.10 p.m.	SOS lines 0.14.a. 00 to 0.14.c. 07. — CAVALRY FARM. Batteries still keeping up to 500 RPG	
		9:58 p.m.	SOS lines 0.14.d.45 to 0.14.d.82 — ROBART FACTORY CAPT PERKINS LIAISON OFFICER	
WANCOURT	25/7		LT SPOOL relieves LT SHIELDS as F.O.O. guns Nr 5144 + 4578 + 2231 condemned for sundry ammunition expended 6.12 noon 6999. In addition five rounds troops are being ... a very fine day, ammunition fresh. the 6" Bty fired on second pattern of the enemy with good results.	

WAR DIARY or INTELLIGENCE SUMMARY

Army Form C. 2118

Place: WANCOURT

Date	Hour	Summary of Events and Information	Remarks and references to Appendices
26/9		40th Bde R.F.A.	57B N.W.3 1/10000 GUEMAPPE
	10.30pm	The day was fine. WANCOURT was shelled during the day with 4.1"s & 5.9"s. and firing was on any observed enemy movement on our front. There was not much to report. Bombardment of CAVALRY FARM & the neighbourhood commenced 10.30pm. The Bde opened up with 3 minutes intense fire at 10.33pm that lifted & rested on hostile O14a till 10.36pm + then lifting onto LANYARD TRENCH. Ahd the attack was unsuccessful on account of the FARM. Ammunition expended up to 12 noon 1488.	
	[illegible]	The S.O.S. firing for the night were 150 yds west of the line O14d00 – O14d 52.7. No further attack. ROBART FACTORY The 4.4 + 4.5 Hwy Bdes carried out the above attack.	
27/9	4.45am	This day the 1st Army + 17 Corps are on our left are to continue the advance and along the front. Barrage was put up to deceive the enemy as to the front of the attack at 4.25 we barraged O20a 8+5+ to O14a 8+8+ lifting at the rate of 100 yds every 4 minutes reaching the rear of the Bde front on the line O14a 6.32 – O14d 23 programme was again the Bde fired on the mobile[?] price bhd. the muddible[?] zone prod. searching back SOO yds tooks up 36 rounds per battery. SOS line O14cB0 – B[?]to O.14 central Ammunition expended to 12 noon 4823.	
28/9		This morning through the Colonel, who had been ill for 2 days went down to ARRAS. B.Q. Behrman saw the Colonel before the attack was on to the Colonel began. Major C. Vickery D.S.O. came to take up. The commencement of the 15th Div heavy artillery districts sent enemy returned to in the 56th Div. [illegible] relief of the 15th Div. heavy artillery districts sent enemy returned to in the 56th Div. slight enemy movement N.E. of ROBART FACTORY. O16 a 63. lost front so much. Sgt. ful Gunner stelled minutely. Ammunition expended 3694 in shortly CAMBRAI ROAD WANCOURT to GUEMAPPE stelled minutely to prevent the enemy tapping on 36 rds for night for him N15 6&. 24 rds for night firing O14 Central	
	7.30pm	SOS fire for the night O14c80 – [illegible] O63 – O14 central	
29/9	11.15am	A fine sunny day Major Vickey DSO's reconnoitres new positions in N16a & . Ammunition expended 4-12 noon 2196 rounds. fired on small enemy movements in LANYARD TRENCH probably lows CAMBRAI ROAD N16 + N11a WANCOURT TOWER GUEMAPPE N16a + [illegible]	
	6.30pm	stuttel SOS line O14c90 – O14c7.4	

WAR DIARY
or
INTELLIGENCE SUMMARY

Army Form C. 2118

Place	Date	Hour	Summary of Events and Information	Remarks and references to Appendices
WANCOURT	30/7/17		40th Bde R.F.A. 51 B NW 3 1/10000 GUEMAPPE	
			This day's work repeated 22.5.B. The enemy shelled GUEMAPPE, MONCHY + CAMBRAI ROAD leaving Towards the afternoon. During the afternoon evening the front in HANYARD TRENCH. 014c90 - 0142 y.4 and was SOS by East. M189 r.C. The 6 + 23 + 25% advanced moving into their positions. The 6th Bty having on	
		7.0pm	they were shelled on their way out – did nor fire no casualties to personnel on gun were killed another guns no casualties to personnel or equipments.	

WAR DIARY.

40th. Brigade. R. F. A.

3rd. DIVISION.

MAY. 1917.

WAR DIARY or INTELLIGENCE SUMMARY

Army Form C. 2118

WM 33 40th Bde R.F.A. 1st – 31st May 1917

Place	Date	Hour	Summary of Events and Information	Remarks and references to Appendices
MANCOURT	1/5	4pm	First day in preparation for the battle the Bde Hq move to the 49 & 26 Bn Dugouts and many of the unpaid sheltering the headquarters moves. Battle front line reached at N.2.a.62. The cellars etc line at N16.f.18. Leaving behind at N18a.46 & N18.b.15.	57 B S.W.2. 57 C N.W.3.
		7pm	The 49th & 130 Bty move into position at N18a.46 & N18.b.15. Ammn expended 2741.	
	2/5		This day the Brigade continued digging in their new positions & the Hqs settled in Army HQ.	
		8.30pm	The 130 Bty near the Bois du VERT with lethal & lachrymatory shell preparatory to the attack.	
		9.45pm	Ammunition expended 1509.	
		7pm	All batteries in their new position as reported.	
	3/5	3.45am	The Barrage opened.	
		8am	The line from CAVALRY FARM CAMBRAI ROAD in fact as O15.c.10.80 and Kernel S to the COJEUL RIVER the 167 Bde have now advanced at all & the 14th Div reported to be EAST of CHERISY.	
		11am	Lt WRIGHT FOO reports from CAVALRY FARM Enemy massing for counter attacks S of BOIS du VERT. Brigade Commander turned on batteries 232 F.A. Brigade 110 Bde RFA – 41st Bde RFA supported.	
		12.30pm	14th Div men counter attacked & forced back to their original line.	
		1pm	Reported that 169 Inf Bde also have been flanks unsupported.	

Army Form C. 2118

WAR DIARY
or
INTELLIGENCE SUMMARY
(Erase heading not required.)

Place	Date	Hour	Summary of Events and Information	Remarks and references to Appendices
WANCOURT	3/5	1pm	The 167 Inf Bde reported attached front to ourselves when enjoined. From 1am we maintained the protective barrage throughout the remainder of the day & night. One battalion of the 23rd Bde being kept in reserve in our battery front at minimum. TOOL & PIT TRENCHES. The 3 Coy shelled ROMART FACTORY, TOOL & LANYARD TRENCHES & PONT A TRDIS QUEULES. Enemy munitions persistent and mainly distributed barrage fire during the day & night speaking up from time to time. The raining of the guns altered during the night. Counterbattery experience 2 hours from 6-18 pm 2-3am. 2nd Lt BAGG & 4 O.R.s wounded. 1 Lt 49 Bty for duty. Major MEYNELL + 1 O.R. of 232 Bde wounded. Ammunition expended by the Bde. 5678 by M.A. – 6/232 – 563.	

WAR DIARY or INTELLIGENCE SUMMARY

Army Form C. 2118

Place	Date	Hour	Summary of Events and Information	Remarks and references to Appendices
VINCOURT	4/5/17	7.20 pm	2nd Lt SPOOR from from trench P.C. sent slip off as ammunition wagon gone to hospital. Took slip for #/2/r & 6/2/r1 asked to withdraw 6" & 4.9" btys over their dumps. The batteries were ordered over by steady fire during the night. Ammunition Expended SOS 6	
	5/5/17		This day 2nd Lt STAGG goes to rest hospital.	
		10.30 pm	SOS signals reported from 42nd Div on our right O.P. She wore rangefinder reported fire on Mui SOS lines went at 10.45 pm all reported gone to 1554.	
		4pm	Rounds expended SOS and O14.C.70 – O14d 7.5 determining line happy up. Kneyham the day 500 yds East of SOS lines. Observed rounds by 130° OP on VIS-EN-ARTOIS will procure effect. The taking positions was cleared with the whole during the night party shell demolishing this day and eastern the french mortar trigger partly shell demolishing the new O.P. in the BROWN LINE at Ammunition Expended 334. . ROHART FACTORY & LANYARD TRENCH shelled during the day. Also the entrance to VIS-EN-ARTOIS by the CAMBRAI ROAD. Showing little enemy movement.	
	6/5/17 4pm-6			
	7/5/17	12.30 pm	This day. The 6" btys shot at an Enemy Balloon behind VIS EN ARTOIS and open sights at GOOD targets. Rounds expended 1572. Following points registered O22a 8.9. O21d 4.6.2. little enemy movement observed & no change in the situation	

WAR DIARY
or
INTELLIGENCE SUMMARY
(Erase heading not required.)

Army Form C. 2118

Instructions regarding War Diaries and Intelligence Summaries are contained in F. S. Regs., Part II. and the Staff Manual respectively. Title Pages will be prepared in manuscript.

Place	Date	Hour	Summary of Events and Information	Remarks and references to Appendices
	8/5/17		This day no change in the tactical situation. Ammunition expenditure normal. Artillery fire below normal	
	9/5/17		This day no change in the tactical situation. Ammunition expenditure normal. Artillery fire normal	
	10/5/17		This day Colonel MAIR return to the Bouleaux Wd. No change in the tactical situation. Ammunition expenditure normal. Artillery fire normal	
	11/5/17		This day ammunition expended 1650 rounds. 640 rounds fire sent at the position. Very little hostile movement observed during the day.	
	12/5/17	8.30pm 8.31	Bombardment for 20 minutes was carried out. Took Trench concentration held during the night. SOS dispatched at the rate of 24 rounds per gun on hostile movement. Ammunition expended 3295 rounds the greater portion on the Boulevard last night. Bullets firing at 016.a.8.6. 030.c.2.7. fired on by the 130" Battery	
		6.45pm	All hostile arms fire by orders until 6 pm	
		SOS 10.3		

WAR DIARY or INTELLIGENCE SUMMARY

Army Form C. 2118

(Erase heading not required.)

Instructions regarding War Diaries and Intelligence Summaries are contained in F.S. Regs., Part II. and the Staff Manual respectively. Title Pages will be prepared in manuscript.

Place	Date	Hour	Summary of Events and Information	Remarks and references to Appendices
	13/5/17		Fairly fine day. Raining in the evening. The batteries were heavily shelled but there was no damage. After dark the 23rd Battery machines opened on F.N.6.c.9.3. machine gun nests and caused casualties from their forward position during the night & on day 14". Received a considerable bombardment. The great part of the 15th Army howitzer ammunition. The following batteries fired on 0186 & 6 - on 03 b 03. 05 a 00 65 & 030 a 27. See inventory of artillery positions was 030 b 03. 05 a 00 65 & 030 a 27. See inventory of artillery of 1148 rounds shewed intermittently all night.	
	14/5/17	6.30pm 7.10am 1pm	Rain now & then all day. Late by moving up we Batteries in the Brown line on N.17e & N.18d twenty shelled during the night. Hostile balloon behind Vis en ARTOIS was sent to N.18.b destroyed by one of our aeroplanes. Hostile planes in our neighbourhood. 2nd our aeroplanes fired on to frontiers N.16 a 6.4. 4.9. 49" Battery ammunition 5 February we expt of great orders orders for no night firing tonight. Rounds expended 1036 rounds to 49" Battery withdrew to position in N.16 a 27. 52. This move has been necessitated by the too advance of the line & was expected when they moved into the forward position the Battery got away without casualties which was very lucky as the neighbourhood was steadily shelled all night. S.O.S. lines for tonight O 14 d 00 to O 14 d 58.	
	15/5/17		Wet + dull	
	16/5/17			
	17		No change	

Army Form C. 2118

WAR DIARY
or
INTELLIGENCE SUMMARY
(Erase heading not required.)

Instructions regarding War Diaries and Intelligence Summaries are contained in F. S. Regs., Part II. and the Staff Manual respectively. Title Pages will be prepared in manuscript.

Place	Date	Hour	Summary of Events and Information	Remarks and references to Appendices
	18th	9.20pm	Attempt was to explode TOOL TRENCH hole by COPSE nr O8 central. Intent bullets report heavy rifle fire. Heavy fire was reported and continued later. Several bombs have been thrown, but it appears that the enemy counter attacks.	
		10.30p	Report from armed detachment times 10.30p m follows. Within the party sends following report which we learn has been completed about 10 pm. Ceaseable machine gun and rifle and some strongly held the trenches installing a considerable number of grenades. Have to support this attack.	
		10.47p		
		11.50p	Report receives that J party have withdrawn from TOOL TRENCH North of the BLOCK at O8c.2.2.	
	19th		CAPT PERKINS, Lt O'KEEFE, Lt HARKER 2nd Lt LLOYD all killed by 5.9 shell burst in the dugout at Hd Qtrs Mines. Attack on North half of TOOL TRENCH by 167' Bde & 6 DEVILS TRENCH BOIS DES AUBRINES by 87th	
	20	9r	Bde. 29" Div. 40 Bde cooperated by installing in the vicinity of LANYARD TRENCH.	

Place	Date	Hour	Summary of Events and Information	Remarks and references to Appendices
	26	12.40am	Situation still obscure. According to information received from 97. Inf Bde it is thought that we go must hold DEVILS TRENCH & Le BOIS DES AUBÉPINES. Two wounded men of 167 Bde. night platoon stated that (ten minutes there they tried) to hold BLOCK in TOOL TRENCH. They were ordered about 10 minutes afterwards [to] retire & from a bombing party should appear there have consequently built & hold BLOCK.	
		1.0am	Message from advanced HQ times 12.3 am states no attack have occurred yet, but from reports between trenches some doubt on the success of the attack. Bns going in to TOOL TRENCH and tunnel on either side of Tunnel are being attacked by supporting company by Houdain up TOOL TRENCH from BLOCK.	
		1.25am	Situation on left still obscure but it is thought that the L Bde on our left, which is on its right, have established themselves in TOOL TRENCH North of the tunnel & are pushing bombing parties South hold until further intelligence	

Army Form C. 2118

WAR DIARY
or
INTELLIGENCE SUMMARY
(Erase heading not required.)

Instructions regarding War Diaries and Intelligence Summaries are contained in F. S. Regs., Part II. and the Staff Manual respectively. Title Pages will be prepared in manuscript.

VIS-EN-ARTOIS

Place	Date	Hour	Summary of Events and Information	Remarks and references to Appendices
	20	2 AM	Enemy shelling SADDLE & SPADE TRENCHES & GORDON ALLEY 40' tr's Bde retaliates on PIT & FACTORY TRENCHES.	
		8.15 AM	Counter-battery work ordered by artillery on enemy hows in section 40' Bde retaliates on PIT TRENCH & FACTORY TRENCH.	
			Announce expected A 1030 Ax 1256 Bx 997	
	21		O.8c again visits the enemy. Failure flatly charges in the fact that our new attack started together. The whole question that bonding put about 5 elk flank. There is no doubt that we needed TOOL TRENCH N.pile LOPSE but that even as actual, many flank bondings strike by the enemy on the loss of two officers. Sh have wounded and in the trenches. W. L. Sop. causalties hardings. Hostile fire round.	
	22		2nd LT BISCOE transferred to 6th Bn.	

WAR DIARY
or
INTELLIGENCE SUMMARY
(Erase heading not required.)

Army Form C. 2118

Instructions regarding War Diaries and Intelligence Summaries are contained in F. S. Regs., Part II. and the Staff Manual respectively. Title Pages will be prepared in manuscript.

Place	Date	Hour	Summary of Events and Information	Remarks and references to Appendices
	22		7o' + 1'" Bdes do not report. 62° & 63° Bdes the enemy attacked N. of our Bde. have been the left sub group. 130° Bde were heavily shelled with R and >59 about 6 am to 10.30 pm. At 10.30 pm enemy came up about unknown. They were repeatedly walked back until 3 am. No damage done that we know of.	(LGA)
	23		No change. 2nd Lt JOHNSTON posts to Bty from Bde.	
	24		25° Bdy front. 23° Bty one section at N.16.a.a.9 40.30 one section at N.11.d.5.2. Bn Subs group the one at N.11.d.5.2.	
	25		No change. 2nd Lt HAWKER posts to 50° Bty from Bde. 2nd Lt WRIGHT posts to 45° Bty from DAC. 25 — 9.30 am — 9.30 pm one to N.22.a.9.2	
	26	10 am	Battle. He set about shelling enemy on pits mostly heavily — N.17. Our wind hit station. Zeppelin Heavy Villas which 130° Bde. N.11.a.4 + N.12.a were reportedly shelled.	

Army Form C. 2118

WAR DIARY
or
INTELLIGENCE SUMMARY
(Erase heading not required.)

Place	Date	Hour	Summary of Events and Information	Remarks and references to Appendices
	26(cont)		...59" thought to be a German dump — SUPPORT FACTORY at 5.30 p.m. Enemy raids.	
	27		Situation normal. Patrols sent out during the night. Occasional bombardment by German artillery and Minenwerfer throughout the day — our reply	
	28		at 3.15 p.m. Shrapnel shells in rapid succession (3 pt and 4.9) were put into PIT TRENCHES at N16 c.7. Small artillery activity. Guns reserved for retaliation.	
	29		HOOK TRENCH (at abt. 7.30 p.m.) 2	
			2nd Lt WATSON joins Bn H.Q.	
	30th		Intermittent shelling of our trenches throughout the day by 4.2s and 5.9s but not heavy. During the night 29th/30th another attack was ordered on HOOK TRENCH, without artillery preparation, but was postponed. The only heavy shelling by the enemy occurred in the early morning when retaliation B was given. Orders received for attack on the HOOK TRENCH, with artillery preparation. Barrage commenced at 11.30 p.m.	
	31st		Attack on HOOK TRENCH continued during night of 30th-31st. Objective gained, but had to be relinquished. Our artillery fire was slackened	N.F.A

1875 Wt. W593/826 1,000,000 4/15 J.B.C. & A. A.D.S.S./Forms/C. 2118.

WAR DIARY

or

INTELLIGENCE SUMMARY

(Erase heading not required.)

Army Form C. 2118

Place	Date	Hour	Summary of Events and Information	Remarks and references to Appendices
	31st	about 1.30 a.m.	The remainder of the day has been quiet. Orders received at 6.0 p.m. that all guns are to be manned during the night.	

Lieut Colonel
Comdg 40th Brigade
RFA

WAR DIARY.

40th. Brigade R.F.A.

3rd. DIVISION.

JUNE. 1917.

Army Form C. 2118

WAR DIARY
INTELLIGENCE SUMMARY
(Erase heading not required.)

40th Bde RFA
1st – 30th June 1917.

Vol 34

Place	Date	Hour	Summary of Events and Information	Remarks and references to Appendices
	1917 June 1st		Brigade H.Q. N11a 5.2 – 6th Battery – N15d 6.8 – 23rd Battery N10c 5.2 – 49th Battery N16a 3.8 130th Battery N22a 9.2 – Personnel of 6th Battery resting in Battery wagon lines. Very quiet throughout the day, the WANCOURT–FEUCHY Line being intermittently shelled.	
	2nd		Relief of 111th Brigade 37th Division by 184th Brigade 61st Division commenced. Relief of 111th Brigade 37th Division by 184th Brigade 61st Division completed during the night in the evening which was completed during the night. Relief of 111th Brigade by 184th Brigade complete. Infantry Bde H. headquarters shelled with 8" during the afternoon. Hostile aircraft more active than usual, especially between 7 a.m. and 10 a.m.	
	3rd		Quiet throughout the day with the exception of consistent enemy shelling of N.23.a. from direction of REMY. Hostile aircraft fairly active in early morning.	
	4th		N11a shelled from 6.15 a.m. till 9.0 a.m. Direct hit on an oven stairway, which smashed up one end of the Officers mess. Lieut. Colonel Bolton and Captain Thomas of the Gloucesters are attached to the Brigade for 3 days. Captain T. Thomas is attached to the 6th Battery and Colonel Bolton to Brigade H.Q.	

Army Form C. 2118

WAR DIARY
or
INTELLIGENCE SUMMARY
(Erase heading not required.)

Instructions regarding War Diaries and Intelligence Summaries are contained in F.S. Regs., Part II. and the Staff Manual respectively. Title Pages will be prepared in manuscript.

Place	Date	Hour	Summary of Events and Information	Remarks and references to Appendices
	5th		Fairly quiet day, but a certain amount of shelling in N11a, which continually cut wires from Bde I.E.Q. H ostile aircraft have been less active to-day, and one hostile aeroplane was brought down about 9.0 p.m.	
	6th		Also quiet all morning and afternoon. At 7.25 p.m. in reply to rather heavy shelling of our front and support lines just south of the COJEUL river retaliation was given with good effect.	
	7th		Still quiet. Two more infantry officers are attached, Major Green to 130 Bty and Lieut Robinson to 494, and Colonel Bolton & Capt Thomson having rejoined their units yesterday.	
	8th		Very little shelling of back areas during the day. Our fire is continuous at about 14 rounds per hour for each Bty. Our aeroplane activity has greatly increased.	
	9th		A little more shelling in the morning. The GUEMAPPE valley receiving some attention, but quieter again in the afternoon. Major Green and Lieut Robinson rejoin their units this afternoon.	
	10th		Very quiet 24 hrs. Not a shot was fired by hostile infantry or artillery between 2.30 a.m. and 8.30 a.m. Visibility has been poor lately.	

1875 Wt. W593/826 1,000,000 4/15 J.B.C. & A. A.D.S.S./Forms/C. 2118.

WAR DIARY or INTELLIGENCE SUMMARY

Army Form C. 2118

(Erase heading not required.)

Instructions regarding War Diaries and Intelligence Summaries are contained in F.S. Regs., Part II. and the Staff Manual respectively. Title Pages will be prepared in manuscript.

Place	Date	Hour	Summary of Events and Information	Remarks and references to Appendices
	11th		Gas shell bombardment carried out from 11 pm to 3 am on night of 10th/11th. The weather being very favourable for this. Continuous firing by day and night is still being carried out.	
	12th		Continuous bombardment of enemy trenches carried on throughout the day. Hostile artillery still quiet but slightly more active than yesterday on our support trenches. Gas shell bombardment started at 10 pm but has to be stopped on the gas on leaving back on to our own infantry, but without inflicting any casualties. Hostile artillery is more active on back areas. Orders have been issued that HOOK & TOOL TRENCHES and the high ground of INFANTRY HILL will be taken on morning of 14th.	
	13th		No gas shell bombardment during night 13th-14th.	
	14th		Attack takes place at 7.20 a.m. HOOK TRENCH being occupied without any artillery preparation, a barrage is put down at Z zero + 1½' and gradually slackened till it ceases at about 9.0 a.m. The morning and afternoon are quite till 5.30 pm when the enemy puts down a heavy barrage on our trenches to the west of the BOIS DU VERT and attempts a counter attack which is dispersed by our artillery.	
	15th		Hostile artillery more active especially on our communication trenches and	

Army Form C. 2118

WAR DIARY
or
INTELLIGENCE SUMMARY
(Erase heading not required.)

Instructions regarding War Diaries and Intelligence Summaries are contained in F.S. Regs., Part II. and the Staff Manual respectively. Title Pages will be prepared in manuscript.

Place	Date	Hour	Summary of Events and Information	Remarks and references to Appendices
	16th		the area between MONCHY and the CAMBRAI road. Heavy firing south of our divisional front from 9.0 p.m. to 10.40 p.m. and from 11.10 p.m. till 11.45 p.m.	
		2.30 a.m	At 2.30 a.m this morning the enemy put down a heavy barrage on LONG and HOOK trenches. The barrage slackened about 3.0 a.m and ceased at 3.45 a.m. our batteries having put down a barrage from 2.31 am till 3.0 a.m. at 9.15 a.m in retaliation. A was given in reply to hostile shelling of our trenches.	
	16th	2.30 pm	It appears that the enemy attempted a counter attack with about 600 men however succeeded in retaking our advanced post at the MOUND. H.e. however succeeded in retaking our advanced post at the MOUND.	
	17th		Enemy shelling normal during the morning was normal. In the afternoon HOOK and LONG TRENCHES were rather heavily shelled.	
	18th		At 1.0 a.m on night 17th–18th the front trenches in the zone on our left were heavily shelled, and in reply to this, the enemy fired on the western edge of the BOIS DU VERT. Apparently no movement was made by the enemy.	

WAR DIARY or INTELLIGENCE SUMMARY

Army Form C. 2118

Place	Date	Hour	Summary of Events and Information	Remarks and references to Appendices
	19th		Hostile artillery very quiet. Orders are received that the Bde will take over a new Z one north of our present Zone at 5 p.m. tomorrow.	
	20th		Fire is carried out on our old zone during the day, but each battery registered the new zone during the morning, using an O.P. in HUZZAR LANE at N12c 85 55. At 5 p.m. the Bgde took over the Zone, came under the command of C.R.A. 12th Division and with the 62nd Bde formed the right Group under the command of Lt.Col. C.T. Main D.S.O.; covering 36th Infantry Brigade from O.8.d. 1.9.5.6. O.8.d. 2.0.4.8. The 40th Div R.P.s on Z are extends from O.3.c. 10.50 to O.8.d.5.9.	
	21st		Fire is carried out on the new Z one with an allotment of 200 rds per 18 pdr, and 100 rds per Howitzer battery per 24 hrs. At 3 p.m. 6.4.2 fell in the Bde O.P. in the railway cutting; killing 2nd Lt Pudelle, who was on duty there.	

Army Form C. 2118

WAR DIARY
or
INTELLIGENCE SUMMARY

(Erase heading not required.)

Instructions regarding War Diaries and Intelligence Summaries are contained in F.S. Regs., Part II. and the Staff Manual respectively. Title Pages will be prepared in manuscript.

Place	Date	Hour	Summary of Events and Information	Remarks and references to Appendices
	22nd		It still shelling on back areas has been no heavier than usual to-day but three retaliations have been given by the Brigade. One at 10.40am in reply to shelling of LONG TRENCH and one at 5.20pm and 6.30pm on a hostile T.M. firing from O9a66. Orders were received at 8.0pm to the effect that the Brigade will withdraw on night 23/24	
	23rd		Night O.P. officers observed from old O.P. in BROWN LINE last night instead of from O.P. at in HUZZARLANE. Batteries cannot fire at 5.0p.m but did not withdraw until after 9.15p.m. to their wagon lines. Rest of the	
	24th		At 11.a.m the Bde passed the starting point, ACHICOURT CHATEAU and marched to BERNEVILLE via ARRAS-DOULLENS road, arriving at about 1.0.p.m. The Bde was sent to BERNEVILLE for a short rest and in order to refit.	
	25th		Brigade in rest	

WAR DIARY or INTELLIGENCE SUMMARY

Army Form C. 2118

Place	Date	Hour	Summary of Events and Information	Remarks and references to Appendices
	26th		Bde in rest	
	27th		Bde in rest. Lt BURNE joins 23rd Battery from 42nd Brigade	
	28th		Brigade in rest. Brig General Olivant inspects Batteries.	
	29th		Brigade in rest.	
	30th		Brigade in rest. Orders have been received that Bde will proceed to BAPAUME district on the first July.—	
			Brigade joins the starting to	

Stewart Blair C.
O.C. No 4th BDE RFA

WAR DIARY.

40th. Brigade R. F. A.

3rd. DIVISION.

JULY. 1917.

Army Form C. 2118.

WAR DIARY
or
INTELLIGENCE SUMMARY.
(Erase heading not required.)

July 1917
40th Bde RFA
Vol 35

Instructions regarding War Diaries and Intelligence Summaries are contained in F. S. Regs., Part II. and the Staff Manual respectively. Title pages will be prepared in manuscript.

Place	Date	Hour	Summary of Events and Information	Remarks and references to Appendices
BAPAUME	July 1st		Brigade passed the starting point in BERNEVILLE at 7.15 a.m. and proceeded to BAPAUME by BEAUMETZ – RANSART – ADINFER – AYETTE – ABLAINZEVELLE – ACHIET-LE-GRAND – BAPAUME. A halt of 2 hours being made at ABLAINZEVELLE. The Brigade arrived in BAPAUME at 3.30 p.m and bivouaced for the night, south-east of BAPAUME in H 34.	
	2		At 2.30 p.m. the Batteries resumed the march and proceeded via BANCOURT to HAPLINCOURT and bivouaced in I 10. Brigade H.Q. bivouaced in I 10.A.	
	3		Brigade H.Q. proceeded to HAPLINCOURT at 10.30 am and bivouaced in I 10 30 am and	

WAR DIARY

INTELLIGENCE SUMMARY

July 1917 — 40th Bde. RFA

Place	Date	Hour	Summary of Events and Information	Remarks and references to Appendices
	4th		Brigade remains at LE APLINCOURT. The battery positions are moved so as to form a Brigade in 4 mi. facing East.	
	5th		Battery wagon lines are inspected by General Geddes.	
	6th	6 am	At 6 pm the command of the new zone passes to O.C. 40th Bde R.F.A. from O.C. 2nd Australian Field Artillery Brigade. The Batteries do not take over until after 9.30 pm owing to the unreadiness of moving before dark. The 6th Battery of 40th Bde relieved the 5th Battery in T.35.a.5.2 / T.36.a.9.2 / T.35.c.0.3 and T.34.a.0.6. / T.35.c.0.3 and T.34.a.0.6. / T.27.D.2.8.
			The 23rd Battery of 40th Bde relieved the 4th Battery in T.35.c.0.3 and the 49th Battery of 40th Bde relieved the Battery in J.27.D.2.8 and the 130th Battery of 40th Bde relieved the 102nd Battery in J.35.a.5.2. Brigade H.Q. are situated in the sunken road in T.20.c.4.9.	
	7th		Batteries register the new zone in the morning. Night firing is carried out according to future R.A. orders.	

Army Form C. 2118.

WAR DIARY
or
INTELLIGENCE SUMMARY.
(Erase heading not required.)

July 1917
40th Bde R.F.A.

Place	Date	Hour	Summary of Events and Information	Remarks and references to Appendices
	8th		Owing to poor visibility the batteries fired a certain no. of rounds in excess of the usual daylight allotment. Hostile artillery was quiet, no intensive shelling being reported.	
	9th		Firing last night was normal, no retaliation on S.O.S signals being received.	
	10th		At 10.25 pm 12,18 rdn @ 6.4.5 IF can concentrated on K15 c 5 2 for 3 mins at 3 R.P.G. per minute. T.M. at K28a15.30 fired on with about 80 rounds. Party of 8 from Brigade proceed to AMIENS on 1 days leave. 2nd Lt Morgan is attached to 49th Battery. 2nd Lt Rollins to the 130th from the D.A.C.	
	11th		A/9th Battery shelled with 5.9's and 8" from 8.30 till 3.30 pm, 1 gun overturned and trail bent, but otherwise no casualties. Hostile artillery more active on back areas than usual. Night firing normal again. Colonel Main goes to 2nd D.A. as C.R.A. Hostile artillery normal again.	
	12th		General Clivant proceeds on leave to-day. Major H aird becomes Bde Commander.	as 153 D.A. orders

WAR DIARY or INTELLIGENCE SUMMARY.

July 1917 Army Form C. 2118.

40th Bde RFA

Place	Date	Hour	Summary of Events and Information	Remarks and references to Appendices
	12th		2nd Lt DEWING is posted to the Brigade and 23rd Battery from "attached".	
	13th		Hostile artillery activity above normal, especially during the night.	
	14th		A shoot concentration was carried out from 12 midnight until 1.35 am this morning, the Company H.Q. and area in K 9 6 and 6 during bombarded with chemical shell. The usual night firing was also carried out.	
	15th		Hostile artillery normal again. About 20 rds 5.9. on 49th By. position between 11.0 and 11.30 am. Night firing as usual.	
	16th		Hostile artillery was normal. At 10.20 pm Shrapnel Concentration No 3, a gas shell bombardment of K 15 6 and K 9 d., was carried out	
	17th		Hostile artillery was slightly more active to day. Situation unchanged.	
	18th		Hostile artillery normal. Capt. C.E. Bde M O Capt Clark, R.A.M.C. leaves	

WAR DIARY

Army Form C. 2118.

July 1917
40th Bde RFA

Place	Date	Hour	Summary of Events and Information	Remarks and references to Appendices
	18th		Bde, being relieved by Capt Henderson R.A.M.C.	
	19th		Hostile artillery much below normal. Major Vickery takes over the command of the Brigade from Major Heard.	
	20th		Hostile T.M. firing from SLAGG Street on to our fronts & fired on intermittently throughout the day without much success, at 10.25 p.m. enemy put down a heavy barrage on our trenches north of the canal. Suffolk "Z" gun until 11.0 p.m. Detached section of 6th Bty withdrawn to W.L.	
	21st		at 2.55 am this morning the enemy made a raid on R9 but was held up by a small bombing force, and took no prisoners. From 3.0 am till 3.45 am the Brigade fired Concentration "C" with no 3 Btys and concentration "B" with no 15 Bty. The remainder of the day was quiet. Orders received for change of gun.	
	22nd		a quiet night. The Brigade is going to cover the 8th Inf Bde front, and for this purpose the batteries will move to the vicinity of POIGNIES	

Army Form C. 2118.

WAR DIARY
or
INTELLIGENCE SUMMARY.
(Erase heading not required.)

JULY 1917

40th Bde R.F.A.

Place	Date	Hour	Summary of Events and Information	Remarks and references to Appendices
	23rd		on night of 23rd/24th or 24th/25th. The 6th Bty moved 1 section to S.16.c.1.7 and 1 section to S.15.c.8.4 on night of 21/22nd. Hostile artillery quite. During night of 23/23rd the 130" Battery moved 1 section to S.16 c 25.15.	
	24th		During night of 23rd/24th the 23rd Battery moved 1 section to S.21.c.05.95. At 5 p.m. on 24th the Brigade took over the new Zone, covering the 8th Infantry Brigade between K.7.d.6.5 and D.24.a.6.6.	
	25th		During night of 24th/25th the move was completed 15 section of the 130th Bty, remaining at T.35.a.5.2 and forming a 4 Gun Battery with one section of D/211 Battery. The comprote Battery being understrength Burtinchh 210th Bde R.F.A.	

July 1917

40th Bde R.F.A

WAR DIARY
or
INTELLIGENCE SUMMARY
(Erase heading not required.)

Army Form C. 2118.

Place	Date	Hour	Summary of Events and Information	Remarks and references to Appendices
	26th		The positions of the Batteries are now as follows:-	
			6a J.15.c.8.4. and J.16.c.1.7.	
			23rd J.15.c.23.80 and J.21.c.05.95	
			49a J.26.d.85.80. and J.27.d.25.90	
			130a J.16.a.40.55 and J.16.c.25.15.	
			and the Brigade O.P. at J.5.c.	
	27th		Major Vickery D.S.O. leaves the Brigade to command the 74th Brigade R.F.A. and Major Laurel commands the Bde in Colonel Mann absence	
	28th		Hostile artillery very quiet	
	29th		At 3 a.m this morning a test S.O.S signal was sent up by the infantry and was replied to in 15 secs by the artillery. One round per gun being fired.	
	30th		Poor visability. Trial W.Z. fired in 45 secs by 23rd By at request of the infantry	

Army Form C. 2118.

WAR DIARY
or
INTELLIGENCE SUMMARY.
(Erase heading not required.)

July 1917   40th B.W.P.A.

Place	Date	Hour	Summary of Events and Information	Remarks and references to Appendices
	31st		At 3.0 am a red & white rocket was observed from the O.P. and "Concentration B" sent down to the Batteries. This was altered to concentration "C" after two minutes. At 3.20, the infantry sent up an SOS signal from post 8, and in reply to this Concentration D" was put down and fire was continued till about 3.50am. It appears that the enemy made a raid on post 8, and successful in taking one prisoner, killing two men, and wounding eight.	

Jas L. Laird
Major Comdg 40th Bde
13 P.A.

WAR DIARY.

40th Brigade. R. F. A.

3rd. DIVISION.

AUGUST. 1917.

WAR DIARY
or
INTELLIGENCE SUMMARY

40th Brigade R.F.A
From 1st to 31st August 1917 (inclusive)

Vol 36

Army Form C. 2118.

Place	Date	Hour	Summary of Events and Information	Remarks and references to Appendices
BEAUMETZ	1 AUGUST		Visibility very poor and rain throughout the day. Infantry sent TESTND to 130th Battery at 4.4 a.m., which was replied to in 4.5 secs by Concentration "D". 49th Battery were a 2nd Lieut into their forward position.	
	2nd		Movement of small parties and parties as large as 50 men continually being reported, between MOEUVRES and BOURLON. These were fired on by the 18 prs. Visibility still very bad.	
	3rd		Weather improving slightly but character practically unfavorable during most of the day.	
	4th		Hostile artillery very quiet. a working party of 50 men were dispersed at 8.30 a.m. near trench in K3 & 9.1. The Colonel returned at 10.30 a.m. and takes over the command of the Brigade from Major Laird.	
	5th		Colonel Rowan-Robinson is attached to the Brigade for instructional purposes. At 10.36 p.m. S.O.S signals went up on Concentration W.X. which was fired on till 11.58 p.m. At 12.8 a.m. S.O.S signals again went up but on Concentration W.Z, fired on till 12.30 a.m. The remainder	

Army Form C. 2118.

WAR DIARY
or
INTELLIGENCE SUMMARY

(Erase heading not required.)

Instructions regarding War Diaries and Intelligence Summaries are contained in F. S. Regs., Part II. and the Staff Manual respectively. Title pages will be prepared in manuscript.

Place	Date	Hour	Summary of Events and Information	Remarks and references to Appendices
	5th		of the night was quiet	
	6th		It appears that the enemy attempted a raid well on the left of our front last night, but failed to enter any of our posts. Weather is much better to-day, and the visibility greatly improved.	
	7th	2.43 am	23rd Battery fired "Trial C1" Fire being opened 1 min 45 sec after message was sent from infantry. There was a slight increase in hostile artillery activity	
	8th		Visibility again poor. Nothing of importance occurred during the day At 10 pm a raid was carried out on the crater at D.30.a.9.9.3.6. but it was found unoccupied	
	9th	12.5.0 am	the raiding party sent up 2 red lights showing that they were returning. No artillery support was required during the raid.	
	10th		Visibility much better, and increased aerial activity; otherwise nothing of interest. During the period, then harder	

(A7093). Wt. W12830/M12935. 750,000. 1/17. D. D. & L., Ltd. Forms/C.2118/14

WAR DIARY
or
INTELLIGENCE SUMMARY.

(Erase heading not required.)

Army Form C. 2118.

Instructions regarding War Diaries and Intelligence Summaries are contained in F. S. Regs., Part II. and the Staff Manual respectively. Title pages will be prepared in manuscript.

Place	Date	Hour	Summary of Events and Information	Remarks and references to Appendices
	11th		Hostile artillery was very quiet. Trench C.2 was received by 23rd Battery from the infantry at 7.20½ p.m, and gun fire at 7.22½ p.m.	
	12th		Nothing of any interest occurred to-day	
	13th		Visibility exceptionally good, but hostile movement below normal.	
	14th		J.3.5.c and J.3.6.a intermittently shelled with 4.2s, from 8 am to 10am and from 4pm to 6pm. Otherwise hostile artillery was quiet 2/Lt Tucker was attached to 23rd Bg.	
	15th		Visibility again good, but little movement. Hostile fire markedly nil	
	16th		Colonel Milliman of Munsty of M'intains [?] visits the Brigade and Batteries	
	17th		Nothing to report	
	18th		A raid carried out about 12.30am this morning on an enemy post at K.8.a.5.6. for the purpose of obtaining identification, was unsuccessful in obtaining any prisoners, no artillery support however was required.	
	19th		8.15 p.m – 1.30 p.m the 6th Battery position at J.16.c was shelled	

Place	Date	Hour	Summary of Events and Information	Remarks and references to Appendices
			with 2.2" from [?] the direction of GRAINCOURT. One gun pit was hit and a gun slightly damaged. Otherwise no casualties	
	20th		The enemy commenced shelling the Divisional Front during the morning. From about 2.30 to 4.15 p.m. a single gun hostile in J.3.b., was shelled with 5.9's, with aeroplane observation. No damage was done.	
	21st		The Battery of this Brigade registered on the enemy Rifle Pits in K.8.a., in preparation for a raid to be carried out at some future date, probably night 2.5/26.	
	22nd		The rifle pits in K.8.a. were subjected to a heavy bombardment from 11.0 pm to 11.10 pm late night. Aeroplanes have been very active to-day.	

Army Form C. 2118.

WAR DIARY
or
INTELLIGENCE SUMMARY.
(Erase heading not required.)

Place	Date	Hour	Summary of Events and Information	Remarks and references to Appendices
	23rd		In the last 3 days all the officers and men of the Brigade have been through the gas chamber at FREMICOURT to test the box respirators. At 12.0 am this morning the rifle fire in K 8 a was again bombarded for 10 minutes.	
	24.		Hostile fire was again below normal, and slow owing to a high wind during the day.	
	25.		Normal day; nothing of interest occurred.	
	26.		Early this morning the rifle pits in K 8 a were made the objective of a raid; Zero hour being 2.0 am. The raiders were unsuccessful in obtaining any identification and	

WAR DIARY
or
INTELLIGENCE SUMMARY.
(Erase heading not required.)

Army Form C. 2118.

Place	Date	Hour	Summary of Events and Information	Remarks and references to Appendices
	27th		We suffered 5 casualties 1OR being killed and 5 wounded. Enemy movement above normal. J26 d & J35 were reported to have been shelled with 8" during the morning. Aeroplanes were inactive owing to a violent gale blowing. 2nd Lt LOVE of 23rd Battery is accepted as an observer in the R.F.C and leaves the Brigade. Wind still very high	
	28			
	29th		2/Lt AETURPIN of 23rd Battery is posted to the 58th Division as a signalling officer and proceeded to-day. Wind has decreased very slightly. The 293 Army F.A Bde was withdrawn last night, and the front covered	

WAR DIARY

Army Form C. 2118.

Place	Date	Hour	Summary of Events and Information	Remarks and references to Appendices
	30th		by this Bde is now covered by 121st Bde. At 3 hours of 42nd Bde. The 6th Bty of 40th Bde comes under the orders of the 42nd Bde and covers part of that Bde front.	
	31st		Hostile artillery activity showed a slight increase on our front system. Major Newland DSO joins the Brigade and takes command of the 6th Battery.	
			Hostile artillery normal again, and bad weather continues, it is reported that last night the enemy but down a barrage well to the right of our front and attacked, but no further particulars are available.	

Rwman
Lieut-Colonel
Comdg 40th Bde RFA

WAR DIARY.

40th. Brigade R. F. A.

3rd. DIVISION.

SEPTEMBER 1917.

WAR DIARY or INTELLIGENCE SUMMARY

Army Form C. 2118.

40th Bde RFA From 1st to 30th September 1917

Vol 37

Place	Date	Hour	Summary of Events and Information	Remarks and references to Appendices
BEAUMETZ	1st Sept.		There are now only 2 18 pdr batteries and 1 4.5" How battery covering each Brigade Front: About 6 a.m. a hostile aeroplane flew over the Brigade wagon line at HAPLINCOURT and dropped 3 bombs, wounding a horse and a mule, otherwise no damage was done.	
	2nd Sept		Last night the one remaining gun of 130th Battery, forming the Contalmaison battery was withdrawn and put into DOIGNIES with the remainder of the 130 Battery.	
	3rd Sept		Orders are received that the Division is to be relieved shortly, but a definite date for the relief of the artillery has not been stated.	
	4th Sept		Aerial activity has increased considerably otherwise a normal day	
	5th		The Brigade is to be relieved on the night of 6/7th and 7/8th by the 240th Bde RFA of the 56th DA. The CO and Battery commanders of that Bde go round the Battery positions	

WAR DIARY
or
INTELLIGENCE SUMMARY

Army Form C. 2118.

Place	Date	Hour	Summary of Events and Information	Remarks and references to Appendices
	6th		After Dusk one section of each of the Batteries of the 40th Bde R.F.A. is relieved by 1 section of the batteries of the 230th Bde., the remaining sections to be relieved on night of 7th, 8th.	
	7th 9th to 14th		The command of the Brigade Zone passes to 280 Bde R.F.A. at 6 p.m. On rest. On the 13th the Adjutant, Capt G.M. Fisher was taken away from the 3rd Div Arty and went to Hospital.	
	15th to 16th		40th Bde R.F.A. detrained at HOPOUTRE SIDING near POPERINGHE and marched into camp at WATOU on evening of 15th and morning of 16th. Batteries of 40th, 84th 2nd Bdes. form Sub Group commanded by O.C. 40th Bde R.F.A. under 55th D.A.	
	17th		Night of 16th, 1st Sections of batteries took up position close to WELTJE Night of 17th remaining sections took up position. Bde H.Q. dugout close to POTIJZE CHATEAU	

WAR DIARY
or
INTELLIGENCE SUMMARY.

(Erase heading not required.)

Army Form C. 2118.

Place	Date	Hour	Summary of Events and Information	Remarks and references to Appendices
	18th		Normal day. Hostile artillery was fairly active on our back areas near POTIGZE	
	19th	9am to 12 noon	Bombardment of enemy front line system. 6pm to 9pm harassing fire on enemy front system. 9pm to zero hour heavy bombardment of enemy front system.	
	20th		Barrage started	
		6.30am	Hostile barrage of 15cm commenced on our front line, but very weak.	
		7.26am	Hill 35 reported captured and strongly held.	
		9.215am	Enemy reported to be counter attacking in large numbers, but the attack eventually faded away.	
		11.55am	S O S.	
		12.30pm	Our line reported as follows. GREENLINE from D.2.13.37 to D.13.a.8.4. YELLOW LINE from D.13.6.2 to D.14.c.10, DITCH TRENCH, S of HILL 37 GALLIPOLI and LENS, and CLUSTER HOUSES.	

Army Form C. 2118.

WAR DIARY
or
INTELLIGENCE SUMMARY.
(Erase heading not required.)

Instructions regarding War Diaries and Intelligence Summaries are contained in F. S. Regs., Part II. and the Staff Manual respectively. Title pages will be prepared in manuscript.

Place	Date	Hour	Summary of Events and Information	Remarks and references to Appendices
	20th	6.45 hm	Enemy counter attack from HILL 37 to D14 a 31.	
		6.55 hm	Enemy reported quiet	
			SOS signals were sent up at 7.10 hm, 7.12 hm, 7.15 hm and 7.35 hm. Further enemy attacks were unsuccessful and situation reported quiet at 8.15 hm.	
	21st	10 am	Our line reported as follows. CLUSTER HOUSES, SCHULER GALLERIES, DIS(used) GALLIPOLI Fm. KEIR Fm, The CAPITOL, GALLIPOLI COPSE, THE SNAG, TULIP COTTAGES, Strong points are held in rear of this line. SCHULER FARM in our hands.	
		4.0 hm	SOS sent up west of SCHULER FARM at 6.50 hm and dfront HILL 35 at 7 hm. Batteries continued firing at 1 RPG hm till 7.55 hm.	
	22nd	6.10 am	Heavy hostile shelling of HILL 35 and SCHULER Fm. Enemy fire slackened.	
		6.22 ..	The remainder of the day was normal, hostile artillery showing no unusual activity	

Army Form C. 2118.

WAR DIARY
or
INTELLIGENCE SUMMARY.
(Erase heading not required.)

Instructions regarding War Diaries and Intelligence Summaries are contained in F. S. Regs., Part II. and the Staff Manual respectively. Title pages will be prepared in manuscript.

Place	Date	Hour	Summary of Events and Information	Remarks and references to Appendices
YPRES. POTIJZE	2° 23rd		At 5.0 am batteries fired on their SOS lines but no infantry attack materialised and by 5.10 am all was quiet. Hostile artillery was fairly quiet throughout the morning up till 11.30 am, when the area round CAMBRIDGE ROAD was shelled with 15 cm and 21 cm. During the afternoon the detachments of the 40th and 45th Brigades took over the guns and positions of the 295 and 296th Brigades R.F.A. in the area just east of CAMBRIDGE ROAD, the 295 + 296th Brigades taking over the guns of 40th + 45th Bdes. near WIELTJE. The positions of the batteries are as follows. 6th Battery I 5 d 21, 23rd Battery I 15 d 1 2, 49th Battery I 5 c 9.9, 130th Battery I 11 b 0 8, 29th Battery I 5 d 7.2, 41st Battery I 5 a 9.1, 45th Battery I 5 d 8.3, 139th Battery I 5 d 5.0, 49th Battery moved 4 of their guns forward about 150x to avoid the CAMBRIDGE ROAD. During the night a few gas shells were fired	
	24th			

Army Form C. 2118.

WAR DIARY
or
INTELLIGENCE SUMMARY.
(Erase heading not required.)

Place	Date	Hour	Summary of Events and Information	Remarks and references to Appendices
	26th		into the Neighbourhood of CAMBRIDGE ROAD O 23 d Bde H.Q. moved from	
		"	POTIZSE to the ramparts in YPRES	
		25th	Hostile artillery more active. Orders for the resumption of the offensive are received.	
			Major Glynn 42nd Parapet was wounded in the leg while proceeding to the O.P.	
		4.20am	Preliminary bombardment for attack begins.	
		5.50am	Zero hour. Intense bombardment began.	
		7.10am	Reported that first objective has been taken on divisional front. The enemy put down a barrage, which was not very strong on our front at 6.15 hrs. Then barrage slackened off still further at 9.45 am	
		10.0am	A map dropped by the R.F.C. at 9.0 am shews our line as follows	
			BLUE LINE from Right of DIV 6 ZONNEBEKE Stat. railway. Thence 100x west of road from STATION to JACOBS HOUSE	
		10.5	F.00 reports that we have not got ZONNEBEKECHURCH.	

WAR DIARY
or
INTELLIGENCE SUMMARY

Army Form C. 2118.

(Erase heading not required.)

Place	Date	Hour	Summary of Events and Information	Remarks and references to Appendices
		11.15pm	We are in touch with the Australian division on our right and our line runs BLUE LANE from right boundary to about D.21.d.8.2, shell holes on road between D.21.d.5.4. and D.21.d.0.9. and VAN ISACKERE FARM	
		2.45am	3rd D.A. ordered S.O.S. as all 4 Group fronts, an enemy are reported to be advancing through railway cutting in D.17.c. and from a line D.16.c.55 — D.16.d.85..	
		3.57	Enemy counter attacking between HILL 40 and ZONNEBEKE Church but the attack apparently did not develop.	
		6.50	Barrage for a second attack on HILL 40 is commenced, (right of 3rd Brigade). But this attack was unsuccessful	
	27th		During the morning and afternoon the enemy shelled our trenches from ZONNEBEKE to TOKIO intermittently and also the MENIN ROAD. Our line is practically unchanged since	

WAR DIARY
or
INTELLIGENCE SUMMARY

(Erase heading not required.)

Army Form C. 2118.

Place	Date	Hour	Summary of Events and Information	Remarks and references to Appendices
	27th	11.15 am	yesterday.	
	28th		S sending barrages comment out during the day on enemy's front system. Hostile artillery Normal. At 6.10 pm SOS went up on 3 Division front and a counter attack against hill 40 was early beaten off.	
	29th		A quiet day. Hostile artillery was slightly more active on our forward areas, on enemy reinforcements shooting. E A were more active in bathing roads than usual.	
	30		At 12.5 am and 4.50 am enemy shelled our front line for about 5 minutes with 77 mm and 105 mm. Hostile artillery was normal throughout the day.	

Signed [signature]
O.C. 40th Bty R.F.A.

WAR DIARY.

40th. Brigade R. F. A.

3rd. DIVISION.

OCTOBER. 1917.

Army Form C. 2118.

WAR DIARY
or
INTELLIGENCE SUMMARY.

40th Brigade R.F.A.
1st to 31st October 1917

Place	Date	Hour	Summary of Events and Information	Remarks and references to Appendices
YPRES	Oct 1st		Practice Barrage fired at 6.15am. and 8.15am. Enemy left us intermittent barrage during the day on the front of the corps on our right. Groups and Counter Zones have been reconstituted. No.1 Group under Lt Col OT Main, now consists of the 40th and 64th Brigades R.F.A and covers our front from the YPRES-ROULERS railway as the Northern boundary to _____ as the southern boundary. Orders are received that the batteries will move forward to morrow. Hostile artillery fire has been below normal to day.	
	2nd		Batteries moved to area C.30.d. during early morning. 7¾3am. 5.0 pm.	
	3rd		Practice barrages fired at 7¾.15 am. and 1.30 pm. Forward position reconstituted in neighbourhood of ZONNEBEKE REDOUBT.	

WAR DIARY
or
INTELLIGENCE SUMMARY.

Army Form C. 2118.

Place	Date	Hour	Summary of Events and Information	Remarks and references to Appendices
YPRES	4th	6.0am	Zero Hour. No Preliminary Bombardment was carried out for this attack.	
		6.50am	OP reports a fairly heavy hostile barrage from D.26 c.5.3 & - 14	
		7.25am	BREMEN REDOUBT. was reported to be in the RED LINE, and also the Division on our right, hostile barrage is still light except at an enemy M.G. D.22a and c, which is being heavily shelled will 5.9s from the direction of PASSCHENDAELE. Examination of German prisoners shown that enemy intended to attack this morning at 7am (Army Time), in order to recapture ZONNEBEKE. For this purpose he was employing the guards Division.	
		12.15	Battalion noted consolidation proceeding on consolidating line, Report being turned 12.5 hrs. SOS signals were sent up by the infantry at 12.15 hr, 3.8 hrs, 6.52hr, 9.55 hrs, 10.56 hrs, <s>12.58</s> 7am, but all counter attacks	

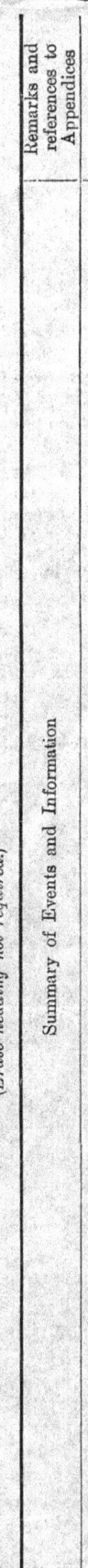

WAR DIARY
or
INTELLIGENCE SUMMARY

Army Form C. 2118.

Place	Date	Hour	Summary of Events and Information	Remarks and references to Appendices
	4th		officers to have been killed up by our artillery and rifle fire.	
	5th		Hostile artillery showed little increased activity on back areas. The enemy infantry attacked without success at 12.30 am, 3.40 am, 6.52 am, 2.30 pm and 7.5 pm. Orders were received that the Brigade will have to move into the area D26 d. 3 manned by 3rd Aust-Div hand to 66th Division. Weather still very bad, and roads becoming steadily worse.	
	6th		During the day the Battns. move forward, in relation at a time to the forward position. All ammunition has to be taken up by pack. Rain all day. Brigade HQ move from YPRES to SQARE FARM in C.30.d. Our aeroplanes have been very active during the morning.	
	7th			

Army Form C. 2118

WAR DIARY
or
INTELLIGENCE SUMMARY
(Erase heading not required.)

Instructions regarding War Diaries and Intelligence Summaries are contained in F.S. Regs., Part II. and the Staff Manual respectively. Title Pages will be prepared in manuscript.

Place	Date	Hour	Summary of Events and Information	Remarks and references to Appendices
	8th		Weather slightly improved. Hostile artillery has been normal. From 6 pm 6th until No. 16 rent. has been composed of 40th and 42nd Brigades R.F.A., under Lt Col G.T. Mann ; the 64th AFA Brigade forming No. 4 G rent. Orders are received that the attack will be resumed tomorrow.	
	9th	5.20 am	Barrage commences.	
		8.30 am	Orders received from 3rd Australian D.A. that Protective Barrage will not start at 9.10 am as ordered, but will continue at 1 R P G per minute; It appears that the infantry started the attack about 50 minutes late and were left by our barrage.	
		9.50 am	Report timed 8.0 am that infantry are consolidating the RED LINE.	
		11.0 am	F.O.O. reports 17th and 20th Battalions within 150x of final objective at 8.40 am.	
		1.0 pm	Enemy MG at D 18 central, which our troops appear to have	

Army Form C. 2118

WAR DIARY
or
INTELLIGENCE SUMMARY
(Erase heading not required.)

Instructions regarding War Diaries and Intelligence Summaries are contained in F. S. Regs., Part II. and the Staff Manual respectively. Title Pages will be prepared in manuscript.

Place	Date	Hour	Summary of Events and Information	Remarks and references to Appendices
	10th		We have retired slightly from VIENNA COPSE, to conform with the Brigade on our Flank. The centre of our front line is vague.	
			S.O.S. sent up at 6.0 hm. 6.45 hm and 9.45 hm.	
	11th		Quiet night, except for some shelling of battery positions in D.26.d. 66th Division in line relieved by 3rd Australian Division. Hostile artillery activity above Normal. Battery positions in D 26 shelled throughout the day. Capt LEE of 29th Battery killed. Attack will be resumed to-morrow.	
	12th	5.25	Attack commences. Enemy put down a fairly heavy barrage about half an hour before zero and was apparently expecting our attack	
		6.10	We are ordered to be in the RED LINE and in the BLUE LINE	

WAR DIARY
or
INTELLIGENCE SUMMARY

(Erase heading not required.)

Army Form C. 2118

Place	Date	Hour	Summary of Events and Information	Remarks and references to Appendices
	13th		at 10.30am, but the position is not at all clear. It appears that we reached the REDLINE at times, but were late in reaching the BLUELINE while the division on our left never got to the BLUE LINE. The enemy then all to swing heavy Machine Gun fire to bear from the flanks, and we were forced to retire slowly back to the original jumping off line. S.O.S. signals sent up at 5.30 pm and 6.10 pm, but apparently no attack. Hostile artillery considerably above normal. Vicinity of the batteries was shelled with 8" from 11.0 am to 2.30 pm and with 5.9 from 3.45 pm to 4.55 pm, receiving 1200 litres.	

WAR DIARY
or
INTELLIGENCE SUMMARY
(Erase heading not required.)

Army Form C. 2118

Place	Date	Hour	Summary of Events and Information	Remarks and references to Appendices
	14th		Hostile artillery still active, seems on whole front, and in neighbourhood of batteries. EA were also active flying low over battery position.	
	15.		Battery position shelled throughout the night. 2nd Lt WARBURTON killed on the position. Hostile artillery were intermittently active against battery position throughout the day.	
	16th		In the morning B.C. of 2nd Canadian Field Artillery, who was relieving the 3rd D.A., reconnoitred the position. 1 section 2.0 hrs and remaining 2 sections to battery at 6.0 hrs. Personnel only were relieved, guns being handed over to in situ	

Army Form C. 2118

WAR DIARY
or
INTELLIGENCE SUMMARY
(Erase heading not required.)

Instructions regarding War Diaries and Intelligence Summaries are contained in F.S. Regs., Part II. and the Staff Manual respectively. Title Pages will be prepared in manuscript.

Place	Date	Hour	Summary of Events and Information	Remarks and references to Appendices
	17th		40th Bde personnel withdrew to wagon lines and take guns of Bde CFA.	
	18th		40th Batteries march under battery arrangements to WATOU area. Bde in rest at WATOU.	
	19th		Brigade marches to GODWARESVELDE about 12 noon.	
	20th 21st		Bde in rest at GODWARESVELDE.	
	22nd		at 5.0 hours battery entrains for BAPAUME.	
	23rd		10.0 am entraining of Brigade complete. On arrival at	

WAR DIARY or INTELLIGENCE SUMMARY

Army Form C. 2118

Place	Date	Hour	Summary of Events and Information	Remarks and references to Appendices
BAPAUME	24th		Batteries march to GOMIECOURT	
	25th		Bats in rest at GOMIECOURT. B.C.s go up to reconnoitre positions to be taken up on from 310th Bde R.F.A. 62nd D.A.	
	26th			
	27th		1 Section goes into action relieving 1 section of 310 Rot clock 7.0 hrs. Remaining section goes into action in morning. 1 command of D merged.	
	28th		Gun passes to O.C. 40th Bde R.F.A at 6.0 hrs. Registration of new gun carried out.	
	29th		Quiet day.	
	30th		Valley west of NOREUIL shelled at various intervals throughout the day by 5.9".	
	31		Nothing to report.	

Duncan Kinloch Bland
O.C. 40th Bde R.F.A.

WAR DIARY.

40th. Brigade. R. F. A.

3rd. DIVISION.

NOVEMBER 1917.

40th Bde RFA
From 1st to 30th November 1917

Vol 39

WAR DIARY
or
INTELLIGENCE SUMMARY.
(Erase heading not required.)

Army Form C. 2118.

Hour, Date, Place	Summary of Events and Information	Remarks and references to Appendices
VAUX. 1st Nov.	U.23.c was shelled by hostile T.M's and field guns at 1.20 pm for about 5 minutes.	
2nd Nov	Corps Concentration carried out. Lt. NASH and 2 Lt. JENKINS from Brigade from D.A.C, and are attached to 23rd and 130th Batteries respectively.	
3rd	Hostile fire NIL 2/Lt JENKINS temporarily attached to 6" Batty.	
5th 6th 7th	Hostile fire practically nil. Walking to what was a successful raid by 13th King's Liverpool regt. 1/7th in vill'd 3 prisoners were taken.	
8th	Major Thompson and Captain Bevin proceed to England to attend course of Instruction. Hostile fire Normal on our front lights.	

Army Form C. 2118.

WAR DIARY
or
INTELLIGENCE SUMMARY.
(Erase heading not required.)

Place	Date	Hour	Summary of Events and Information	Remarks and references to Appendices
		9ʰ } 10ʰ	Visibility very poor. Hostile artillery active.	
		11ʰ	Certain movement observed on HENDECOURT DURY ROAD otherwise activity normal.	
		12ʰ	Infantry report transport can be heard any night very close to the front line South of RIENCOURT.	
		13ʰ 14ʰ } 15ʰ	Nothing to report.	
		16ʰ	Hostile field guns slightly more active against our front line	
		17ʰ } 18ʰ	Visibility very poor on night of 17ʰ/18ʰ Batteries more than guns were to be able to fire as far east as U.21. For the hours 6ʰ Battery moves all 6 guns into position at #C.15.6.4.7.29ʰ. Battery down to full 4 gun out of these pits, there no change to reconnoy.	

Army Form C. 2118.

WAR DIARY
or
INTELLIGENCE SUMMARY.
(Erase heading not required.)

Place	Date	Hour	Summary of Events and Information	Remarks and references to Appendices
	19th		Nothing to report	
	20th	6.20 am	At 6.20 am the 2nd Division co-operating in an attack by 3rd Army captured BOVIS TRENCH from U21b 12 52 to U22c 50 50. For the purpose a barrage was put down on BOVIS trench from Zero to Zero + 8'. Enemy barrage which was put down at Zero + 4' was very weak and only lasted for about 2.5. minutes. During the remainder of the day, hostile artillery fire was about normal.	
	21st	3.45 pm	At 3.45 pm SOS signal was sent up but no attack developed. Night was quiet on our front. Hostile artillery slightly more active than usual especially against	

WAR DIARY or INTELLIGENCE SUMMARY

Army Form C. 2118.

Place	Date	Hour	Summary of Events and Information	Remarks and references to Appendices
North of BULLECOURT.	22		Visibility very poor. Hostile artillery normal, nothing larger than 4.2 being fired on the front. 2Lts YOUNG, McGREGOR and [?] from the Brigade.	
	23		Visibility much reduced. Balloons covered throughout the morning in INCHY EN-ARTOIS and MOEUVRES. Slight shelling of valley west South West of MOEUVRES.	
	24		Visibility still good and enemy movement much above normal especially in the vicinity of HENDECOURT	
BULLDOG TRENCH.	25		Enemy are stated to have moved on to be only holding very lightly the trench from U.22.d.80.90 to U.21.d.60.60. Posts	

WAR DIARY
or
INTELLIGENCE SUMMARY.
(Erase heading not required.)

Army Form C. 2118.

Place	Date	Hour	Summary of Events and Information	Remarks and references to Appendices
	26th		are now held from these points to our original front line	
	27th		Hostile artillery more active. No attacks nor fronts. Hostile artillery still active. Batteries take on their normal zones and all guns are replaced in their pits. 6" Battery having 6 guns at C.15.d.4.7.	
	28th		Nothing to report acceptably intermittent shelling of NOREUIL VALLEY.	
	29th		A large number of hostile batteries were reported active between 7.30 am and 10.30 am. About 30% of these being new positions. At 10.30 hrs. enemy shelled NOREUIL and valley to the west with 77 mm and 4.2, 15 and gas	

WAR DIARY
or
INTELLIGENCE SUMMARY.

Place	Date	Hour	Summary of Events and Information	Remarks and references to Appendices
	30		From 2.15am to 5am NOREUIL and valley were shelled with 77mm HE and gas. During the day both artillery was abnormal and at 10.15pm NOREUIL was again shelled with gas. On night 29/30 the 3rd Divison extended to night flank to D.21.d.7.4. The 9th Brigade coming in on the right of the 8th Brigade. The 9th Brigade are covered by three batteries of 56" D.A.	

Sinnen Lieut Colonel
O.C. 40th Bde R.F.A.

1/XII/7-

WAR DIARY.

40th. Brigade, R. F. A.

3rd. DIVISION.

DECEMBER. 1917.

WAR DIARY
or
INTELLIGENCE SUMMARY.
(Erase heading not required.)

Army Form C. 2118.

40th BdeRFA
Decr. 1917.

Place	Date	Hour	Summary of Events and Information	Remarks and references to Appendices
	1st Dec		3.50am to 5.0am NOREUIL shelled with Gas 77mm and 4.2".	
			6.30am to 7.30am our Trenches in U 22 d were heavily shelled with 77mm, 4.2 and 5.9.	
	2nd 3rd		Nothing of importance to report. Hostile artillery not heavy. active	
	4th		4.15pm 30 rds BCBR on U B4 and 30 rds on V A 3.	
	5th		Nothing to report	
	6th		Major Howard of 28th Bty temporarily commands the Brigade, the Colonel have gone sick. Postern for defence of Intermediate and Coates lines sketched.	
	7th		The Brigade is to form a group of 5 Btys under Col. Macdonnell. A/281 Bty is going to action in the 6th Bty war position in C 15 c 9.	

Army Form C. 2118.

40'OTL RFA
Dec. 1917.

WAR DIARY
or
INTELLIGENCE SUMMARY.
(Erase heading not required.)

Place	Date	Hour	Summary of Events and Information	Remarks and references to Appendices
	9th		Brigade HQ moves from VAULX to Sunken Road in C9d. Enemy is becoming more active against NOREUIL valley particularly at night.	
	10th 11th		Enemy is increasingly active and a great deal of movement is reported by aeroplanes. 8th I. of Bde is relieved by 9th Bde in night.	
	12th		At 6.30 am the enemy attacked from about BULLECOURT to GOOLE AVENUE, and succeeded in gaining a footing in the APEX from BUNNY HCG to about RIPONLANE. But not in PUDSEY SUPPORT. Throughout the day	

Army Form C. 2118.

WAR DIARY
or
INTELLIGENCE SUMMARY.
(Erase heading not required.)

Place	Date	Hour	Summary of Events and Information	Remarks and references to Appendices
	13th		The enemy put down barrages about once every 2 hours on our front and support lines and on RAILWAY RESERVE. By means of bombing, the enemy gained 2 whary Support blocks being established 50x west of BUNNY HUG. By 6:30 pm and at the junction of RIPON LANE and the front line. The night was correspondingly quiet. During the night the division on the right took over part of our front as far as HOBART AVENUE, inclusive. At 5.50 am two SOS rockets were sent up from	

WAR DIARY or **INTELLIGENCE SUMMARY**

Army Form C. 2118
40 R.F.A
1917

Place	Date	Hour	Summary of Events and Information	Remarks and references to Appendices
	14		U.29.b. but no attack followed. Barrages were again put down as yesterday but no attack developed though S.O.S. was sent up from bombardment "M" at about 3.50 p.m. During the night 13/14th one section of A/281 is relieved by 1 section of a battery of 18th Army Field Artillery Brigade, who are relieving the 281st Bde. During the afternoon NOREUIL Valley was shelled with about 20 "8". Col. Clark, comdg. 18th A.F.A. Bde. takes over the command of the groups from Col. MacDowell. During night 14/15th relief of 281st Bde. by 18th Bde. is completed. The 40th Bde. plus 1 Bty. of 18th Bde. R.F.A. is in turn as a group under 18th Bde. H.Q.	

Army Form C. 2118.

40th Bde RFA
Decr, 1917

WAR DIARY
INTELLIGENCE SUMMARY
(Erase heading not required.)

Place	Date	Hour	Summary of Events and Information	Remarks and references to Appendices
	15		Battery H.Q. are moved from neighbourhood of BEUGNATRE to BEHAGNIES, 6th and 23rd Batteries going into standings, 49th and 130th into the open. Administration of 40th Bde is carried on from Temporary H.Q. at VAULX.	
	16.		H.Q. W.L. move to BEUGNATRE. BEHAGNIES.	
	17, 18, 19, 20, 21.		No change.	
	22.		40th Bde. H.Q. established at BEUGNATRE. BEHAGNIES.	
	23. to 31.		No change.	

J C Watson 2Lt.
F. O. C. 40th Bde RFA

3RD DIVISION
DIVL. ARTILLERY

40TH BRIGADE R.F.A.

~~1918~~

1918 JAN — 1919 FEB

Army Form C. 2118.

40th Bde RFA

WAR DIARY
or
INTELLIGENCE SUMMARY.
(Erase heading not required.)

From 1st to 31st January 1918

Place	Date	Hour	Summary of Events and Information	Remarks and references to Appendices
HENDECOURT SPECIAL SHEET PARTS 51B S.W, SE 57C NW, NE	1/1/18		Batteries of the Brigade still in action in NOREUIL VALLEY grouped under H.Q. 156th (Army) Brigade R.F.A.	
	19/1/18		H.Q. 40th Bde R.F.A. out of the line at BEHAGNIES	
		11.AM	H.Q. 40th Bde R.F.A. relieve 156th (Army) Bde R.F.A. and resume tactical command of the Batteries of the Brigade. Major J. M. David M.C. R.F.A. commanding the Brigade in absence of the Brigade Commander on leave.	
	22/1/18		Divisional Artillery assisted by 1 6" How. Battery, bombard new German Trench running South from COPSE TRENCH V.16.c Both Batteries fired 75 rounds on V.16.c.40.25	
	23/1/18		German Trench Mortars meeting many than Divisions opposite our sector to be on the alert. Following precautionary measures taken on our part. Anti-Tank Gun (18pr of 64 Battery) in forward position at C.10.9.5.5 manned 1/2.h. before dawn by 1 Officer and 5 O.R. Guards preparations carried out by	
		6.20 AM	the Brigade on orders from CRA from 6.20 AM - 6.30 AM and 6.40 AM & 6.50 AM Enemy retaliated with trench mortars but nothing further observed	
	24/1/18	11.30 AM	Experimental Anti-aeroplane barrage fired by 18 pdrs. bursts at 100, 200 & 300 ft. above our front line at low thought that enemy aircraft flying 250 over our trenches might be dealt with in this way. Good results obtained	

Army Form C. 2118.

WAR DIARY
or
INTELLIGENCE SUMMARY.
(Erase heading not required.)

Instructions regarding War Diaries and Intelligence Summaries are contained in F. S. Regs., Part II. and the Staff Manual respectively. Title pages will be prepared in manuscript.

Place	Date	Hour	Summary of Events and Information	Remarks and references to Appendices
	25/1/18	7 P.M. to 10 P.M.	NOREUIL and valley subjected to gas shell contaminant. No casualties reported	
	29/1/18	Noon	Old H.Q. at NOREUIL closed down and new H.Q. at B.24.D opened. Return of Brigade Commander.	
			Throughout the month we carried out day and night harassing fire averaging 1000 rounds per battery per 24 hours. During the last 10 days there were clear nights and a good moon and hostile aircraft were very active bombing back areas and back areas.	

1st February 1918.

E. Morgan
4 Rgt
for Captain 4th Bn R.75

Lieutenant Colonel
O.C. 40th Bde R.F.A.

Army Form C. 2118.

40th Bde RFA
From 1st to 28th February 1918

WAR DIARY
or
INTELLIGENCE SUMMARY.
(Erase heading not required.)

Place	Date	Hour	Summary of Events and Information	Remarks and references to Appendices
VAULX	1st		Ref sheet 57c	
	to		Battery still in action in NOREUIL VALLEY. HQ at VAULX.	
	6th		No events of great importance.	
	7th		Forward section changed from 76th Battery to	
			carry out trench 25 in, from 29th Bgde to 53rd Dvn.	
	8th		HQ 40 Bde relieved by HQ 295 Bde.	
			Remaining sections relieved by sections of 295th Bde.	
			Battery joined up with HQ at BEHAGNIES.	
	9th		HQ 40 & 23rd Batteries move to MOYENNEVILLE. 49 Bde	
			moves to FIENEUX. 130 Battery moves to BOISLEUX-AU-MONT	
	10th		Training	
	11th		"	
	12th		"	
	13th		"	
	14th		"	
	15th		"	
	16th		"	
	17th			
	18th			
	19th			

2nd Lt FELTON joins from 3rd DAC

Army Form C. 2118.

WAR DIARY
or
INTELLIGENCE SUMMARY.

(Erase heading not required.)

Place	Date	Hour	Summary of Events and Information	Remarks and references to Appendices
Ref sheet 57 C			February 1918	
	20		Training 130 Battery moves to FICHEUX	
	21		Training	
	22		"	
	23		"	
	24		"	
	25		"	
	26		"	
	27		G.O.C. inspection. D. sub inspection.	
	28			

2/3/18

[signature] Lieutenant
OC 40th Bde RFA

[signature] Captain RFA
OC 140 Bde RFA

3rd Divisional Artillery

40th BRIGADE R. F. A.

MARCH 1918

Army Form C. 2118.

40th Bde RFA
Vol 43

WAR DIARY
INTELLIGENCE SUMMARY

Place	Date	Hour	Summary of Events and Information	Remarks and references to Appendices
FICHEUX			Ref sheet 51c S.W. MARCH 1918	
	1st		Bryde. hrs. at. W.L.s at MOYENNEVILLE to W.L. at FICHEUX. All Batteries in answer endeavour taken	
			WANCOURT. Bryde grouped under 42nd Bryde. 18th AFA Bryde. Nothing except S.O.S firing.	
	2nd		Construction of reserve position under Capt H.K.A. BURNE	
			being.	
	3rd		No change.	
	4th		HQ moved up to vicinity of MERCATEL. (M 36 c 91)	
	5th		23rd Battery gone into whole reserve at M22b.8.5	
	6th		No change. Work on reserve position continues	
	7th		" "	
			" "	
	8th		H.Q. moved to a town the new 40 Bde position.	
			That completes Centre Group. HQ situated at	
			40 Bde goes over the B. Infanty. Bryde.	
	9th		No change. Lt E.W. RAYNOR & Lt A.T. HARVEY Rtnd 6.35 for DAC	
	10th			

40ᵗʰ Bde RFA

WAR DIARY
or
INTELLIGENCE SUMMARY.

Army Form C. 2118.

Place	Date	Hour	Summary of Events and Information	Remarks and references to Appendices
	11ᵗʰ		holdings	
	12ᵗʰ		" "	
	13ᵗʰ		" "	
	14ᵗʰ		" "	
	15ᵗʰ		" "	
	16ᵗʰ		" "	
	17ᵗʰ		Carried out registration for ssos of all calibres —	
	18ᵗʰ		" " WANCOURT TOWER.	
	19ᵗʰ		" "	
	20		" "	
	21ˢᵗ	5pm	Enemy barrage opened with discharge of gas projectors, directed on either flank of the Division's front. Fire was chiefly intense in the vicinity of BULLECOURT and MONCHY. There was also Heavy shelling of batteries + especially HENINEL valley. Shell seemed to be gas + H.E. from guns of all calibres. There was a delay in response of 4.2's. Shower Platform and O.P. were out 15 minutes after S.O.S. was sent R.Q Hqrs + visual being heavily shelled with Mustard + 4.2's.	

WAR DIARY or INTELLIGENCE SUMMARY

Army Form C. 2118.

40th Bde R.F.A.

Place	Date	Hour	Summary of Events and Information	Remarks and references to Appendices
	22nd		There was practically no shelling of CENTRE GROUP batty positions. Communication was maintained with WEST O.P. (O.31c2.) and EGRET O.P. (N.30.b.7.1.) until about 5.12 a.m. and 7.00 a.m. at their O.Ps respectively. No station as above.	
		7.45am	A runner from EGRET O.P. reports enemy fire ceased at 6.30 a.m. Response at 6.45 a.m. No S.O.S. signal seen on Divisional front. Fire on our front stopped. Slight.	
		9.30am	Report by runner from Liaison Officer states that enemy batteries restarting T.M. range on our front. Infantry report situation quiet. Slight S.A. shelling of following areas:- Royd S. Sft report all quiet on 'B' Bgne front. A few S.A. enemy seen talking back from shell holes in front of Poelcapelle.	
		10.10am	During the afternoon several heavy attacks were made on the Division front against the 3/4 Bgne on the right by 3 gns and support of regiment of O.C. 42ⁿᵈ Bgne on the left by 3 gns. The G.O.C. Divn. was finally obliged to fall back slightly on the original line 34. Divisional however remained.	

40th Bde R.F.A.

Army Form C. 2118.

WAR DIARY
or
INTELLIGENCE SUMMARY.
(Erase heading not required.)

Place	Date	Hour	Summary of Events and Information	Remarks and references to Appendices
	21st	6.0pm	Report of enemy movements in front of CHERISY. This report was afterwards contradicted by aeroplane report however dropped at 6.30pm. This states that enemy was visible not only in our trenches, but that there was now signs of concentration.	
		7.50pm	8" Bde front is that 9" Bde front runs in following :- SWIFT SUPPORT NW along FIRST AVENUE - CURTAIN SUPPORT - BROWN SUPPORT. Intermittent hostile fire during the night. - not heavy. During the day batteries were turned on the open in 028 029 ~ 034.	
	22nd	1.15am	S.O.S. from 9" Brigade front. Artillery response given by battalions up to S.O.S. (HE mixed with shrapnel) and 2" system BATTLE ZONE. Situation still remained quiet being it with the 9" Bde heavily attacks from the S.E. and fell back HIND SUPPORT.	
		12.30p	9" Bde heavily attacks from the S.E. and fell back HIND SUPPORT and 2" system BATTLE ZONE.	
		3.25	OP reports several hundred of the enemy massing W of CHERISY - VIS road in 027b. H.A. on 18" & H Bde started firing.	

Army Form C. 2118.

40th Bde RFA

WAR DIARY
or
INTELLIGENCE SUMMARY.
(Erase heading not required.)

Instructions regarding War Diaries and Intelligence Summaries are contained in F. S. Regs., Part II. and the Staff Manual respectively. Title pages will be prepared in manuscript.

Place	Date	Hour	Summary of Events and Information	Remarks and references to Appendices
	22nd	4.40p	Infantry report a Bosch cavalry [?] enemy massing on HENDECOURT - BURY road on UBC. Flying [?] to tea [?] enemy CHERISY.	
		4.55pm	G/B.Cdpk [?] concentration on [?] - SUN QUARRY SENSEE [?] valley. HA [?]	
		5.0p	2nd Gds Bgde updated Infy 3rd Sysm Rwly BURY-BEG PUERE UF	
		6.40p	Enemy reported massing in front of SWIFT SUPPORT	
		6.58p	SOS from Right Coy [?] J14/3 Sec. 40 Sec [?] at 41/3 Sec	
		10.45p	Infantry reserve [?] for 16/34 Bsc - no withdrawal	
			to 2 Spectus Bstry Comdr now Survey[?] room [?] 50.	
	23rd	1 am	Own shelling from DA 10 withdrawal [?] batteries the place[?] batteries as follows:	
			L/3 Bty to M13 D 2.4	
			49/3 Bty to N19 a L.8	
			1/36 Bty to M.24 central	
			42"/3 Sec to [?] under 40th Sec	
		2.30 pm	HQ move back to BOISLEUX-AU-MONT with HQ 41st Sec and	

40th Bde RFA

WAR DIARY
INTELLIGENCE SUMMARY

Place	Date	Hour	Summary of Events and Information	Remarks and references to Appendices
		5 AM	8.I.F Bde. All Batteries in action [in] their positions.	
		8.0 AM	Batteries moved forward by sections. Btys at dusk to positions as under :—	
			6th Btty to S.3.d.9.6	
			48th Btty to S.3.a.9.2	
			130 Btty to S.4.c.8.2	
			When 6th Bty Bgde [went to] read S.4.g.2 and N.31.c.0.0. Both the O.P.s manned. Only night [written?] in installation [of?] new battery O.P.s. [Advanced] report centre established in the day at MPT (H.25)	
		5.0 P	Enemy [put?] smoke on front & Right centre & left Bgn [Brigade?] sector [our] front lines but no damage to Ken [Menin?]	
		8.15 P	23 Btty reports the Bugger from S.3.d.9.3 [&] S.3.d Sgt [9.5.23] at Sgt [9.5.23]	
		10.10 P	[Infantry?] report considerable movement in T 4 & T 5 @ S.10.3 From [Btty] & Bde. have opened up on described.	

40th Bde RFA   Army Form C. 2118.

WAR DIARY
or
INTELLIGENCE SUMMARY

Place	Date	Hour	Summary of Events and Information	Remarks and references to Appendices
	24th	5.40am	Heavy enemy barrage reported from O.P. - M35	
		10.45pm	Enemy Howitzers left corner of Bois-du-F.M. in full swing	
		11.20pm	SOS from 8th (gp). Between 11.20pm & 1 am enemy made determined attempt to penetrate our new advanced line but did not succeed.	
			H.V. Guns also shelled area during the evening. Barrage fire 35' times repeated. Sharp rifle + MG fire coming from many Q.3.b. + B2.c. + 3.a. Considerable movement during day through (?) just S of 8th (?) Wood also South of Guards Lines along twilight.	
			GREEN ARMY LINE	
	25th		[On return by runners to HQ at daylight 2nd Div. 40 HQ more back during the evening to S.H. 40. Battalion with brass Durgate left at 8am. t-M27c58.]	

Army Form C. 2118.

40th Bde R.F.A

WAR DIARY
or
INTELLIGENCE SUMMARY.
(Erase heading not required.)

Place	Date	Hour	Summary of Events and Information	Remarks and references to Appendices
	25th		1st Battery to M.33.c.02.22 2nd Battery to M.22.b-93.02 4th Battery to M.27.c.30.60 13th Battery to M.33.a.24.50	
	26th 3am to 8am		SE Enemy shelled heavy fire on batt. areas. No casualties (?) The enemy reports were very heavy. T.9. T.14. & T.15. The hostile shelling was intense as we could see — There were however no registrated movement of enemy till evening when the 9am — 10pm Divisional front was — counter attacked 5pm to 7pm Si's hour was however repulsed with effect situation Quiet night. Wessex R.B.(16ers) shone light O.P (R.31) 6N.69 I Wessex R.B.(16ers) shone light to E.57.B etc	
	27th			

40th BdeRFA

WAR DIARY
or
INTELLIGENCE SUMMARY.
(Erase heading not required.)

Army Form C. 2118.

Place	Date	Hour	Summary of Events and Information	Remarks and references to Appendices
	27th	10.30am	Hostile artillery shewed some activity in T.21.D - shells continually movement in T.21.C. Slightly affected ayg?	
		1.5pm	Small parties seen about in S.17.D trenches informed.	
		11.35pm	Riflemen, K.S.L.I. sent to retaliation on Russia T.26 & Inverness + plug with. Batteries C & D opened fire on the enemy T.21.D & T.15.C. B.att. on enemy's front line trench were generous were directed at — Y D/181 concentrated on R.ght. & enemy C/181 " L " 1.20 30.70 D/181(sec) L " 1.20 30.70 M.33.a.53.85 (1.30 31 minutes)	
	28th	3am	Enemy fired a steady bombardment, that front line — stood Goods had to move, thing in the way 40 been refilled with slow concentrated fire was enemy preparation.	

40th Battery

WAR DIARY
or
INTELLIGENCE SUMMARY.
(Erase heading not required.)

Army Form C. 2118.

Place	Date	Hour	Summary of Events and Information	Remarks and references to Appendices
	28-		The S.O.S. signal was sent up about 7.30 am. by 3rd Bde at the junction of 2nd and 3rd Bdes. Fire was continually without any response.	
		9.55AM	"B" Bde front reports that tanks are in fact 9" Bde reports their own tanks fallen back slightly to their right. Heavy fire at Battn report enemy through our front line & trench line from N32 central to S6c . Steady rate of fire maintained by infantry & sent to inform to GREEN ARMY LINE	
		1.50p	2nd I. Scot. through the GREEN LINE. RSR and KSLI fight to hold it.	
		2.0p	Fire ordered to prevent hurt.	
		2.30p	A shell of the enemy communications unable to reach our O.P. but owing to cloud over the enemy ground observation impossible. Patrols to give warning extended unless our batteries and MG's steadily opened fire.	
		After 3.0	considerable movement was observed	

40th Bde R.F.A.

Army Form C. 2118.

WAR DIARY
or
INTELLIGENCE SUMMARY.
(Erase heading not required.)

Place	Date	Hour	Summary of Events and Information	Remarks and references to Appendices
	29=		T.4 a. T.12 a. & T. 17. T.9 a. Enjoy? on possible will attack Henry Ditch. 90.90 the gradually tightens. b/ unit map 1st Bathers emp'ment Henry Ditch. Westerning Henry Curpis from line between Dawn. Brigade in 3 Bie. Commencing J.6 Causing Fea Box - Werks Bie. - battery posterin will arise to take over a forest 90% Command movements shall be after - clothy or Sous trench - Eng? 70 who provide Reg. Relief of Sectors by 15th Canadian Bde.	
		6.35 " relieves by 15th Canadian Bde	
		23" " 25" "	
		49 " " 16" "	
		1.30 " " 22" "	
		Sectors afterwards used South. E/191. + sector of 3/181 known to posters in vicinity of R 23 b and 2 OC 18.1 Bde.	
		D.A. - Groups of H.Q. Hillers. A.D Bde (for event - Arte? 4, 6 CFA B)	
		Right Group - (181, 1Bde)	
4"			Sectors: afterwards — E W - ARTOIS

40th Bde RFA Army Form C. 2118.

WAR DIARY
or
INTELLIGENCE SUMMARY.
(Erase heading not required.)

Place	Date	Hour	Summary of Events and Information	Remarks and references to Appendices
	29		Left Gouy — {4th Bde (– personnel) & "C"FA Bn } {18' AFA Bde }	
			Q.1 + Bde relieved by 5th Canadian Bde + 19th FA Bde	
	30	5 am	Relief of 40th Bde sections complete and with 181' Brigade.	
		10.30 am	Attack on Quesnoy front. Resistance given by flank batteries. Stood down.	
		4.45	Following section H.Q. CRA Bde ordered up	
		7.30	Communication from 4th AC 40 Bde to tactical CRA Bde	
		10.00	Batty relief complete	
			HQ and batteries moved to GOUY-en-ARTOIS	
	31		Brigade in rest at GOUY-en-ARTOIS.	

W.J. North Capt.
Adjutant 40 Bde RFA

SECRET.

CENTRE GROUP ORDER NO. 127.
-:-:-:-:-:-:-:-:-:-:-:-:-:-:-

Reference Map WANCOURT Special Sheet 1/10,000.

1. The 7th K.S.L.I. will raid the enemy's front line at about O.26.c.38.58 on the night 17th/18th March 1918.
2. Artillery Co-operation will be as follows :-
   From Zero minus 5' to Zero.

Right Group   Active Postns. 2 18-pdrs. O.26.a.75.10 to O.26.a.60.00
      "   " 4 18-pdrs. O.26.c.80.70 to O.26.c.50.32
Centre Group 49th Bty. 4 guns O.26.a.60.00 to O.26.c.80.70
     "   "   2 guns Support Line O.26.c.50.32 to
                                          O.26.c.50.05
           6th Bty. 3 guns O.26.c.50.05 to O.26.c.24.14
     "   "   3 guns O.26.c.24.14 to O.32.a.15.90

From Zero until "All In".

Right Group. 3 guns O.26.a.75.10 to O.26.a.60.00
               4 guns O.26.c.80.70 to O.26.d.00.90
Centre Group. 49th Bty. 4 guns O.26.a.60.00 to O.26.c.80.70.
     "   "   2 "   O.26.c.70.40. " O.26.c.75.25.
      6th. "   3 "   O.26.c.50.05. " O.26.c.24.14.
       "   "   3 "   O.26.c.24.14. " O.32.a.15.90.
    130th. " ....O.26.c.75.05.
                            O.32.a.40.80.
                            O.26.d.38.51.
                            O.26.b.21.00.
                            O.26.d.30.95.
                            O.26.d.32.90.

3. Rate of fire:-

       From zero minus 5 to zero, 1/2 S.O.S. rates.
       From zero to "withdrawal signal" 2 R.P.G. per min.
       From "withdrawal signal" to "all in" signal,
                                                      1 R.P.G. per min.

4. Ammunition.

       18-pdrs. H.E. (106 fuze as desired).
       The 130th Battery will not fire 106 fuzes where the western extreme of 100 per cent zone is within 300 yards of our front line.

5. The signal for "Withdrawal" will be a golden rain rocket fired from our front line at O.26.c.05.95 and the signal for "All In" will be 2 Green and 2 White Lights fired from the same place.

6. The Brigade Signal Watch will be sent to Batteries between 8 p.m. and 10 p.m. to-night in order to synchronise watches.

7. Zero hour will be notified later.
8. ACKNOWLEDGE.

17/3/18.   Captain R.F.A.

Copies to 6th, 49th, & 130th)   Adjutant Centre Group.
        Batteries   )
    Right & Left Groups.
    8th Inf. Bde.
    7th K.S.L.I.

SECRET.

ARTILLERY PROGRAMME.

Artillery co-operation will be as follows :-

From Zero minus 5' to Zero.

    Right Group. Active Positions 2 18-pdrs. O.26.a.75.10. to
                                                              O.26.a.60.00.
       "   "   4 18-pdrs. O.26.c.80.70. to
                                                            O.26.c.50.32.

    Centre Group. 49th Bty. 4 guns O.26.a.60.00. to O.26.c.80.70.
       "   "   2 guns Support Line O.26.c.50.32. to
                                                    O.26.c.50.05.
               6th Bty. 3 guns O.26.c.50.05. to O.26.c.24.14.
       "   "   3 guns O.26.c.24.14. to O.32.a.15.90.

From Zero until "All in".

    Right Group. 2 guns O.26.a.75.10. to O.26.a.60.00.
                  4 guns O.26.c.80.70. to O.26.d.00.90.

    Centre Group. 49th Bty. 4 guns O.26.a.60.00. to O.26.c.80.70.
       "   "   2 " O.26.c.70.40. to O.26.c.75.05.

               6th Bty. 3 guns O.26.c.50.05. to O.26.c.24.14.
       "   "   3 " O.26.c.24.14. to O.32.a.15.90.

               130th Bty............ O.26.c.75.05.
                                      O.32.a.40.80.
                                      O.26.d.58.51.
                                      O.26.b.21.00.
                                      O.26.d.30.95.
                                      O.26.d.32.90.

2. Rate of fire:-

    From Zero minus 5 to Zero -   ½ S.O.S. rates.
    From Zero to "withdrawal signal" 2 R.P.G. per min.
    From "Withdrawal Signal" to "all in" signal 1 R.P.G. per min

3. Ammunition.

    18 -pdrs. H.E. (106 fuze as desired).
    The 130th Battery will not fire 106 fuzes where the western extreme of 100 per cent zone is within 500 yds. of our front line.

D.K. 401.

Right Group.
Left Group.
6th.   )
49th.   ) Batteries.
130th.)
8th. Infantry Brigade.

:-:-:-:-:-:-:-:-:-:-:-:-:

Reference Centre Group Order No.127 of to-days date:-

Amendment
Para(1)

(a) Zero hour will be 2-15 a.m.
(b) The signal for "withdrawal" will be 3 golden rain rockets sent up at 2-25 a.m.   *2 green & white*
(c) The signal for "all in" will be 3 blue rockets instead of the lights laid down in paragraph 5.
(d) The Infantry would be grateful if the Right and Left Groups would give instructions for the 2-10 a.m. bombardment ordered in G/2325/7 to continue until 2-25 a.m.

Captain R.F.A.

17/3/18.   Adjutant Centre Group.

3rd Divisional Artillery

[WAR DIARY]

40th BRIGADE R. F. A.

APRIL 1918

3rd Divisional Artillery

Army Form C. 2118.

40th Brigade R.F.A.

From 1st to 30th April 1918

WAR DIARY
or
INTELLIGENCE SUMMARY.
(Erase heading not required.)

Instructions regarding War Diaries and Intelligence Summaries are contained in F. S. Regs., Part II. and the Staff Manual respectively. Title pages will be prepared in manuscript.

Place	Date	Hour	Summary of Events and Information	Remarks and references to Appendices
			40th Brigade R.F.A.	
GOUY EN ARTOIS	April 1st		Brigade leaves GOUY at 9.30am and marches via BARLY - AVESNES-LE-COMTE — BUNÉVILLE to VERLOINGT, arriving at 6.30pm. Night spent in VERLOINGT.	
GAUCHIN VERLOINGT	2nd		Brigade leaves VERLOINGT at 9.0am and marches to MARLES-LES-MINES arriving at 3.0pm.	
MARLES-LES-MINES	3rd		Brigade at MARLES-LES-MINES.	
	4th		at 9.0am Brigade marches to BARLIN under 1st Canadian Division and becomes Corps Reserve.	
BARLIN	5th 6" 7" 8"		Brigade in rest.	
	9th		Orders received at 4.0pm. that Brigade is to go into action to-night, under HOHENZOLLERN GROUP, 11th D.A., on	

Army Form C. 2118.

WAR DIARY
or
INTELLIGENCE SUMMARY.
(Erase heading not required.)

Instructions regarding War Diaries and Intelligence Summaries are contained in F. S. Regs., Part II. and the Staff Manual respectively. Title pages will be prepared in manuscript.

Place	Date	Hour	Summary of Events and Information	Remarks and references to Appendices
LABOURSE	10"		a reinforcing Brigade. Batteries are to be in the neighbourhood of ANNEQUIN. Lt SHARP and 2Lt MORRIS posted to 11" Divisional Artillery. Lt RAYNOR rejoins 3rd D.A.C. Batteries in action by dawn as follows: 6" Bty. G.5.c.7.5. 23 Bty G.4.c.7.6. 480" Bty G.3.c.9.7. 49" Bty u detached from the HOHENZOLLERN G redoubt and comes into action under CAMBRIN G redoubt at F.22 d 3.6. 6", 23 and 130" Batteries form Subt. Group. under HOHENZOLLERN G redoubt. Hostile Artillery inactive. Registration.	
	11"		Orders received at 11.30 am that Brigade will come out of action at 1.30 pm and rendez-vous at LABEUVRIERE.	
	12"		B. C. to report at mess 3rd D.A.C at OBLINGHEM. Portion recommended in the neighbourhood of LANNOY. 8 Ohm Batteries	

WAR DIARY or INTELLIGENCE SUMMARY

Army Form C. 2118.

Place	Date	Hour	Summary of Events and Information	Remarks and references to Appendices
BELLERIVE	13th		in action as follows:- 6ᵃ Battery W13c 70 50, 23ʳᵈ Battery W13c08 49ᵗʰ Battery V18c 98.10, 130ᵗʰ Battery V18c 10 80. Wagon lines at L'ABEUVRIERE, with advanced W.L. at L'ABBAYE. 70ᵗʰ Brigade, covering 76ᵗʰ Inf. Brigade front. Hostile artillery inactive, but a lot of enemy movement engaged.	
	14th		During the evening 11ᵗʰ Inf Brigade, 4ᵗʰ Division, relieved 76ᵗʰ I.Bde. A great deal of hostile movement was engaged throughout the day. 7.0 hrs to 7.10 hrs. 18 pdrs put down a creeping barrage to support an attack by the 11ᵗʰ Inf Brigade to take the line Q 32 c 00 – R 19 Z 2. DU VINAGE – Q 19 c 60. The operation is successful, 150 prisoners being taken. 8 pm E. enemy reported to be counter attacking but attack unsuccessful. During the day orders have been received that 1 section per battery	

WAR DIARY
or
INTELLIGENCE SUMMARY

Army Form C. 2118.

Place	Date	Hour	Summary of Events and Information	Remarks and references to Appendices
			will be relieved to night by 1 section Hv Battery of A 251st Bngde 50th D.A. completing One section Hv Bty of 40th Brigade RFA to go into action NE of BETHUNE, in positions selected by Major V.H. THOMPSON MC. R. Staff of one section Hv Battery complete by 9.30 am. when command passes to OC 251st Bde R.F.A.	
	15"		40th Bde HQ move to BETHUNE (E5c 65.45) and 1 section Hv Battery came into action by dawn as follows 6" Bty E11d 95.95 23rd Bty X1 L 7.5, 49th Bty W30d 7070, 130th Bty F7 a 8070. C and D Batteries 250th Brigade are attached to 40th Brigade and are in action as follows C/250 at X1L 30 30. The 6 Batteries D/250 at X1L 30 30. The 6 Batteries and cover the 9th Inf Bde Fr. front until 06.25.0 nets W30d 2050 night Covent.	

WAR DIARY
or
INTELLIGENCE SUMMARY.
(Erase heading not required.)

Army Form C. 2118.

Place	Date	Hour	Summary of Events and Information	Remarks and references to Appendices
	15		Registration. Command of group hours to O.C 40" Brigade at 9.30am when morning this ation for Battery of 40" Bde Batteries are in action.	
	16"		Capt WILSON 130" Bty hosted to 5" Army Brigade RFA Quiet night. During the day enemy is fairly active against our front line but hostile artillery fairly quiet. 20/mm 49" Bty barely shelled for about 5 mins, this was repeated times during the afternoon. During the night 49" Bty moved to a new position at E.12.a.10.70.	
	17"		Enemy artillery active with harassing fire during night day. 40" Bde HQ moves from to E.4.b.70 and 9" & I. BdPs Two prisoners captured by Division say that the enemy	

Army Form C. 2118.

WAR DIARY
or
INTELLIGENCE SUMMARY.
(Erase heading not required.)

Instructions regarding War Diaries and Intelligence Summaries are contained in F. S. Regs., Part II. and the Staff Manual respectively. Title pages will be prepared in manuscript.

Place	Date	Hour	Summary of Events and Information	Remarks and references to Appendices
	18th		will attack from GIVENCHY to ROBECQ to-morrow morning. During the early night enemy artillery was active. Enemy shelled our front line heavily from 3.0am to 5.0 am but no infantry attack followed. The Division on either flank was shelled from about 7.0am till 9:30 am and then attacked. The attack on the left by PACAUT WOOD was unsuccessful and some prisoners were taken. On the right at 10.0 am enemy was reported to have entered GIVEN CHY at several points.	
		10.20am	Our line reported by Bde on right to run as follows. A7.9.8 – WINDY CORNER – HITCHIN ROAD to West of FESTUBERT.	
		10.45	1st Div reported slight advance in line from GIVENCHY to PLANTIN	

Army Form C. 2118.

WAR DIARY
or
INTELLIGENCE SUMMARY.
(Erase heading not required.)

Instructions regarding War Diaries and Intelligence Summaries are contained in F. S. Regs., Part II. and the Staff Manual respectively. Title pages will be prepared in manuscript.

Place	Date	Hour	Summary of Events and Information	Remarks and references to Appendices
			Situation no change in front.	
		From 3.0 am till 10.45 am Batteries fired on our SOS lines at the rate of one round of 5 mins every 15 mins.	
		10.45 am all quiet in Brigade front.	
		2.30 pm	23rd Bty 1.30 pm Bty and 9/250 Bty put down a barrage on the front of the Brigade on our right, to assist in a counter attack.	
		3.0 pm	Counter attack started to have regained nearly all ground lost this morning.	
		8.55 pm	Our line reported as follows. Unchanged on 3rd and 4th Divn fronts. 1st Divn on right. Enemy have held trenches and high ground N and NE of GIVENCHY KEEP. We have lost FESTUBERT KEEP and ROUTE A KEEP. Otherwise no change.	

Army Form C. 2118.

WAR DIARY
or
INTELLIGENCE SUMMARY.
(Erase heading not required.)

Instructions regarding War Diaries and Intelligence Summaries are contained in F. S. Regs., Part II. and the Staff Manual respectively. Title pages will be prepared in manuscript.

Place	Date	Hour	Summary of Events and Information	Remarks and references to Appendices
	19"		9th Inf Brigade relieved by 8th Inf Bde. Lt Danaher 49" Battery posted to 130" Battery as 2/C ptain. Hostile artillery was inactive throughout the day. At about 8.0am this morning we retook FESTUBERT and ROUTE A Kts.	
	20"		No change. At 8.0pm enemy put down a heavy barrage on the front of Div on right but no attack followed. E A considerably more active flying lower.	
	21st		It in. rotated to D. in echelon. Harassing fire was carried out by the enemy throughout the night	
	22d		E A again active. 2 prisoners captured by Danaher. On days enemy will attack due to .... morning and our	

WAR DIARY
or
INTELLIGENCE SUMMARY.

Army Form C. 2118.

Place	Date	Hour	Summary of Events and Information	Remarks and references to Appendices
	23rd		will not. At 12 midnight 23rd Bty and C/250 Bty put down a barrage in the front of the Bde Brigade on our right to assist in a minor operation against Rads 'A' KEEP which was unsuccessful. Hostile artillery was normal throughout the day. A little TM fire from MESPLAUX Farm in reply against our front line. During the evening our section in the battery of 6", 2 of C/250 and D/250 Batteries was relieved by section the Hq of 230 Brigade RFA 46th Div. Guns were handed over in situ, detachments only being relieved. The sections of 6" and 23rd Batteries hitherto manned by ...lord of A/250 and B/250, at	

Army Form C. 2118.

WAR DIARY
or
INTELLIGENCE SUMMARY.
(Erase heading not required.)

Place	Date	Hour	Summary of Events and Information	Remarks and references to Appendices
	24"		at W.28&9.1 and W.27&16.3 respectively, and continuing the updating of the 42nd Brigade R.F.A. covering the 76th Inf. Bde front.

At 4.0am 23rd & C/250 Batteries reported the damage had greatly (?) for the Brigade on right) to enable attack on Redt A Redt, which was retaken. —

Remaining sections of 6" and B/250. About an hour after the relief was completed, orders were received that A and C/250 would return to action immediately and 6" and 23rd Batteries proceed to own Wagon Lines at LABEUVRIÈRE.

At 9.0pm command of Group passes to O.C. 230 Bde R.F.A. so that Group consists of 230 Bde R.F.A. and 49 & 130 Batteries, remaining 139th 2 Brigade of the 46th Division. 40th Bde R.F.A. 149 proceeds to | |

Army Form C. 2118.

WAR DIARY
or
INTELLIGENCE SUMMARY.
(Erase heading not required.)

Instructions regarding War Diaries and Intelligence Summaries are contained in F. S. Regs., Part II. and the Staff Manual respectively. Title pages will be prepared in manuscript.

Place	Date	Hour	Summary of Events and Information	Remarks and references to Appendices
	25"		LABEUVRIÈRE.	
			At 6.0am. 49" and 130 Batteries pull out from their positions and moved to LABEUVRIÈRE.	
			Fog 9.0am 40" Bde. RFA + C & D/250 Bdes are out of action in W.L at LABEUVRIÈRE.	
			3" Division came under orders of XIII Corps and batty positions were reconnoitred during the day, in the vicinity of LANNOY and ODLINGHEM to cover the front from LA PANNERIE to AVELETTE to present held by 11" Brigade 4" Division.	
			During the evening one section two Battery gas into action as follows:	
			6" B.g during 27" Rty 4" DA. 23rd Rty W20a.83, 49" Rty W20c.73, W13 d 35\	
			130" Bg W20c.54, C/250 Rty W13c.36 D/250 Rty W13d1.2 during 134" Rty 4" DA.	

Army Form C. 2118.

WAR DIARY
or
INTELLIGENCE SUMMARY.
(Erase heading not required.)

Place	Date	Hour	Summary of Events and Information	Remarks and references to Appendices
	26th		Registration by section in action.	
			30mm 23rd and 49th Batteries shelled. During the evening remaining sections of the battery go into action. 23rd Battery moves to W20k82.	
			49th Bty to W.14.c.02.5. D/250 Bty has guns at W.19.c.00.90 and 4 at W.13.d.12.	
			11th Bde, 4th Divn HQ move to W.27.c.51.9 and take over command of	
			40th Bde HQ move to W.27.c.51.9 and take over command of	
			LEFT GROUP 3rd D.A, covering 76th Inf Bde.	
			Hostile artillery was very active during the night shelling the vicinity of battery position with HE and Gas.	
	27th	12.15 am	The vicinity of 130th Bty position was heavily shelled for about a few minutes.	
			Night firing is carried out by a detached section of each battery, which	

WAR DIARY or INTELLIGENCE SUMMARY

Army Form C. 2118.

Place	Date	Hour	Summary of Events and Information	Remarks and references to Appendices
	28th		...ments at dusk to a position some distance from the battery and returns to the battery position before dawn. 130 Battery moves to a new position at W.25.d.80.60 during the night. At 12 noon C.O. and Battery Commanders of 47" Brigade R.F.A. 14" R.A. report at H.Q. to reconnoitre positions, as 47" Bde are to relieve 250? R.F.A. C and D Batteries, 250" Bde R.F.A, and also put in two extra batteries. During the evening location for Bty of 47" Bde R.F.A. come into action as follows: A Battery at W.13.5.6.?, V.18.d.6.3., W.13.a.1.0, C Battery W.13.c.5.6, D Battery W.13.d.3.3 (4 How.) and W.13.d.05.30 (2 How.) The 130 Bty is ordered to move from W.25.d.80.60, as it is considered to be too close to a mine shaft. The Battery moves during the night to a position at E.2.c.7.8.	

Army Form C. 2118.

WAR DIARY
or
INTELLIGENCE SUMMARY.
(Erase heading not required.)

Place	Date	Hour	Summary of Events and Information	Remarks and references to Appendices
	29ᵗʰ		HQ of 47 Bde established at V30a02. 47ᵗʰ Bde R.F.A forms a Sub Group under the Left Group. Hostile artillery was active regarding HINGES church. Owing to the enemy menacing two sectors the battery of 47ᵗʰ Brigade R.F.A came into action & C and D Batteries 250ᵗʰ Brigade R.F.A. return to their wagon lines and moved under orders of 50ᵗʰ DAGAMETTES. Night firing carried out by detached section of 49ᵗʰ and 130 Batteries slick from main position of 6ᵗʰ and 23ʳᵈ Batteries.	
	30ᵗʰ		Hostile Artillery Fire was normal during the night, but was normal throughout the day. HINGES being heavily shelled from 1.30 hm to 3.30 hm.	

Stewart Hulbolmel
OC 40ᵗʰ Bde R.F.A.

```
    6th  )
   33rd  )
   49th  ) Batteries                           D.K. No. 514.
  C/350  )
   42nd Bde. R.F.A. )
  275th Bde. R.F.A. )
    8th Inf. Bde.   ) For information.
    3rd Div. Arty.  )
```
-:-:-:-:-:-:-:-:-:-:-:-:-:-:-:-:-:-

1. Mutual Support between 40th Bde. R.F.A. and flank Bdes. R.F.A. will be as follows :-

   (a) <u>42nd Bde. R.F.A. in support of 40th Bde. R.F.A.</u>

      I 18-pdr. Bty.   X.7.c.75.35   to X.7.d.60.40
      I 18-pdr. Bty. (2 guns)   X.7.d.60.40   to X.8.c.20.50
                (4 guns)   X.8.c.20.50   to X.8.c.75.65

   (b) <u>40th Bde. R.F.A. in support of 42nd Bde. R.F.A.</u>

      6th & 49th Btys.   X.8.d.00.50   to X.8.c.45.65
      6th Bty. will take the right half and 49th Bty. the left half.

   (c) <u>275th Bde. R.F.A. in support of 40th Bde. R.F.A.</u> (SUPPORT MAROON).

      I 18-pdr. Bty.   X.23.a.00.90 to X.16.d.50.00
      I 18-pdr. Bty.   X.16.d.50.00 to X.16.d.00.40

   (d) <u>40th Bde. R.F.A. in support of 275th Bde. R.F.A.</u> (SUPPORT LOIGNE).

      33rd & C/350th Btys.   X.23.a.65.80 to X.16.d.80.00
      33rd Bty. will take the right half and C/350 Bty. the left half.

2. Rates of fire for the above will be as ordered by this office.

3. Please (ACKNOWLEDGE).

20/4/18.   Captain R.F.A.
                                            Adjutant 40th Brigade R.F.A.

40th Bde RFA

Army Form C. 2118

WAR DIARY or INTELLIGENCE SUMMARY

From 1st to 31st May 1918

Place	Date	Hour	Summary of Events and Information	Remarks and references to Appendices
Ref Sheet 36A S.E. 1/20000	May 1st		Hostile artillery activity was slightly above normal during the day. We carried out continued harassing fire on the enclosure at W11a&b.	
	2nd		Hostile activity normal except for two heavy concentrations on OBLINGHEM. 40° Bde HQ move from W27c5.9 to CHATEAU L'ABBAYE. Major EU BODY 130" Battery wounded to hospital. 2Lt CARPENTER attd 6" Bty returns to DAC, and 2Lt COWAN joins 6" Battery.	
	3rd		130 Battery move one section into an advanced position at W21c.7.4. Enemy put heavy concentration on the OBLINGHEM area during the day, but was normal in forward areas. 2Lt COWAN attached to 42nd Bde RFA from 6" Battery. 2Lt BOYLES attd 6" Battery, and 2Lt DURBIN 49" Battery from 3rd DAC.	
	4th	2.30 am	Left Group (?) assisted by Right Group put down a barrage for an attack on an enclosure in W11a&b by 1st Gordon Highlanders. The attack was successful the 2 MG's and 40 prisoners being captured. Hostile artillery was active against LANNOY and OBLINGHEM at intervals	

WAR DIARY
or
INTELLIGENCE SUMMARY.
(Erase heading not required.)

Army Form C. 2118.

Place	Date	Hour	Summary of Events and Information	Remarks and references to Appendices
	5		During the day 6.0 how 6" Bty and D/47 Bty were shelled. During the night 6" Battery moves 2 guns to W13d 8.8 and 4 guns to W15 a 6.6.	
			During the night 76 Inf Bde were relieved by the 9" Inf Bde. About 3.0 a.m. enemy made an attack on the 9 relief. S.O.S. was sent up and the attack driven off. During the night a raiding party obtained four prisoners.	
	6		Throughout the afternoon the enemy shelled the Canal Bank in W16 L and W17 a. In retaliation the Bosses in W5c and the Practice Trenches were engaged. Hostile artillery was normally active.	
	7		HAZEBRUCK. Calm normal. L+Col Noble attacked by 40 Bosses. RFA fire instructions in regards hired warfare. Battery started return amount of faulty ammunition in sepect of which gun [illegible] short rounds.	
	8		Enemy artillery was very active against our forward areas from 3.30 am to 4.30 am but [illegible] normal throughout the day. During night 7/8 6" Battery moves 4 guns to position at W14 d 3.1.	

Army Form C. 2118

WAR DIARY
or
INTELLIGENCE SUMMARY.
(Erase heading not required.)

Instructions regarding War Diaries and Intelligence Summaries are contained in F. S. Regs., Part II. and the Staff Manual respectively. Title pages will be prepared in manuscript.

Place	Date	Hour	Summary of Events and Information	Remarks and references to Appendices
	9th		Night quiet till 1.30 am when enemy commenced harassing fire till 5.0 am. Hostile artillery below normal during the day except in the vicinity of the Canal Bank. During the night special bombardments were carried out on a prisoner had stated that enemy would attack. 4.9" withdrew low fired from to main position.	
	10th		Enemy again harassed from 1.30am till 4.30am using HE and gas, but was quiet during daylight. EA activity was slightly above normal.	
	11th		Quiet day except for some shelling of the Canal Bank.	
	12th		From 2.0am to 4.30am enemy shelled our battery areas with Yellow cross gas shell. 9.0 pm to 9.30 pm and intermittently throughout the night the detached section of 6" Battery was shelled with 4.2s and 5.9's. Night was quiet.	
	13th		Detached section of 6" Battery shelled from 16.0 am to 3.0 pm and one gun put out of action. During night remaining gun was put into action at W14 d 3.4.	

* D. D. & L., London, E.C.
(A8204) Wt. W1771/M2 31 750,000 5/17 Sch. 52 Forms/C2118/14

Army Form C. 2118.

WAR DIARY
or
~~INTELLIGENCE SUMMARY~~

(Erase heading not required.)

Instructions regarding War Diaries and Intelligence Summaries are contained in F. S. Regs., Part II. and the Staff Manual respectively. Title pages will be prepared in manuscript.

Place	Date	Hour	Summary of Events and Information	Remarks and references to Appendices
	14th		H A matin. Major WOLFF joins 40th Brigade RFA and takes over, the command of 150 Battery, ivce Major BODY, invalided to England. Wind enemy harassing fire during night. Visability was very good throughout the day.	
	15			
	16th		Canal Bank on left Battalion front was shelled from 7.0 am &	
	17th	9.0 am.	Hostile artillery below normal during day. Enemy work at W11b and W12a was engaged with bursts of fire during the night. On the vicinity of the 181st Battery was shelled with Yellow cross Gas shell during the night. During the night the 6" Battery hit the guns at W21a 20 80.	
	18th 19th 20th		Normal day. At 3.0 am. the enemy turned a heavy gas bombardment of HINGES, and HINGES WOOD, with YELLOW CROSS. The bombardment ceased about 5.15 am. about six or seven thousand rounds being fired	

* D. D. & L., London, E.C.
(A8004) Wt. W1771/M2 31 750,000 5/17 Sch. 52 Forms/C2118/14

WAR DIARY
or
INTELLIGENCE SUMMARY.

(Erase heading not required.)

Army Form C. 2118

Instructions regarding War Diaries and Intelligence Summaries are contained in F. S. Regs., Part II. and the Staff Manual respectively. Title pages will be prepared in manuscript.

Place	Date	Hour	Summary of Events and Information	Remarks and references to Appendices
	21st 22nd		Lt Col NASH + 2/Lt CH BISCOE and OSMOND were gassed and evacuated, also 8 OR Signallers. Weather very good, and excellent visibility in the enemy. Raining night of 22nd, not 23. Battery were 4 guns from W.20.6.7.2 to W.25.d.2.2.72.	
	23rd		Normal Day.	
	24th		At 1.30 am the 2n Suffolks made an enemy transder at W.5c.20.80 but are unsuccessful. (Order attached.)	
	25th		From 8.0am 25th to 8.0am 26th No telephones are used in XIII Corps area. Hostile artillery was quiet.	
	26		At 1.20am the enemy opened a heavy gas bombardment of the area SW of HINGES and of LANNOY with Yellow Cross, Blue Cross and Phosgene. This bombardment slackened at 2.45am. Ceased at 3.30am. Lt BULCOCK, Hans Furlow from 40th Bde R.F.A. in show column.	
	27		Lt Col Main present on a weekly leave. The Left Group. 3 ~ D.A. + Theofon	

Army Form C. 2118.

WAR DIARY
or
INTELLIGENCE SUMMARY.
(Erase heading not required.)

Place	Date	Hour	Summary of Events and Information	Remarks and references to Appendices
			commanded by Lt Col. Maisle, Agrahir R.H.A. Hostile fire was above normal throughout the day. Coy. Concentrations were carried out during the night 26/27".	
		28" 29"	Hostile artillery continued active. Nothing of importance to report. HV Guns which had been active against LA BEUVRIERE shelled the Bengal	
		30	Wagon Lines at 5.00am. Wagon Lines therefore moved further into the wood.	
		30" 31"	Indiscriminate shelling of battery areas with blue cross gas shell during the night	

J B Watson M/
For O C 40" Bde R.F.A.

SECRET.

:- LEFT GROUP ORDER No. 162. -:-

Reference LOCON 1/10,000.

1. During the night May 3rd/4th, 1918 1st. Gordon Highlanders will attack the Orchard in W.11.a. & b.

2. The 1st. Gordon Highlanders will assemble half an hour before Zero at the following points:-
       W.11.a.8.2. to W.11.a.9.1.
       W.11.a.7.3. & W.11.a.4.5.

and will creep up as close to the barrage as possible.

3. At Zero hour the posts of 8th. K.O.R.L. and 2nd. Suffolk Regt. now at W.10.b.95.70. will advance 150 yards along the road and dig in at about W.11.a.15.90.

4. Artillery co-operation will be as follows:-

(A). Zero to zero plus 5'.
    40th. Brigade R.F.A.

3 18-pdr. batteries (less 1 section).	W.11.a.60.72. to	W.11.a.93.32.
1 Section.	W.5.c.85.75. "	W.5.c.95.68.
Right Group.		
2 18-pdr. batteries.	W.11.a.93.32. to	W.11.b.51.30.
47th. Brigade R.F.A.		
2 18-pdr. batteries.	W.5.c.85.05. "	W.11.b.22.71.
1 18-pdr. battery	W.5.d.08.40. "	W.5.d.40.10.
4.5" Hows.		
130th. Battery R.F.A. area;	W.5.c.28.27. - W.5.c.65.25. - W.5.c.80.55. -	
	W.5.c.40.60.	
D/47th. -"- area;	W.5.c.76.47. - W.5.c.36.52. - W.5.a.50.00. -	
	W.5.b.00.00.	
1 Section Right Group.	W.12.c.15.55.	

Heavy Artillery.

1 Battery 6" Hows.	Defensive lines in W.5.b.	
1 " " "	Enclosures and houses in W.6.a. and W.6.d.	
1 " " "	Enclosures and houses in W.12.a. and W.6.c.	
1 " " "	VERT BOIS FARM and enclosure in Q.35.d.	

(B). From Zero plus 5' to Zero plus 9'.
    40th. Brigade R.F.A.

3 18-pdr. batteries (less 1 section).	W.5.c.85.05. to	W.11.b.22.68.
1 Section.	W.5.c.85.75. "	W.5.c.95.68.
47th. Brigade R.F.A.		
3 18-pdr. batteries.	W.5.d.05.42. "	W.11.b.65.75.
4.5" Hows.	———— AS IN (A) ————	
Heavy Artillery.	———— AS IN (A) ————	

(C). From Zero plus 9' to Zero plus 1 hr.
    40th. Brigade R.F.A.

3 18-pdr. batteries.	W.5.d.05.42. "	W.11.b.65.75.
4.5" Hows.	———— AS IN (A) ————	
Heavy Artillery.	———— AS IN (A) ————	

5. Rates of fire.
    18-pdrs. Zero to zero plus 9' - 4 R.P.G. per minute.
             Zero plus 9' to zero plus 1 hr - 1 R.P.G. per minute.
    4.5" Hows. :- Zero to zero plus 9' - 2 R.P.G. per minute.
             Zero plus 9' to zero plus 1 hr. - 1 R.P.G. per 2 min

6. Ammunition:- 18-pdrs. Zero to zero plus 9' H.E. only.
Zero plus 9' to zero plus 1 hr. 75% Shrapnel, 25% H.E.
4.5". Hows. 50% 106 fuzes except 130th. Battery R.F.A. which will fire 101 fuzes only.

7. On completion of the operation and until further orders S.O.S. lines for the Left Group will be as follows:-

      40th. Brigade R.F.A.
3 18-pdr. batteries,   W.11.b.65.75 to W.5.d.05.42.
1 4.5". How. battery,   W.5.d.28.76. " W.6.c.00.00.

      47th. Brigade R.F.A.
2 18-pdr. batteries,   Concentrations "K" and "L".
1 18-pdr. battery,   W.5.c.45.20. to W.5.d.00.40.
1 4.5". How. battery,   Concentrations "I" and "J".

8. The signal for the Heavy Artillery to commence firing will be the opening of the 18-pdr. barrage.

9. Watches will be synchronised at Left Group H.Q. (W.25.a.00.85) at 11 p.m. tonight. Right Group & 47th. Brigade R.F.A. will please detail an Officer to attend at that hour.

10. Zero hour will be 3-30 a.m. on 4th. May.

11. Acknowledge.

                          Captain R.F.A.

3/5/18.   Adjutant Left Group.

        Copies to :-   6th. Battery R.F.A.
                           23rd.   -"-
                           49th.   -"-
                           130th.   -"-
                           47th. Brigade R.F.A. (5 copies).
                           Right Group. (4 copies).
                           76th. Infantry Brigade.
                           1st. Gordon Highlanders.
                           Office File.

SECRET

:- LEFT GROUP ORDER NO. 196 -:-

Reference Map LOOON I/10,000, Edition S.

1. The 2nd Suffolk Regt. on the night 23rd/24th May, 1918, will raid the enemy's post about W.5.c.90.80, for the purpose of obtaining an identification.
2. Artillery co-operation will be as follows :-
   (a) From zero to zero plus 5'

   18-pdrs. 40th Brigade R.F.A.
           23rd Bty.   W.5.c.60.47 to W.5.c.45.62
           49th "   W.5.c.45.62 to W.5.c.90.80
           6th   "   W.5.c.90.80 to W.5.a.10.00

   47th Brigade R.F.A.
           W.5.a.10.00 to W.4.b.92.90

   4.5" Hows.
   40th Brigade R.F.A.
       3 guns area W.5.a.79.00-W.5.a.87.35-W.5.central.
       4 guns Area W.5.a.92.43-Q.35.d.15.00-W.5.b.55.41.
   47th Brigade R.F.A.
       Practice trenches N. of line W.5.c.90.80 to
       W.5.c.62.79.

   (b) From zero plus 5' to zero plus 20'
   18-pdrs. 23rd Bty.   W.5.d.05.74 to W.5.c.87.94
           49th "   W.5.c.87.94 to W.5.a.68.13
           6th   "   W.5.a.68.13 to W.5.a.50.32
           47th   ) W.5.a.50.32 to W.5.a.36.40
           Bde. R.F.A) W.5.a.00.20 to W.4.b.92.90

   4.5" Hows.
   40th Bde. R.F.A. ——— As in (a) ———
   47th Bde. R.F.A. ~~Practice trenches N. of line~~ Road
       ~~W.5.a.60.60 to W.5.a.75.00~~ W.6.a.90.25

   (c) Zero plus 20' ——— CEASE FIRE ——— W.5.a.86.25

3. Rate of fire :- 18-pdrs. Zero to zero plus 5' - Intense.
       Zero plus 5' to zero plus 10' - 5.R.P.G. per minute.
       Zero plus 10' to zero plus 20' - 3 R.P.G. per minute.

   4.5" Hows. + Half above rates.

4. Ammunition:- Zero to zero plus 5' - H.E. only.
       Zero plus 5' to zero plus 20' - 75% Shrapnel.

5. The Heavy Artillery will gas hostile active batteries on Left Brigade front from zero minus 5' to zero plus 20'.
6. The Signal to withdraw will be given by means of a gas rattle. There will be no "All in" Signal.
7. Zero hour will be 1-30 a.m. 24th May, 1918.
8. The 47th Brigade will send a Signal watch to Group H.Q. at 9-30 p.m. to-night to be synchronised. A watch will be sent round to Batteries of the 40th Brigade R.F.A. by orderly, between 9-30 p.m. and 10-30 p.m. to-night.
9. ACKNOWLEDGE.

23/5/18.
                                   2/Lieut. R.F.A.
                                     a/Adjutant Left Group.

Copies to - 6th Bty. R.F.A.   23rd Bty. R.F.A.
           49th " "   130th -"-
           47th Bde. R.F.A.   42nd Bde. R.F.A.
           2nd Div. Arty.   76th Infantry Brigade
           2nd Suffolk Regt. 8th Kings Own.

```
  6th  )                                            D.K. 555.
 23rd  )
 49th  ) Batteries
130th  )
 47th Brigade R.F.A.
 43nd    —"—
 76th Infantry Brigade     )
  8th K.O.R.L.             ) For information.
  3rd Divl. Arty.          )
```

Reference Left Group Order No. 194 of 29/5/18 :-

1. Table for Field Artillery Co-operation is cancelled and the attached substituted.

2. The raid will take place on night 1st/2nd June.

3. Please ACKNOWLEDGE

31/5/18.   [signature]   Captain R.F.A.
                                                     Adjutant Left Group.

FIELD ARTILLERY CO-OPERATION.

	Time.	Unit.	18-pdrs.	4.5"Hows.	Target.	Rate of fire.	Remarks.
A.	Zero to Zero plus 3'	40th Bde. R.F.A.	6. (6th Bty)		W.II.b.50.85 to W.II.b.42.77.	4 R.P.G. per minute.	H.E. only. 106 Fuze **not** to be used.
			6. (40th Bty)		W.II.b.42.77 to W.II.b.35.84 to W.II.b.54.105		
			6. (23rd Bty)		W.II.b.65.10 to W.II.d.73.20		
				2 2 2	W.S.d.60.90. W.II.b.64.30. W.II.b.65.95.	2 R.P.G. per minute.	
		42nd Bde. R.F.A.	6.		W.II.b.45.90 to W.II.b.54.07.	4 R.P.G. per minute.	
			6.		W.II.b.54.07 to W.II.b.50.55.		
				2 2	W.II.b.80.05 W.II.d.80.60	2 R.P.G. per min.	
		47th Bde. R.F.A.	18.		W.II.b.43.90 to W.II.b.60.45 to W.II.d.73.80	4 R.P.G. per minute.	Shrapnel only.
				4.	W.12.x.W.35 to W.12.a.50.70	2 R.P.G. per min.	NOT 106 Fuzes
B.	Zero plus 3' to Zero plus 15'.	40th Bde. R.F.A.	6. (6th Bty) 6. (40th Bty) 6. (23rd Bty)		—As in A.— W.II.b.70.50 to W.II.b.70.50 —As in A.—	2 R.P.G. per min.	All H.E. 106 fuzes **not** to be used.
				As in A.	—As in A.—	1 R.P.G. per min.	
		42nd Bde. R.F.A.	As in A		—As in A.—	2 R.P.G. per min.	
				As in A	—As in A.—	1 R.P.G. per min.	
		47th Bde. R.F.A.	As in A		—As in A.—	2 R.P.G. per min.	
				As in A	—As in A.—	1 R.P.G. per min.	

ZERO PLUS 15' — CEASE FIRE

Army Form C. 2118.

40th Brigade R.F.A.

From 1st to 30th June 1918

WAR DIARY
or
INTELLIGENCE SUMMARY.
(Erase heading not required.)

Vol 46

Place	Date	Hour	Summary of Events and Information	Remarks and references to Appendices
	June 1st		Hostile artillery normal	
	2		At 12.30 am a barrage was put down for a raid by 8th K.O.R.L which was successful 1 Officer and 10 OR being captured. Hostile artillery normal.	
	3		Hostile artillery slightly less normal. Lt D ROBBINS wounded by a Bn Crow gas shell whilst at the afternoon of 23rd Bty. Lt D.E.L. RELTON and D.E.L RELTON 1" Bty. gassed.	
	4		Lt D.E.L RELTON died of wounds at No 6 CCS Lt LANHAM 1" Bty. rejoined from attachment to 3. D.A 14Q	
	6		About 12.5 am the enemy attempted to raid an op. our post in W.1/c but was unsuccessful leaving one wounded person in our hand. Lt.Col G.T.Mair Lt BRYDONE JACK M.C attached took over command of the Group from Lt.Col Murfile. 2Lt BROWN attached 2.5" Bty, 2Lt PICK UP 49" Bty, 2Lt MARSDEN 130. Bty from 3. D.A.C. 2Lt JACK attached 23" Bty from 49" Bty.	
	7		No change. Harassing fires on enemy units at night	
	8		"	
	9		"	
	10		"	
	11		"	
	12		During the night the batteries of 331 Bde RFA came into action under order	

Army Form C. 2118.

WAR DIARY
or
INTELLIGENCE SUMMARY.
(Erase heading not required.)

Instructions regarding War Diaries and Intelligence
Summaries are contained in F. S. Regs., Part II.
and the Staff Manual respectively. Title pages
will be prepared in manuscript.

Place	Date	Hour	Summary of Events and Information	Remarks and references to Appendices
	13" 14"		of O.C. left Groush No Change [struck through] During the night 14/15 T&s (?) advanced in line to a depth of 1000 yds NW of S. Canal. At 11.45 hrs barrage for the attack opn (OOs attacked).	
	15		Attack repulsed initially successful. 200 prisoners and many M.G.s were brought in. Our line now runs Q34 d 1020, W5 a 3525, W12 a 05, 60. AAA Hostile retaliation was slight. AA	

Army Form C. 2118.

WAR DIARY
or
INTELLIGENCE SUMMARY.
(Erase heading not required.)

Place	Date	Hour	Summary of Events and Information	Remarks and references to Appendices
	16, 17, 18		No change. Hostile artillery slightly above normal. On night 16/17" B 31 Bd. withdrawn from active service to their W.L.	
	19"		An epidemic of fever being about 4 day, is rend. was become fairly prevalent in the Brigade. B/47 and D/47 Batteries ordered to left Group, go out of action and proceed to CAMBLAIN CHÂTELAIN for training. A and C/104 Brigade take over SOS lines and concentrations of Bond D/47 but remain in their former positions in 4 Rue Anne.	
	20, 21"		Hostile artillery normal. Prisoners' statements that an attack is to be made on this front.	
	22"		Prisoners captured in early morning state preparation for attack have been made. Hostile artillery below normal. Detached section of 23" Battery at 5.9 during the afternoon, and moves the following night to a position at " ". No change.	
	23, 24, 25, 26, 27, 28"		A heavy lasting 3 minutes is put down by all batteries at 6.0am to assist in an operation which is being carried out by the Corps on our left. 250 rounds	

Army Form C. 2118.

WAR DIARY
or
INTELLIGENCE SUMMARY.
(Erase heading not required.)

Place	Date	Hour	Summary of Events and Information	Remarks and references to Appendices
	29"		Hostile artillery more active in battery areas.	
	30"		No change.	

J B Watson 2/Lt
Fu OC 40° Bu REA

SECRET.

:- LEFT GROUP ORDER No. 202. -:

Reference LOCON 1/10,000 Edition 8.

1. The 3rd.Division is attacking on a front from W.18.b.75.73. to LA PANNERIE W.4.a.95.80 on the night 14th./15th.June,1918.
  The attack will be carried out by the 9th.Infantry Brigade in the Centre with 1 Battalion and by the 76th.Infantry Brigade on the Left with 2 Battalions.
2. The bombardment by Field and Heavy Artillery will commence at Zero hour which will be notified later.
3. The Artillery covering the 3rd.Division will be re-grouped into 3 Groups on completion of the Infantry relief on the night 13th./14th.June, the Left Group being composed of the 40th.Brigade R.F.A. with B. and D. Batteries of the 47th.Brigade R.F.A.
4. The 66th.Divisional Artillery is placed under the orders of the 3rd.Division for the above operation and will go into action on the night 13th./14th.June, and remain in action until the night 16th./17th.June, both nights inclusive.
5. The attack will be supported as follows:-

Right Group 3rd.D.A.   )
Centre Group 3rd.D.A.   )   Under tactical command of Lieut.Col.C.M.H.
330th.Brigade R.F.A.   )   Stevens D.S.O., covering 9th.Infty.Brigade.

Left Group 3rd.D.A.   )
One Group 4th.D.A.   )   Under tactical command of Lieut.Col.G.T.Mair,
331st.Brigade R.F.A.   )   D.S.O. covering 76th.Infty.Brigade.

46th.D.A.   Co-operating on 8th.Infantry Brigade front.

6. The XIII Corps Heavy Artillery assisted by 1 Corps Heavy Artillery are neutralising hostile batteries which normally fire on the front of the attack and are engaging selected targets.
7. Details of Left Group Programme is shown on attached Time Table.
8. Concentrations, S.O.S.Lines, Counter Preparations and Mutual Support as issued in Group Orders Nos. 165 & 170 and D.K.531 will be cancelled at Zero Hour.
9. Concentrations, S.O.S.Lines and Counter Preparations for use when the operation is completed will be published in a subsequent Group Order.
10. Prior to Zero Hour, harassing fire will be carried out as at present.
11. One Officer per Battery will attend at Left Group H.Q. between 7 p.m. and 8 p.m. on 14th.instant to synchronise watches.
12. The Roster for Night O.P. and Liaison duties will be issued later. from 14th.instant
13. ACKNOWLEDGE.

                                              Captain R.F.A.
11/6/18.   Adjutant Left Group.

        Copies to - / 6th.Battery R.F.A.
                     23rd.   -"-
                     49th.   -"-
                     130th.   -"-
                     47th.Brigade, R.F.A.
                     B/47 Battery R.F.A.
                     D/47   -"-
                     76th.Infantry Brigade.
                     331st.Brigade R.F.A.
                     4th.D.A. Group.

LEFT GROUP TIME TABLE FOR 18-pdrs. TABLE 'A', 1st PHASE.

Group Letter.	Bty.	Time.	Target.			Ammunition.	Rate of fire.
A.	6th. 23rd. 49th. B/47.	Zero to zero plus 8' -	W.5.d.50.08 W.5.d.20.22 W.5.c.91.38 W.5.c.62.53	to " " "	W.5.d.20.22 W.5.c.91.38 W.5.c.62.53 W.5.c.30.70	H.E.	Rapid.
B.	6th. 23rd. 49th. B/47.	Zero plus 8' to zero plus 12'	W.5.d.63.20 W.5.d.34.37 W.5.d.04.52 W.5.c.74.68	to " " "	W.5.d.34.37 W.5.d.04.52 W.5.c.74.68 W.5.c.44.83	ditto	ditto
C.	6th. 23rd. 49th. B/47.	Zero plus 12' to zero plus 16'	W.5.d.33.78 W.5.d.48.50 W.5.d.17.67 W.5.c.88.82	to " " "	W.5.d.48.50 W.5.d.17.67 W.5.c.88.82 W.5.c.58.98	ditto	ditto
D.	6th. 23rd. 49th. B/47.	Zero plus 16' to zero plus 20'	W.5.d.90.48 W.5.d.60.64 W.5.d.30.80 W.5.d.00.97	to " " "	W.5.d.60.64 W.5.d.30.80 W.5.d.00.97 W.5.a.71.13	ditto	ditto
E.	6th. 23rd. 49th. B/47.	Zero plus 20' to zero plus 24'	W.6.c.05.60 W.5.d.73.78 W.5.d.43.95 W.5.b.13.10	to " " "	W.5.d.73.78 W.5.d.43.95 W.5.b.13.10 W.5.a.85.26	ditto	ditto
F.	6th. 23rd. 49th. B/47.	Zero plus 24' to zero plus 28'	W.6.c.05.60 W.5.d.80.83 W.5.b.58.11 W.5.b.27.23	to " " "	W.5.d.80.83) W.5.b.58.11) W.5.b.27.23) W.5.a.98.40)	50% H.E. & Shrapnel H.E.	ditto
G.	6th. 23rd. 49th. B/47.	Zero plus 28' to zero plus 32'	------ As in F. ------ ------ ditto ------ W.5.b.11.58 W.5.b.41.41	 to "	)) W.5.b.41.41) W.5.b.11.55	50% H.E. & Shrapnel. H.E.	Normal ditto Rapid ditto
H.	6th. 23rd. 49th. B/47.	Zero plus 32' to zero plus 36'	------ As in F. ------ ------ ditto ------ ------ As in G. ------ W.5.b.41.41 to W.5.b.23.70			50% H.E. & Shrapnel	Normal ditto ditto Rapid
I.	6th. 23rd. 49th. B/47.	Zero plus 36' to zero plus 60'	------ As in F.) Protec- ------ ditto) tive ------ As in G.) Barrage. ------ As in H.)			ditto	Normal

2nd PHASE.

Group Letter.	Bty.	Time.	Starting Line.	Finishing Line.	Ammunition.	Rate of fire.
J.	6th. 23rd. 49th. B/47.	Zero plus 1 hr.8' to zero plus 1 hr.9'	Protective Barrage		50% H.E. & Shrapnel	Rapid
K.	ditto	Zero plus 1 hr.17' to zero plus 1 hr.18'	ditto		ditto	ditto
L.	ditto	Zero plus 1 hr.25' to zero plus 1 hr.26'	ditto		ditto	ditto
M.	6th. 23rd. 49th. B/47.	Zero plus 2 hrs. to zero plus 2 hrs.9' *1.45 am. to 1.54 am.*	Protective Barrage Lifting 100 yards at zero plus 2 hrs. 1' and continuing to lift 100 yards every minute to a total depth of 800 yards.	W.6.b.18.76 to Q.36.c.95.05. Q.36.c.95.05 to Q.36.c.72.35. Q.36.c.72.35 to Q.36.c.52.60 Q.36.c.52.60 to Q.36.c.33.85.	ditto	ditto
N.	ditto *2.15 am. to 2.24 am.*	Zero plus 2 hrs.30' to zero plus 2 hrs.39'	ditto	ditto	ditto	ditto
O.	ditto *2.45 am. to 2.54 am.*	Zero plus 3 hrs. to zero plus 3 hrs. 9'	ditto	ditto	ditto	ditto
P.	ditto *3.25 am. to 3.34 am.*	Zero plus 3 hrs 40' to zero plus 3 hrs.49'	ditto	ditto	ditto	ditto

LEFT GROUP TIME TABLE FOR 4.5" Hows. TABLE 'C'.

Group Letter.	Bty.	Time.	Target.	Rate of fire.	Ammunition.
A.	130th.	Zero to zero plus 8'	House W.6.c.20.25 " W.6.c.32.32 " W.6.c.37.25 Bridge W.5.d.88.32 " W.5.d.85.42 " W.5.d.82.53.	Rapid	101 fuzes.
	D/47.		W.5.d.30.81 to W.5.a.72.13		106 fuzes
	D/331.		W.5.a.72.13 to Q.35.c.25.00		ditto
B.	130th.	Zero plus 8' to zero plus 12' -	Bridge W.5.d.73.80 " W.5.d.72.88 W.6.c.05.60 to W.5.d.43.94. W.5.d.43.94 to W.5.a.83.27. W.5.a.83.27 to Q.35.c.40.16	ditto	101 fuzes 101 fuzes 106 fuzes ditto ditto
	D/47.				
	D/331.				
C.	130th.	Zero plus 12' to zero- plus 16' -	W.6.c.20.77 to W.5.b.57.09 Bridge W.5.b.62.25 " W.5.b.58.42 T.M. W.5.b.57.20 T.M. W.5.b.68.20.	ditto	106 fuzes 101 fuzes
	D/47.		W.5.b.57.09 to W.5.a.98.40		106 fuzes
	D/331.		W.5.a.98.40 to Q.35.c.55.30		ditto
D.	130th.	Zero plus 16' to zero- plus 20' -	W.6.c.33.90 to W.5.b.70.23 T.M. W.5.b.57.20 T.M. W.5.b.68.20. W.5.b.70.23 to W.5.b.10.55 W.5.b.10.55 to Q.35.c.70.45	ditto	106 fuzes 101 fuzes 106 fuzes ditto
	D/47.				
	D/331.				
E.	130th.	Zero	W.6.c.33.90 to W.5.b.77.31	Normal	
	D/47.	plus 20'	W.5.b.77.31 to W.5.b.25.70	Rapid	106 fuzes
	D/331.	to zero- plus 24'	W.5.b.25.70 to Q.35.c.70.45	ditto	
F.	130th.	Zero	W.6.c.33.90 to W.5.b.77.31		
	D/47.	plus 24'	W.5.b.77.31 to W.5.b.37.84	Normal	106 fuzes
	D/331.	to zero- plus 37'	W.5.b.37.84 to Q.35.c.70.45		
G.	130th.	Zero plus 37' to zero- plus 4 hrs.	Area W.12.a.60.90 - W.6.c.90.20 - W.12.b.40.80 - W.12.b.00.40. Area W.6.d.10.80 - W.6.b.50.10 - W.6.d.70.70 - W.6.d.20.50. Area W.6.a.10.90 - Q.36.c.20.50 - Q.36.c.80.60 - Q.36.c.80.10		120 rounds per Bty. per hour. 106 fuzes. 4 Bursts per hour searching and sweeping.
	D/47.				
	D/331.				

LEFT GROUP TIME TABLE FOR 18-pdrs. 331st Bde. R.F.A. Table 'B'.

Group Letter.	Time.	Bty.	Target.	Ammunition.	Rate of fire.
A.	Zero to zero plus 8'	A. C. B.	W.5.d.72.30 to W.5.d.00.68 W.5.d.00.68 to W.5.a.40.15 W.5.a.40.15 to W.5.a.12.90	Shrapnel	Rapid
B.	Zero plus 8' to zero plus 12'	A. C. B.	W.5.d.90.48 to W.5.d.20.88 W.5.d.20.88 to W.5.a.61.32 W.5.a.61.32 to Q.35.c.28.00	ditto	ditto
C.	Zero plus 12' to zero plus 16'	A. C. B.	W.6.c.05.60 to W.5.b.33.00 W.5.b.33.00 to W.5.a.75.45 W.5.a.75.45 to Q.35.c.41.17	ditto	ditto
D.	Zero plus 16' to zero plus 20'	A. C. B.	W.6.c.19.77 to W.5.b.46.14 W.5.b.46.14 to W.5.a.90.58 W.5.a.90.58 to Q.35.c.55.30	ditto	ditto
E.	Zero plus 20' to zero plus 24'	A. C. B.	W.6.c.22.82 to W.5.b.60.30 W.5.b.60.30 to W.5.b.04.70 W.5.b.04.70 to Q.35.c.70.45	ditto	ditto
F.	Zero plus 24' to zero plus 28'	A. C. B.	W.6.c.22.82 to W.5.b.75.45 W.5.b.75.45 to W.5.b.20.82 W.5.b.20.82 to Q.35.c.83.58	ditto	ditto
G.	Zero plus 28' to zero plus 32'	A. C. B.	--------- As in F. --------- W.5.b.75.45 to Q.35.d.40.00 Q.35.d.40.00 to Q.35.c.80.55	ditto	Normal Rapid ditto
H.	Zero plus 32' to zero plus 40'	A. C. B.	--------- As in F.)-Protective --------- As in G.) Barrage --------- ditto)	ditto	Normal
I.	Zero plus 40' to zero plus 60'	ditto	--------- ditto ---------	ditto	Slow

2nd PHASE.

Group Letter.	Time.	Bty.	Starting Line.	Finishing Line.	Ammunition.	Rate of fire.
J.	Zero plus 1 hr.8' to zero plus 1 hr.9'	A. C. B.	Protective Barrage.		50% H.E. & Shrapnel	Rapid
K.	Zero plus 1 hr.17' to zero plus 1 hr.18'	ditto	ditto		ditto	ditto
L.	Zero plus 1 hr.25' to zero plus 1 hr.26'	ditto	ditto		ditto	ditto
M.	Zero plus 2 hrs to zero plus 2 hrs.9'	A. C. B.	Protective Barrage lifting 100 yards at zero plus 2 hrs 1' and continuing to lift 100 yards every minute to a total depth of 800 yards.	W.6.b.37.95 to Q.36.c.92.60. Q.36.c.92.60 to Q.36.a.50.17 Q.36.a.50.17 to Q.35.b.92.68	ditto	ditto
N.	Zero plus 2 hrs.30' to zero plus 2hrs.39'	ditto	ditto	ditto	ditto	ditto
O.	Zero plus 3 hrs. to zero plus 3 hrs.9'	ditto	ditto	ditto	ditto	ditto
P.	Zero plus 3 hrs.40' to zero plus 3 hrs.49'	ditto	ditto	ditto	ditto	ditto

WAR DIARY or INTELLIGENCE SUMMARY

40th Brigade RFA
From 1st to 31st July 1918
Army Form C. 2118
Sheet 1. 47

Place	Date	Hour	Summary of Events and Information	Remarks and references to Appendices
Ref 36 A S E 1/20000	1st		No Change	
"	2		"	
"	3		"	
"	4		"	
"	5		"	
"	6		At 9.30am all batteries put down a barrage to cover the Princess on left and raid, which was successful. 3 prisoners being captured	
"	7		A battalion relief is expected to take place attack to take front, during the night. Harassing fire in the fore noon.	
"	8		No change	
"	9		Heavy firing at 1.30am on left in the vicinity of CALONNE	
"	10		Hostile harassing fire during the night – our slightly above normal	
"	11		No Change	
"	12		"	
"	13		"	
"	14		Lt Col C.T. Mair gone to 3° D.A.H.Q as a/CRA the 40° Bde being commanded by Major J.A. WOLFF, 130 Battery	

WAR DIARY
or
INTELLIGENCE SUMMARY.
(Erase heading not required.)

Army Form C. 2118.
40th Brigade RFA
From 1st to 31st July 1918
Sheet 2.

Place	Date	Hour	Summary of Events and Information	Remarks and references to Appendices
	15		Lt LANDON posted to 23 Battery, and 2Lt JACKSON attached	
	16		6" Battery from 3" DAC	
			All batteries in action in a raid by 4" Division, canned out a 2.20 hr. Raid was successful. 29 prisoners being captured.	
	17		During the night 6" Battery move 2 guns to a position at V24.a.9.5.70 a.5-9/How registered + 9" detached section in cover W14.D.	
	18		During the night 4.9" detached section moved onwards, then retire onwards during alternate nights and from 18" onwards, then retire to a different position becoming a main.	
	19		Hostile artillery activity was slightly above normal	
	20		No change.	
	21		6" Battery main gun detached section to W14.c.05.10.	

WAR DIARY
or
INTELLIGENCE SUMMARY.

(Erase heading not required.)

Army Form C. 2118

40th Brigade RFA
From 1st to 31st July 1918

Sheet 2.

Place	Date	Hour	Summary of Events and Information	Remarks and references to Appendices
	22		HV Gun intermittently active on CHOQUES throughout the day.	
	23		Hostile artillery below normal	
	24		No change	
	25		" "	
	26		" "	
	27		" "	
	28		" "	
	29		" "	
	30		" "	
	31		At 12/10am 4.9" Battery comes in a raid carried out by the Brigade on our right; two harrowers being extinned by Lt Col C T Main return to command 40 Bde RFA	

J. B. Water Mr.
For OC 40th Bde RFA

Army Form C. 2118.

40th Bde RFA
From 1st to 31st August 1918

WAR DIARY
or
INTELLIGENCE SUMMARY
(Erase heading not required.)

Place	Date	Hour	Summary of Events and Information	Remarks and references to Appendices
HINGES	1.8.18		Brigade in action in HINGES SECTOR. No change.	
"	2.8.18		No change.	
"	3.8.18		No change.	
"	4.8.18		No change.	
"	5.8.18		Enemy reported to have evacuated posts opposite 4th Div front in vicinity of PACQUAT WOOD. No withdrawal on our front. O.C. 88th Bde R.F.A. visited Bde H.Q. with a view of taking over.	
"	6.8.18		Enemy commenced to withdraw on 3rd Div front. Infantry ordered to maintain close touch with enemy. 23rd Bty held up by MG fire in vicinity of VERTBOIS FARM. VERTBOIS FARM engaged & small parties of enemy seen to move out. Total advance from 300 to 500 yards was accomplished during day. Two Sections Two Sections of Bty relieved by 2 Sections of Bty 88th Bde R.F.A. & marched to W.L's at La Beuvrière.	
"	7.8.18	9 P.M.	Two Sections of Bty & all transport marched from W.L.s to Beuvrière to BAILLEUL-LEZ-PERNES.	
"		11 A.M.	Command passes to O.C. 88th Bde R.F.A.	
BAILLEUL -LEZ-PERNES		8.30 P.M.	Remaining sections relieved by 88th Bde R.F.A. & marched direct to BAILLEUL-LEZ-PERNES.	

Army Form C. 2118.

WAR DIARY
or
INTELLIGENCE SUMMARY.

(Erase heading not required.)

Instructions regarding War Diaries and Intelligence Summaries are contained in F. S. Regs., Part II. and the Staff Manual respectively. Title pages will be prepared in manuscript.

Place	Date	Hour	Summary of Events and Information	Remarks and references to Appendices
BAILLEUL-LEZ-PERNES	8.8.18		Rest & Bty Training.	
"	9.8.18		Bty Training. Gen. BIRDWOOD Commdg V Army visited Bdes.	
"	10.8.18		Bty Training. All guns & Hows of Bde sent to calibration Ranges.	
"	11.8.18		Bty Training. Officers drawing drill under C.R.A. and O.C. Bde.	
"	12.8.18		XIII Corps Horse Show. 138th Bty won Bty Turnout.	
"	13.8.18		Bty Training & Clearing of Camp.	
		8.30 P.M.	Bde marched from BAILLEUL-LES-PERNES, through WAVRANS, S.Pol., FREVENT	
REBRUVRIETTE	14.8.18	7 A.M.	Arrived & billeted at REBRUVRIETTE. 27 mile night march.	
		9.30 P.M.	Bde marched at 9.30 P.M. through SUS-ST-LEGERS HUMBERCOURT.	
HUMBERCOURT	15.8.18	12.30 A.M.	Arrived & billeted at HUMBERCOURT. Rested.	
"	16.8.18		Bty Training	
"	17.8.18		Bty Training.	
"	18.8.18		Bty Training.	
"	19.8.18		Bdr & Bty Commanders reconnoitred BOUZY AREA for battery positions	
LA CAUCHIE	20.8.18	1.30 A.M.	Bdes moved to LA CAUCHIE.	
		5.30 A.M.	Arrived & billeted in LA CAUCHIE.	
		8.30 P.M.	Bty took up positions as follows Bde HQ F.5.a.4.8., 6th Bty F.10.d.3.0 (contd overleaf)	

WAR DIARY
or
INTELLIGENCE SUMMARY.

(Erase heading not required.)

Army Form C. 2118.

Instructions regarding War Diaries and Intelligence Summaries are contained in F. S. Regs., Part II. and the Staff Manual respectively. Title pages will be prepared in manuscript.

Place	Date	Hour	Summary of Events and Information	Remarks and references to Appendices
Near Bouzincourt			23rd Bty F.5.C.0.2, 41st Bty F.5.C.0.1, 130th Bty F.10.b.8.3 (Batt.) 49th Bty F.5.F.9.1.9. (Position of assembly)	
	21/8/18	1.30am	Btys in action.	
		4.55am	"Zero Hour". Bdg did not open fire until Zero + 86'.	
		7am	"Blue line" reported captured by 2nd Div. 3rd Div then passing through & reached the line of the Railway. 49th Bty moved forward to position at A.8.C.1.9.	
		10am	Bty moved forward to Advanced Infantry H.Q. COURCELLES captured & posts established E of Railway. No further operations during day.	
	22/8/18		Quiet day. 36th Bde R.F.A. come into action under orders of 40th Bde R.F.A.	

WAR DIARY or INTELLIGENCE SUMMARY

Army Form C. 2118.

(Erase heading not required.)

Place	Date	Hour	Summary of Events and Information	Remarks and references to Appendices
	23.8.18	3 A.M.	Bde. under command of CRA 2nd Div. Zero hour. Attack on GOMIECOURT. 8th Bde. capture line 500 yds E of railway. 76th Bde. Hrs. through 8th Bde. & capture GOMIECOURT. Attack entirely successful.	
		9.45 AM	Bde. H.Q. moved to 49th Bty position A8c2.2.	
		11 AM	Zero hour for attack on ERVILLERS, BEHAGNIES & SAPIGNIES. Attack carried out as follows 6th Bde. A20.b.8.8. 23rd Bde A21.c.64. 45th Bty A8c.2.2. 130th Bty A20.b.17. 23rd Bde. Bty supports 5 · 2nd Bde. 2nd Div. Btys situated	
		12.50 PM	23 /100 Bty infantry seen going over in G5.d towards G6. Opposition encountered in G4. Small parties of hostile machine gunners in this locality engaged effectively by 23rd Bde Bty.	
		2.45 PM	23rd Bde Bty shoot tanks & infantry held up at Boss trench in G.6.b.21. 23rd Bde engaged parties of enemy G12a 5.8.	
		2 P.M.	40th Bde cease to be under command of OC 42nd Bde & comes under Col. Davies Brownlie 41st Bde R.F.A.	
		4 P.M.	41st Bde supports SAPIGNIES, BEHAGNIES & BIAUCOURT taken also high ground along MORY.	
		7 P.M.	6th & 49th Btys shoot forward to A26.a.2.f. Bde HQ moved to A26.d.9.7.	
		8 P.M.	40th Bde ordered to get into touch with GOC 5th Inf. Bde.	
			40th Bde noted by 41st Bde RFA to cooperate in attack on BEHAGNIES & SAPIGNIES. Orders received & transmitted by telephone to batteries.	
	24.8.18	3:30 AM	Zero hour. 3 Battns 5 & 2nd Bde attacked from W to E under creeping barrage of rate of 100 yds for 4 mins.	
		4:30 AM	1 Batt 2nd Bde attacked SAPIGNIES from N.	

WAR DIARY
or
INTELLIGENCE SUMMARY.

(Erase heading not required.)

Army Form C. 2118

Instructions regarding War Diaries and Intelligence Summaries are contained in F.S. Regs., Part II. and the Staff Manual respectively. Title pages will be prepared in manuscript.

Place	Date	Hour	Summary of Events and Information	Remarks and references to Appendices
	24.3.18		Quiet day	
	25.3.18	8.45 AM	Attack on SAPIGNIES intensely successful. Verbal orders received from 4/1st Bde RFA that 40th Bde to cooperate in an attack by 21st Bde Infantry. Infantry to advance to line H4 e.0 to B27 a 2.0. Attack partially successful. Btys moved to positions as follows. 6th Bty A15c 2.2, 23rd Bty A24 Q 9.9	
		1.30 PM	49th Bty A15d 2.1, 130th Bty A12d 5.0.	
		2 PM	Bde. HQ moved to A23 a 9.6.	
		4.30 PM	S.O.S. sent from 5th KOYLI. Enemy apparently attacked MORY COPSE but was repulsed.	
			Night quiet	
	26.3.18	9 AM	Attack on MORY line in B23 & 29, & 187th Inf Bde. 40th Bde fired smoke barrage on Sunken Road in B23 a & b.	
		2.15 PM	HQ moved to TRIANGLE COPSE	
		3.30 PM	Situation as follows. We hold MORY LINE B23 a 5.0 to B29 a 5.4. Gap between Church from B23 a 5.0 to B16 a 5.5. SOS lines arranged to cover this gap.	
	27.8.18	2 AM	Orders received & transmitted by telephone for attack by 187th Inf Bde on line C13 c 4.5 to SUGAR FACTORY B24 A 7.7.	
		7 AM	Zero hour. Inf. advance under barrage creeping 100 yds for 2 mins.	
		7.45 AM	Objective reported taken.	
		8.45 AM	49th Bty moves forward to B28 c 9.7. To deal with hostile MGs holding up infantry. Targets successfully engaged at ranges of 1400 to 1600 yds. 1 officer from 6th Bty & 1 officer from 23rd Bty detailed to assist 49th Bty in getting information.	
		10.30 AM	All batteries ordered to move forward to cover valley in B.2 DC.	
		12.15 PM	All Btys in action in new position.	

Army Form C. 2118

WAR DIARY
or
INTELLIGENCE SUMMARY.

(Erase heading not required.)

Instructions regarding War Diaries and Intelligence Summaries are contained in F.S. Regs., Part II. and the Staff Manual respectively. Title pages will be prepared in manuscript.

Place	Date	Hour	Summary of Events and Information	Remarks and references to Appendices
	27.8.18	5.P.M	Shelter line swing H54 73 dns S. to H115.1. Then to H11 c1.2.	
		3.PM	49th Bty withdrawn to B20d.	
		10.30PM	40th Bn. transferred to Right Group to come 126th Inf. Bn. immediate for Bn. Breaks down. Supply tank with 1000 rds 18 pdr ammunition for Bn. Breaks down. Wagon lines move forward to COURCELLES - GOMIECOURT area. Quiet night. Harassing fire carried out.	
	28.8.18		Quiet day. No change.	
	29.8.18	3.30PM	Quiet morning. Barrage put down by Bde to watch enemy massing on VAUX - BEUGNATRE Road.	
		5.30PM	Creeping barrage fired to support attack on BANKS RESERVE. Objective gained.	
		6.45PM	Enemy reported massing behind VAULX. Protective barrage put down. No infantry action.	
		7.PM	RIENCOURT HENDECOURT noted to be in our hands.	
		8.PM	40 Bde transferred to Left Group under command of Lt Col H. GOSCHEN DSO.	
	30.8.18	12.45AM	Orders for attack on VAULX - VRAUCOURT at 5AM received & transmitted to Btys by telephone.	
		5.45AM	186th Inf Bde report all objectives gained. 185 Inf Bde report objectives taken except VRAUCOURT SUGAR FACTORY.	
		10.35AM	2nd Div reported to have taken BULLECOURT.	
		11AM	3 Div arrive back at ECOUST in consequence forward move of Btys not sanctioned by Group.	
		1.20PM	Infantry report VAULX not held. VRAUCOURT & SUGAR FACTORY in our hands.	
		1.30PM	Enemy at VRAUCOURT in strength. Counter-Preparation fired by Bdes.	

Army Form C. 2118.

WAR DIARY
or
INTELLIGENCE SUMMARY.

(Erase heading not required.)

Instructions regarding War Diaries and Intelligence Summaries are contained in F. S. Regs., Part II. and the Staff Manual respectively. Title pages will be prepared in manuscript.

Place	Date	Hour	Summary of Events and Information	Remarks and references to Appendices
	30.3.18	3.15 PM	Orders received by wire for attack on Vaulx.	
		5 PM.	Attack cancelled.	
	31.3.18	5 AM	185th Bde attack Vaulx. 15 Feb flys had been sent down on 8270. Replies by runner fwd. dressing fire carried out during night.	Ammunition expended on 40 R Bde RFA

WAR DIARY
or
INTELLIGENCE SUMMARY.
(Erase heading not required.)

Army Form C. 2118.

70th Brigade RFA

From 1st to 30th September 1918 (Inclusive)

Place	Date	Hour	Summary of Events and Information	Remarks and references to Appendices
	1.9.18	5.30AM	Zero hour. 62nd Div. attacked VAULX–VRAUCOURT under a creeping barrage.	
		10AM	Bde ordered to rejoin the 3rd Div. and move to positions near BANKS COPSE, which 74th Bde RFA were vacating at dusk.	
		3PM.	Btys moved at half hour intervals.	
		8PM.	Btys all in action. HQ established 500 yards W of Btys.	
	2.9.18	5.30AM	3rd Div. attacked LAGNICOURT under a creeping barrage. Scant resistance encountered just W of LAGNICOURT where line was established. Lt LAMBERT and 2/Lt JENKINS killed whilst acting as F.O.O.	
	3.9.18	5.20AM	GUARDS Div. passed through 3rd Div. and attacked LAGNICOURT. Bde did not advance as guns were out of range.	
		7.15AM	Bde & Bty commanders went forward to reconnoitre positions N of VAULX. All Btys in action. Owing to silence of hostile artillery Bde & Bty commanders went forward on ascertaining from O.C. 3rd Batt. GRENADIERS that enemy had not been encountered, selected positions E of LAGNICOURT.	
		1PM.	Btys in action. HQ established in EYE COPSE.	
		2PM.	Infantry exploited and met with no opposition until E of BOURSIES	
	4.9.18	11AM	Bde & Bty commanders reconnoitred positions E of LOUVERVAL. Btys moved into action by 2PM. H.Q. in O.P. in Rd N of BOURSIES built by 40th Bde in August 1917. Line slightly advanced during day by GUARDS Div.	
	5.9.18	3AM to 6AM	Enemy put down counter preparation.	
		12noon	Conference held by C.R.A. GUARDS Div. with Bde commanders. After move to WL's at BANKS COPSE. Instructions received that Bde was to withdraw	
		8PM.	Btys withdrew and quarter hour intervals & commenced march at WL's for the night.	
	6.9.18	9AM	Btys marched independently to DOVEHY area to meet vest.	
		12noon	Arrived and in conflict	

WAR DIARY or INTELLIGENCE SUMMARY

Army Form C. 2118.

Place	Date	Hour	Summary of Events and Information	Remarks and references to Appendices
DOUCHY	7.9.18		Brigade in rest.	
"	8.9.18		Brigade in rest.	
"	9.9.18	7 AM	Bde & Bty Commanders went with CRA 62nd Div. to reconnoitre positions near HERMIES	
		11 AM	Orders received for Bde to move up to VAULX - VRAUCOURT.	
		12.30 PM	Brigade marched.	
		4.30 PM	Brigade arrived and camped at VAULX.	
VAULX	10.9.18		Bde Commander reconnoitred Group HQ in HAVRINCOURT WOOD (J.58.9.0). Brigade remains at VAULX.	
HERMIES	11.9.18	8.30 PM	Btys moved to positions in HERMIES. Bde HQ in HERMIES. Group HQ at J.38.9.0 with 186 Inf. Bde. Group consists of 40th, 42nd Bdes & 93rd Army Bde.	
	12.9.18	5.25 AM	186th Inf. Bde carried its objective HAVRINCOURT & FEMY WOOD under creeping barrage.	
			Zero hour.	
		7.50 AM	Infantry reported to be half way through village.	
		8.45 AM	Infantry reported to hold first objective on Eastern side of HAVRINCOURT.	
		10.30 AM	Infantry held up on 1st objective.	
		3 PM	Infantry fell down 300 yds E of MOEUVRES.	
		7.20 PM	S.O.S. sent by Infantry. Enemy apparently counter-attacked but was repulsed. Quiet night.	

Army Form C. 2118.

WAR DIARY
or
INTELLIGENCE SUMMARY.

(Erase heading not required.)

Place	Date	Hour	Summary of Events and Information	Remarks and references to Appendices
HERMIES	13.9.18		Quiet day. No change on front.	
	14.9.18	5.30AM	185th Bde ordered to advance to final objective of 186th Bde of 17th. Orders given by telephone. Zero hour. Infantry attacked under creeping barrage. Operation successful.	
		4PM.	HAVRINCOURT Heavily shelled.	
		4.30PM.	Bde HQ moved to Quarry at J 36.c.1.9. Bdys moved forward to positions as follows 6th & 23rd, K31.d.3.7, 23rd Bty K31.60.9, 49th Bty J 30 d.4.1. 130st Bty K31.6.1.5.	
		5 P.M.	Barrage fired by 130th & 45th Btys to support Infantry attack to link up with Brigade on the right.	
	15.9.18	4.45AM	Suspected counter-attack. Counter-preparation. Creeping barrage fired starting from SOS lines at lifts of 100 yards per two minutes.	
		5.45AM	S.O.S. called for by Infantry. No attack.	
		5.30AM	"	
		6.30AM	Barrage preparation as before.	
		5 P.M.	6th & 23rd Bty's ordered to move back to positions as follows 6th Bty J 30 d.3.2, 23rd Bty J 30 d.2.7.	
		6.P.M.	93rd Bde withdrawn.	
		9.P.M.	186th Bde relieved by 9th Inf Bde. Group Cean R under orders of CRA 3rd Div. GROUP consists of 41st and 42nd Bdes R.F.A.	

Army Form C. 2118.

WAR DIARY
or
INTELLIGENCE SUMMARY.
(Erase heading not required.)

Instructions regarding War Diaries and Intelligence Summaries are contained in F. S. Regs., Part II. and the Staff Manual respectively. Title pages will be prepared in manuscript.

Place	Date	Hour	Summary of Events and Information	Remarks and references to Appendices
HERMIES	16.9.18	3 P.M.	RIGHT GROUP becomes MAIR GROUP consisting of 40th, 44th, 42nd BDES. GROUP Commander moved to new H.Q. at J 23 d 5.0 in HERMIES.	
		9 P.M.	Command passes from G.O.C. 6th Dy. Bde to G.O.C. 2nd N. Bde. Front of GROUP changes to sector of 2nd Inf. Bde.	
"	17.9.18		Bde HQ moved to GROUP HQ. No change on front.	
"	18.9.18	5.20 AM	Smoke barrage fired by Btys to assist in operation by VI Corps.	
		3.30 PM	Heavy concentration by all calibres was put down on the whole Bty area.	
		3.45 PM	Btys opened fire as no news came from infantry.	
		4.15 PM	Barrage brought back on to front line support lines.	
		4.30 PM	Enemy attacked in force & succeeded in penetrating our front line in places.	
		7 P.M.	Hostile shelling eased.	
		9 P.M.	Infantry report line practically restored.	
		11 P.M.	Infantry report line restored and nearly 100 prisoners left in our hands. Night quiet.	
"	19.9.18		No change on front. Wire cutting carried out by 130th Bty. Harassing fire during night.	
"	20.9.18		No change. Wire cutting by 130th Bty. Harassing fire during night.	
"	21.9.18		No change. Wire cutting & harassing fire day & night. Bdr. Commander reconnoitred forward positions.	
"	22.9.18		No change. Wire cutting & harassing fire. Bdr. Commander & B.M. & B.D.A. reconnoitred forward positions.	
"	23.9.18		No change. Wire cutting & harassing fire.	

WAR DIARY
or
INTELLIGENCE SUMMARY.
(Erase heading not required.)

Army Form C. 2118.

Place	Date	Hour	Summary of Events and Information	Remarks and references to Appendices
HERMIES	24.9.18		No change.	
"	25.9.18	10	Wire cutting & harassing fire. Hostile artillery very quiet.	
		10 A.M.	Battery Commanders of 34th Bde R.F.A. reported at HQ and were shown their battery positions in K.20.c.	
			O.C. Bdes attended conference of CRA 3rd Div. & Bde Commanders 42nd, 34th, 76th, 310th & 312th Bdes R.F.A.	
		2 P.M.	Bde Commander 34th Bde reconnoitred his battery positions with O.C. Bde.	
	26.9.18	8 P.M.	6th Bty moved to position E of HERMIES. Orders for attack on FLESQUIERES and HAVRINCOURT given to Btys.	
"			Group HQ moved to dugout in LISLOGNER LANE with 8th Div. Bdr.	
			Bde HQ moved to J.30.a.1.0.	
			Harassing fire carried out during day & night.	
"	27.9.18	3.20 A.M.		
		6 A.M.	Bridge across Canal du Nord reported complete.	
		8.10 A.M.	1st objective taken by 8th Div. Bde.	
		9.55 A.M.	6th & 130th Btys ordered to move forward to positions N of HAVRINCOURT. Btys met Major Thompson at LONE TREE COPSE in K.22.a.	
		11.30 A.M.	6th Bty moved to positions in K.22.a. 62nd Div. 9th passed through 3rd Div. Group of artillery moves to CRA 62nd Div. 34th Bde comes under the orders of Col Mann commanding Mass Group. 130th Bty moved its position in K.22.a. 23rd & 49th Btys ordered to move at once as soon as 5th & 130th Btys and E of Canal.	
		11.50 A.M.		
		12 Noon	23rd Bty moved forward to positions in K.22.a. 49th Bty	

WAR DIARY or INTELLIGENCE SUMMARY

Army Form C. 2118.

Place	Date	Hour	Summary of Events and Information	Remarks and references to Appendices
	27.9.18	2.15 PM	Bde. HQ moved to dugout in WHITEHALL K.22.a. Group HQ moved to K.16.d.6.5.	
		3.30 PM	Enemy reported massing in L.16.b. Target engaged by Bdes.	
		4.20 PM	Our line reported as follows FLESQUIERES (exclusive), SCULL SUPPORT in L.19.a, KAISER TRENCH L.16.d, NIGER TRENCH in L.20.a, PRONY SUPPORT in L.21.a.	
		5.20 PM	Enemy reported massing in RAVINE L.26.b. & L.27.a. Whole Bde fired on these parts for 40 minutes. Hows for 40 minutes	
		5.50 PM	Enemy reported massing in L.26.b. & L.27.d. Bdes engaged targets for 5 minutes.	
		6.35 P.M.	SOS lines for Bdes L.15.c.0.2 to L.15.c.6.2 to L.21.a.8.6.	
		9.0 PM	No change during night. Enemy expected to withdraw & infantry ordered to keep touch.	
		11.30 PM	Orders received for attack by 186th Inf. Bdes on MARCOING & CANAL CROSSINGS.	
	28.9.18	6.30 AM	6th and 130th Btys move forward on reaching limit of range to positions in L.19.a. Infantry attacked under creeping barrage.	
		9 A.M.	Bde's reconnoitre positions in L.20 and L.21.	
		12 noon	MARCOING and E bank of CANAL taken with little opposition.	
		1.45 PM	Btys to move to positions as follows 9/18 Pdr Btys in L.26.c. Hows L.26.c.2.6. Bde HQ to L.19.b.6.5 with GOC 186th Inf. Bde.	
		4.30 PM	Bde H.Q. moved to L.25.b.6.6. Group HQ to L.19.b.6.5 with GOC 186th Inf. Bde.	
		6 PM	Btys all in action. 186th Inf. Bde attacked under creeping barrage to take MARCOING SWITCH and SUPPORT. Operation successful.	
	29.9.18	1.30 AM	Orders for attack by 186th Bde on RUMILLY.	
		7.22 AM	Barrage opened	
		7.30 AM	Infantry attacked	
		11.50 AM	Infantry reported to hold HASNIERES – CAMBRAI ROAD as far as Div Boundary. RUMILLY still held by enemy. Cavalry sent troop sent to reconnoitre G.2 and 3 but unable to get on.	
		12.35 PM	Enemy seen in large numbers in G.B.D. Concentration fired by whole Bde.	
		2.20 PM	Btys ordered to move forward. 186th Bde attack RUMILLY under a creeping barrage. Attack not successful.	
		4 PM	6th Bty in action c.L.28.d.1.0. 130th Bty move to L.28.a.1.5. Bdes HQ to L.27.b.0.5.	

WAR DIARY
or
INTELLIGENCE SUMMARY
(Erase heading not required.)

Army Form C. 2118

Place	Date	Hour	Summary of Events and Information	Remarks and references to Appendices
	29.9.18	6 P.M.	186th Bde again attack RUMILLY under creeping barrage. Southern portion of attack partially successful. Left held up.	
		7.40 P.M.	23rd and 49th Btys move forward to positions as follows 23rd L28d 2.3, 49th L28a 3.6.	
		8.30 P.M.	S.O.S. lines on E. edge of RUMILLY.	
			Night quiet and no change on front.	
	30.9.18	12.30 A.M.	185th Bde ordered to attack at dawn through 186th Bde under barrage by SHERWOOD Grp of 40th Bde to engage movement up to level of attack.	
		10.40 A.M.	Concentration fired on Western outskirts of RUMILLY.	
		11.20 A.M.	About 2000 of the enemy reported moving S.E. in 6, 5, 11 and 17.	
		12.45 P.M.	49th Bty ordered to send forward an officer to works S of the CANAL & obtain information as regards situation E. of RUMILLY.	
		1. P.M.	Group HQ moved to L 20 d 4.4.	
		2.30 to 4.40 P.M.	Barrage fired in support of attack by 185th Bde on RUMILLY support. Attack unsuccessful. Enemy reported holding trench in strength.	
		5.15 P.M.	Btys move to positions in L30a and e S.E. of MARCOING. Bde H.Q. moved to L30 c 16. 23rd and 49th Btys moved in. 6th and 130th Btys moved in.	
		7.30 P.M.	S.O.S. lines G22 a 0.4 to G21 a 7.7, 4.5" Hows on houses in G21 a and to on RUMILLY.	
			Quiet night. No change.	

[signature]
Lieut Colonel
O.C. 40 A. Bde R.F.A.

Army Form C. 2118.

Instructions regarding War Diaries and Intelligence Summaries are contained in F. S. Regs., Part II. and the Staff Manual respectively. Title pages will be prepared in manuscript.

WAR DIARY
INTELLIGENCE SUMMARY.
(Erase heading not required.)

Place	Date	Hour	Summary of Events and Information	Remarks and references to Appendices
	1.10.18	3.20AM	Orders received for attack by 7th Inf. Bde. on RUMILLY.	
		6.0AM	Zero hour. Infantry attacked under creeping barrage.	
		10.30AM	F.O.O. report that 2nd Suffolks driven back on left. Line was along E. edge of RUMILLY.	
		11.15AM	F.O.O. report personally seeing 50 enemy in RUMILLY.	
		11.35AM	Counter attack from direction of SERANVILLERS reported.	
		12 NOON	Batteries ordered to engage enemy roads running from RUMILLY to NIERGNIES, in bursts for 2 hours.	
		2.50PM	Our own men seen in strength in G.27 b & d, G.21 a & c and G.28 a.	
		6.30PM	8th Inf. Bde. attacked in order to establish a line thro' G.10.C and G.17 a x c. attack covered by creeping barrage. 7th Inf. Bde. ordered to clear up RUMILLY. Attack successful.	
		8.35PM	S.O.S. lines G.17.B.7.0 to G.17.B.1.5. Night firing carried out its own consolidation of 8th Inf. Bde.	
	2.10.18		Morning quiet. 8th Inf. Bde. report following line established; road running from G.11 central to G.17 central. Enemy reported holding road from G.12 central to G.6 central.	
		10AM	GROUP H.Q. moved to 3rd Inf. Bde. H.Q. at L.24.C.0.5. Bdr. Commander reconnoitred positions in G.16 and in G.34.	
			3rd Inf. Bde. ordered to push on towards SERANVILLERS.	
		12AM	Infantry had line of road from G.11 central to G.17 central but obliged to withdraw fall back owing to M.G. fire, to trench in G.16 and 23 a. No further operations contemplated for 48 hours. Rest of day quiet. S.O.S. lines G.17.B.7.0 to G.17.B.1.5. Harassing fire carried out during night.	

Army Form C. 2118.

WAR DIARY
or
INTELLIGENCE SUMMARY.
(Erase heading not required.)

Instructions regarding War Diaries and Intelligence Summaries are contained in F. S. Regs., Part II. and the Staff Manual respectively. Title pages will be prepared in manuscript.

Place	Date	Hour	Summary of Events and Information	Remarks and references to Appendices
	3.10.18		Quiet day. Positions West of MASNIERES reconnoitred.	
		10.30am	Our line reported as follows G.16.c.3.9 to G.17.a.1.6 to G.17.d.1.3.	
		10.45am	Harassing fire carried out during night.	
	4.10.18		Quiet day. Btys ordered to move to positions W. of MASNIERES but move cancelled. Night firing carried out.	
	5.10.18		Quiet day.	
		4 P.M.	Report received that enemy withdrawing on IV & V Corps fronts.	
		6.30 P.M.	Enemy shelter trench heavily. Counterpreparation shoot fired down for 10 mins.	
		10 P.M.	34th Bde RFA withdrawn from the Group.	
		5 A.M.	312 Bde RFA comes into the Group.	
	6.10.18		Quiet day.	
		12 Noon	Orders for Batteries to move forward.	
		2 P.M.	Move cancelled. 300 vets per gun to be dumped at positions to be occupied.	
		6 P.M.	Rumour from Corps to effect that Central Powers had asked for armistice. Moved to be engaged & parties advancing under white flag to be made prisoners. Harassing fire carried out all night.	

Army Form C. 2118.

WAR DIARY
or
INTELLIGENCE SUMMARY.
(Erase heading not required.)

Instructions regarding War Diaries and Intelligence Summaries are contained in F. S. Regs., Part II. and the Staff Manual respectively. Title pages will be prepared in manuscript.

Place	Date	Hour	Summary of Events and Information	Remarks and references to Appendices
	7.10.18	9.15am	Batteries ordered to occupy positions W. of MASNIERES, M Batteries to move in by sections.	
		1.15pm	All Batteries in action in new positions.	
		2.30pm.	H.Q. moved to G.24.a.5.5.	
			Orders for attack by Army received.	
			Quiet day and night.	
BROODS				
	8.10.18	4.30am	Zero hour. Infantry advanced under creeping barrage. Vicinity of Btys fairly heavily shelled.	
		6am	Shelling of Battery positions eased.	
		7.10am	Infantry seen in G.19.b & 20.c. New Zealanders on left seen on high ground in G.27.c.	
		7.50am	Report from aeroplane that 1st objective was established at 7am and infantry pushing on to 2nd.	
		8.10am	23rd Bty ordered to send forward 1 section in close support of infantry.	
		8.40am	FOO 6th Bty reported 400 men held up by M.G. W. of NIERGNIES. Tanks seen in G.26. Our men working into NIERGNIES from S.	
		9am.	Second objective thought to be held. 6th Bty ordered to send 1 section forward. Report from FOO 23rd Bty that our infantry seen falling back on left at 8.15am expecting counter-attack. 6th ordered to postpone sending forward of section.	
		9.35am	2nd Objective thought to be held but no confirmation received.	
		9.40am	FOO 23rd Bty report Quentin in A.29.d. has changed hands several times. Now held by enemy.	
		9.45am	3 enemy tanks reported to have held up 2nd Div on 3rd left in H.7.b. N.Z. Div has taken ESNES MILL. 6th & 23rd Btys started teething ordered to shell with Tanks, sent Sections to G.30.e.	
		10.10am	23rd Bty ordered to send one gun forward to hold road in H.20 central. Our infantry reported to hold road in H.20 central.	

Army Form C. 2118.

WAR DIARY
or
INTELLIGENCE SUMMARY.

(Erase heading not required.)

Instructions regarding War Diaries and Intelligence Summaries are contained in F.S. Regs., Part II. and the Staff Manual respectively. Title pages will be prepared in manuscript.

Place	Date	Hour	Summary of Events and Information	Remarks and references to Appendices
	8.10.18	10.15 AM	F.O.O. 49th Bty confirmed report that we held road in H20. 2nd Div ordered to be on 1st objective. SERANVILLERS & LA TARGETTE uncertain.	
		11 AM	Barrage opened as follows: 12.35 PM to 1 PM on LA TARGETTE – CAMBRAI ROAD with Bde Boundary 1 PM shift to 2nd Protective 1.15 PM slow fire.	
		11.40 AM		
		12.15 AM	F.O.O. 130th Bty reported 10.25 AM said 2nd Suffolks held 2nd objective	
		12.25 AM	Suffolks held LA TARGETTE. Barrage at 12.35 PM shot to come S. of H14 d 6.6.	
		12.35 PM	Barrage good. attack not entirely successful.	
		2.15 PM	Bty's ordered to be ready to move forward at short notice. Bde & Bty commanders reconnoitre positions in 830 and 36.	
		3.30 PM	Group HQ moved to G27 d-2.7.	
		4.15 PM	23rd & 49th Btys moved to positions in G36 Q.	
		5.45 PM	6th & 198th Btys moved to positions in G30 6, G36 6.	
		6 PM	HQ moved to G29 C 4.0 in CREVE COEUR.	
			Attack by 76th Inf Bde to clear SERANVILLERS successful. 2nd Div take 2nd objective.	
		7 PM	Lt Col G.T. MAIR DSO Appointed CRA 52nd Div.	
		11.45 PM	SOS lines H16 c 1.2 to H16 d 4.3.	
			Orders received to send out for attack on WAMBAIX by GAVROS.	
	9.10.18	5.20 AM	GAVROS passed thro' 3rd Div. 40th R.F.A. came under orders of CRA GAVROS Div. attack carried out under enemies barrage.	
		2.50 AM		
			F.O.O. 6th Bty reported attack going well. No opposition.	
		9 AM	GAVROS reported to be N.W. of WAMBAIX ways. Orders for 40th R.F.A. sent to move forward that to remain in position of observation.	

Army Form C. 2118.

WAR DIARY
or
INTELLIGENCE SUMMARY.
(Erase heading not required.)

Instructions regarding War Diaries and Intelligence Summaries are contained in F.S. Regs., Part II. and the Staff Manual respectively. Title pages will be prepared in manuscript.

Place	Date	Hour	Summary of Events and Information	Remarks and references to Appendices
	9-10-18	10-10AM	FOO 21st Bty reported our men on Railway and pushing out patrols to CAMBRAI - CAUDRY road. Cavalry seen at 9-15AM crossing railway at about T.19.	
		10-45AM	FOO B/7th Bty report enemy tanks 10 NI.AM Stated hostile artillery shelling railway about H.19.a.8. Infantry advancing without opposition. Group Orders up. 40th Bde came under orders of CRA 3rd Divn. Wagon lines brought up and Btys camped round CREVECOEUR.	
CREVECOEUR	10-10-18	7AM	Btys moved wagon lines to be closer to canal for water. Btys in rest. No changes. Div in 2nd Reserve of Corps.	
"	11-10-18	11AM.	CRA and Bde Commander of 40th, 42nd & 2 Bde's of each R.A. No change.	
"	12-10-18		No changes. Reflet Main DRS. left to join 62nd D.A.	
"	13-10-18		No change. Bdes in rest.	
"	14-10-18		No change. Bdes in Rest.	
"	15-10-18		No change. Bdes in rest.	
"	16-10-18		Bdes & Bty commanders reconnoitred positions E. of QUIEVY. Col. Musgrave D.S.O. took over command of Bde.	
"	17-10-18		No change. Orders received for Bde to move on 18th to positions E of QUIEVY under orders of 62nd D.A.	
"	18-10-18		Bde marched at 8AM. Btys moving out 4 horse intervals. Route SERAINVILLIERS, WAMBAIX, ESTOURMEL.	
		1PM.	Arrived at BEVILLERS at Noon without Wagon lines.	
		4PM.	Btys moved into action to positions as pulls in D9d. Bde HQ established in QUIEVY with 156th Bde R.F.A.	
		8PM.	All Btys in action.	

WAR DIARY or INTELLIGENCE SUMMARY

Army Form C. 2118.

Place	Date	Hour	Summary of Events and Information	Remarks and references to Appendices
QUIEVY	19.10.18		Btys each registered 1 gun. Quiet day. No change. Orders for attack on SOLESMES by 186th Inf. Bde. for 20th Oct.	
"	20.10.18	2 AM	Zero hours. Inf. attacked under creeping barrage.	
		4:20 AM	Barrage for 1st objective stopped.	
		6:30 AM	Infantry report Right Battalion on 1st objective. Battalion on left uncertain. Guppos (on left) reported on Final objective.	
		7:35 AM	FOO 49th Bty reports 2 company's york & Lancs held objective in E7. One company creeping up village 100 yds from its Church. Message timed 6:15 AM.	
		8:30 AM	6th Bty OP Nlent enemy shelling SOLESMES	
		11 AM	Enemy shelled SOLESMES and damaged W25	
		12 noon	Report from F.O.O. 49th Bty that Infantry held Factory in E2C and apparently held up in E2A.	
			Report from Major Cowie 29th Bty that our held moved from W20C 8.7 to W26 5.9.5.	
		12:20 PM	Major Tilowson ordered to reconnoitre positions for Btys in V30 B and C.	
		3 PM	42nd Div (on Right) advised advance back from final objective.	
		4:30 PM	Counter-preparation fired from 6:10 pm to 5:51 in view of suspected counter-attack.	
			Btys ordered to move forward at 9am if Situation is unchanged to positions in V30 B & C.	
		5:20 PM	SOS Signal reported by Bde Bty Pers officer sent for 15 mins. No apparently action taken (final)	
		7:45 PM	Bde ordered not to move till 11AM.	
		10 PM	SOS lines as follows E edge of ROMERIES from W11C 6.2 to W27d 9.2. Harassing fire carried out throughout night.	

WAR DIARY or INTELLIGENCE SUMMARY

Army Form C. 2118.

Place	Date	Hour	Summary of Events and Information	Remarks and references to Appendices
ST PYTHON	21.10.18	11AM	Morning very quiet. Situation unchanged. 6th Bty moved forward to position E of St PYTHON. Rest of Btys moved at ½ hour intervals. HQ established in ST PYTHON D6a 5.5.	
		3PM	All batteries in action. Positions as follows 6th Bty V30a 8.0.2, 23rd Bty V30a 0.5, 49th Bty V30a 0.3, 130th Bty V30d 3.7. Hostile artillery active in ST PYTHON from 11AM until midnight. 2/Lt Young 49th Bty wounded. Harassing fire on roads and approaches carried out by the Brigade during night.	
	22.10.18		No change. Front quiet.	
		10AM	Orders received that 3rd Div. Inf. are to press thro' this 62nd and Reserve attack on 23rd inst. MUSGRAVE GROUP (40th & 42nd Bdes) to be in liaison with 76th Inf. Bde. Orders for attack on ROMERIES, ESCARMAIN & BEAUDIGNIES - CAPELLE road received on morning of 23rd.	
		7PM	Bde HQ moved to HQ 76th Inf. Bde in SOLESMES. Adj. remained in liaison with 185th Inf. Bde till zero hour. Bty positions were shelled during night.	
SOLESMES	23.10.18	12.20AM	Night O.P. opened SOS on 3rd regt. Btys opened fire and stopped at 12.45AM. No infantry action but heavy artillery retaliation.	
		3.20AM	Zero hour. Command passed to 3rd Div. Infantry attacked under creeping barrage. ROMERIES and 1st Objective taken with over 500 prisoners. Attack reported to have gone well.	
		6AM	Major Laird ordered to reconnoitre positions for the Bdes E of ROMERIES in W2 D. if situation was clear.	
		11AM	76th Bde reported to be on 2nd Objective & consolidating. Orders for 42nd Bde to move to positions W of ROMERIES.	
		11.5AM	OC 42nd Bde ordered to support 76th Bde & remain in liaison with GOC.	
		12.15PM	OC 40th Bde to go forward with GOC & Bde on passing through 76 Bde.	

WAR DIARY or INTELLIGENCE SUMMARY

Army Form C. 2118

(Erase heading not required.)

Place	Date	Hour	Summary of Events and Information	Remarks and references to Appendices
	23.10.18	1 PM	Bdys ordered to move to positions already reconnoitred E of ROMERIES, starting at 1.30 PM and moving at ½ hour intervals.	
		1.40 PM	O.C. moved forward to H.Q. 76th & 9th Inf. Batns in ROMERIES	
		2 PM	O.C. moved forward to la TREURSE HINON with G.O.C. 9th Inf. Bde.	
		3 PM	Bn HQ moved & established at la TREURSE HINON.	
		5 PM	C.R.A. wishes O.C. Bn to see G.O.C. 9th Infty about R.O.S. lines & report what they are to do to Bn. Infantry on final objective & pushing patrols forward to ECAILLON river.	
		7 PM	All batteries reported in action in W.22.b and d.	
		9 PM	S.O.S. lines arranged as follows R25.c.7.0 to Q.30.c.8.0.	
		10.30 PM	Orders came from R.A. even flares upon enemy.	
		11.30 PM	Batns all cancelled. Fresh orders to follow.	
	24.10.18	1.45 AM	Orders received & sent out to Btys. Infantry to advance under barrage to take RUESNES and high ground E.S.	
		4 AM	Zero hour.	
		9 AM	Bridges in ESCARMAIN reconnoitred and reported intact.	
		9.30 AM	Battery Commanders ordered to reconnoitre positions in R.25 (N of BEAUDIGNIES) and to meet batteries up, as soon as possible.	
		10 AM	Bn HQ moved up to ESCARMAIN with 9th Inf. Bde. Report to say infantry were in RUESNES at 7.30 AM and meeting with little opposition.	
		1.30 PM	All Btys reported in action. 6 23rd and 4th in R.25, 130th in R.36.d. Situation on night not clear.	
		9 PM	Infantry reported on final objective. 9th Inf. Bde ordered to push out patrols to cover rly railway & establish the line. Night Quiet.	
	25.10.18	7 AM	Post established on BALLEVUE FARM on railway but most of railway held by enemy. Hostile artillery active on RUESNES and high ground to the South. Orders for 3rd Bat Div. to take seven windmills over whole corps front.	

WAR DIARY
or
INTELLIGENCE SUMMARY.

Army Form C. 2118

Place	Date	Hour	Summary of Events and Information	Remarks and references to Appendices
RUESNES	26.10.18		Enemy withdrew to VILLERS POL – ORSINVAL line. Infantry established line as follows, R.2.c.f.2.8. along road to LA CROISETTE, along eastern edge of wood to R.16 central with posts in advance.	
		8 AM.	Bttn HQ established in CHATEAU RUESNES. 8th Inf Bgd HQ in farm R.20.f.2.6. Hostile artillery very active on RUESNES. 120th Bty ordered to move to R.25.f.9.9 with forward section forward to R.19.b.6.4. 23rd Bty to move one section forward to R.19.b.6.4.	
			Hostile artillery active during night. Much gas used.	
"	27.10.18		No change in situation. Several hostile batteries reported & engaged during day. Hostile artillery active morning and at night. 76th Inf Bde took over half of Div front. 2nd DA and 14th Bde RHA reinforced the front. Adjustment of artillery covering front as follows. 2nd DA and 14 Bde RHA covered 76 Inf Bde. 3rd DA (Musgrave Group) and 76 Bde RFA covered 8th Inf Bde.	
"	28.10.18		Hostile artillery active on RUESNES.	
		6.70 AM	Infantry established an advanced line of posts, 300 yds E of the line.	
		8 PM	S.O.S. lines as follows R.11.c.4.1 to R.10.a.5.0 to R.4.a.6.3 to R.4 central.	
"	29.10.18	10 AM	Gross ordered 2nd Div infantry ordered to relieve 3rd Div.	
			Relief to take place as about 6 PM.	
		6 PM	6th Inf field 500 lbs gas from a captured 77 mm gun.	
			Command passed from CRA 3rd Div to CRA 2nd Div.	
		7 PM	Relief of 8th Inf Bde by 6th Bde complete. 6th Inf Bde relieving 8th Bde.	
			Usual night firing carried out on Roads & Tracks.	

Army Form C. 2118

WAR DIARY
or
INTELLIGENCE SUMMARY.
(Erase heading not required.)

Instructions regarding War Diaries and Intelligence Summaries are contained in F. S. Regs., Part II. and the Staff Manual respectively. Title pages will be prepared in manuscript.

Place	Date	Hour	Summary of Events and Information	Remarks and references to Appendices
RUESNES	30.10.18		No change. Btys shelled during night. Usual harassing fire.	
	31.10.18		No change. Orders received for attack by XVII Corps (on left). 23rd & 4th Btys to fire smoke screen.	
		12 noon	Bde & Bty Commanders 6th Bde reconnoitred position for the Bde N of RUESNES.	
			6th Bn R.A. ordered to stand to LA POLIE FARM at 2AM 1st Nov. Artillery cooperation arranged by Bde Commander.	
		4.30pm	6th Bty began moving.	
		6 p.m.	6th Bty in action at R13c7.3. Usual harassing fire including a burst of fire on LA POLIE FARM at 11 P.M.	

A. D. Musgrave
Col. R.A.
O.C. 40th Bde R.F.A.

31.10.18.

Army Form C. 2118.

14

WAR DIARY
INTELLIGENCE SUMMARY.
(Erase heading not required.)

40th Bde R.F.A.
1st – 30th Nov 1918

Place	Date	Hour	Summary of Events and Information	Remarks and references to Appendices
RUESNES	1.11.18	2 AM	Barrage fired in support of raid by 6th Inf. Bde. on LA FOLIE FARM. 9 Prisoners taken. 23rd & 49th Btys fired smoke screen in conjunction with attack by XVII Corps.	
		11 AM.	Warning order from 2nd DA that batteries would have to move forward on 3rd in view of continuing attack by 62nd Div.	
		3 P.M.	Bde Commander reconnoitred positions in R15 a and c (E of RUESNES). Bty Commanders reported to HQ then reconnoitred positions as selected.	
	2.11.18	10 AM	Ammunition dumped at forward positions during night. Usual harassing fire carried out during night. Bde Commander attended conference at R.A.H.Q. 62nd Div. 136th & 187th Bdes of 62nd in line 186th in reserve. 62nd Div on right & Guards on left relieved 2nd Div at 2 P.M.	
	3.11.18	9 AM	Orders received for attack by enemy. Barrages tables & orders sent out at 2 P.M.	
		4 P.M.	Batteries started moving at half hour intervals in following order 23rd, 49th, 130th and 62th.	
		7 P.M.	All batteries reported in action.	
	4.11.18	5:30 AM	Zero hour. Infantry attacked under creeping barrage. Bty positions were shelled during early stages.	
		6 AM	130th Bty report Major M.C. Willis & Hawker wounded by shell, also 1 O.R. killed & 8 O.R. wounded.	
		8 AM.	Inf. report 186th Bde on Blue Line. In touch on Rt with N.Z. Div. & 187th Bde on left.	
		11:15 AM	M.G. officer informed 130th Bty that Green Line held. Bridges met in R12a reported intact.	
		12 Noon	FRASNOY held and coy of Yorks in GREEN LINE.	
		12:30 PM	Gen. Mordacq still advancing. Very many prisoners in LE QUESNOY shelled our infantry from the wood.	
		1 P.M.	Bdes ordered to reconnoitre positions E of ORSINVAL – LE QUESNOY road.	
		2:30 PM	FOO 6th Bty reported success signal fired from RED LINE at 12:45 P.M. Btys started moving forward to positions reconnoitred.	

Army Form C. 2118.

WAR DIARY
or
INTELLIGENCE SUMMARY.
(Erase heading not required.)

Instructions regarding War Diaries and Intelligence Summaries are contained in F. S. Regs., Part II. and the Staff Manual respectively. Title pages will be prepared in manuscript.

Place	Date	Hour	Summary of Events and Information	Remarks and references to Appendices
	4.11.18	3 P.M.	Bde Commander moved forward to LA BELLE MAISON with 187th Inf. Brigade.	
		5 P.M.	6th, 23rd & 48th Bty's reported in action. 130th Bty held up on road.	
		6 P.M.	Bde HQ established in ORSINVAL.	
		8 P.M.	O.C. 130th Bde Bombay visits G.O.C. 107th Bde. for attack on GOMMEGNIES at 6 A.M. 5th	
		10 P.M.	Orders given to Bty's over the telephone.	
		11.30 P.M.	Bde. Commander ordered to bring battery into action in R.A.E. by 5 A.M.	
	5.11.18	5.30 A.M.	130th Bty reported in action.	
		6 A.M.	Zero hour.	
		7.15 P.M.	Barrage reported and infantry pushed on without artillery support.	
		7.45 A.M.	Bde. reported going well with very little opposition. Have cleared GOMMEGNIES.	
		8 A.M.	Bty's ordered to be in vicinity of their forward positions by readiness at 10 A.M.	
		9 A.M.	Bde HQ moved with G.O.C. 187th Inf. Bde. to LE PETIT MENAIS	
		11 A.M.	Infantry reported to have lost touch with enemy & pushing on to region of C.R.A. 6.2nd Div ordered 40th Bde be taken on forced marches in readiness.	
		12 Noon	Bde HQ established in GOMMEGNIES. O.C. Bde in touch with G.O.C. 187th Inf. Bde.	
		12.30 P.M.	Bty's ordered to remain in ORSINVAL and ready to move up to GOMMEGNIES C.B.S.	
	6.11.18	7.30 A.M.	Bty's ordered to send on billeting parties to report at Bde HQ at 9 A.M. Bty's to move at 5 min intervals.	
		9 A.M.	Billeting parties arrived over storm. Sites allotted for Wagon lines.	
		12 Noon	Infantry reported to have taken MECQUIGNIES and advancing to BROWN LINE.	
		12.30 P.M.	Bty's ordered to be prepared to take ammunition from A.R.P. up to Bty's of 42nd Bde Arty covering advance of infantry.	

(A800) Wt. W1771/M691 750,000 5/17 Sch. 52 Forms/C2118/14 D. D. & L., London, E.C.

WAR DIARY or INTELLIGENCE SUMMARY

Army Form C. 2118.

(Erase heading not required.)

Instructions regarding War Diaries and Intelligence Summaries are contained in F. S. Regs., Part II. and the Staff Manual respectively. Title pages will be prepared in manuscript.

Place	Date	Hour	Summary of Events and Information	Remarks and references to Appendices
	7-11-18	5 A.M.	Boys each took 12 wagons of ammunition to 42nds in action N of OBIES.	
		12 noon	Orders received to meet Bde up to vicinity of OBIES.	
		12.30 P.M.	Orders sent to Batteries to meet at 2 P.M. marching at quarter hour intervals in following order 2nd 3rd 42 4th 130th and 6th	
		3 P.M.	Officer from each battery met adjutant near OBIES and arranged billeting.	
		5 P.M.	All batteries in.	
	8-11-18	9.30 A.M.	42nd Bde report infantry have advanced to NEUF-MESNIL (W of MAUBEUGE) without opposition & asked us to join. Small dump in O16. as their batteries were moving. Batteries in P13 (NE of VIEUX-MESNIL).	
		10 A.M.	Adjutant went forward to see 42nd and looked out for camp.	
		11.30 A.M.	Orders sent out for batteries to be ready to move forward at 2 P.M.	
		2 P.M.	62nd D.A. says Brigade will not be moved today.	
		5.30 P.M.	Brigade moving to march at 9 A.M to LE CHEVAL BLANC.	
	9-11-18	6 A.M.	44th Bty moved off immediately followed at 1 hour intervals in following order 130th 6th and 23rd H.Q.	
		6.30 A.M.	Billeting parties met adjutant in LE CHEVAL BLANC.	
			All batteries in by 8 A.M. except H.Q. delayed by Black ... road.	
			Bm ordered to come under command of R.A. 3rd Div.	
			Enemy delegates crossed lines and given till 11 A.M. 11th to accept terms of armistices.	
	10-11-18		C.R.A. brought news of Kaiser's abdication & revolution in Germany. 3rd Div the 3rd Division Guard of 3rd army. Bde ordered up & billeted for long march.	
		7 P.M.	Orders for Bde to move forward to MAUBEUGE received at 11.30 A.M 11th	
	11-11-18	7 A.M.	March cancelled	
		11 A.M.	ARMISTICE with GERMANY began.	

Army Form C. 2118.

WAR DIARY
or
INTELLIGENCE SUMMARY.
(Erase heading not required.)

Instructions regarding War Diaries and Intelligence Summaries are contained in F. S. Regs., Part II. and the Staff Manual respectively. Title pages will be prepared in manuscript.

Place	Date	Hour	Summary of Events and Information	Remarks and references to Appendices
LE CHEVAL BLANC	12-11-18		Brigade in rest. Cleaning up. Bathing area.	
"	13-11-18		No change.	
"	14-11-18		No change. Orders received that Bdys will march 108 4 gun Btys.	
"	15-11-18	7 AM	Guns & Wagons of sections remaining behind forwarded to SOISSONS.	Remaining sections probably report by rail at later period
		9.30 AM	Guns & Wagons ordered to return to Bdy proceed to MAUBEUGE on 16%. Lecture by Rev. educational officer to Officers & NCO's of 40th Bde & 3rd DAC on demobilisation.	
		7 P.M.	Parade addressed by GOC 3rd Div. Sections returned.	
"	16-11-18		Guns & wagons handed in to Ordnance officer MAUBEUGE. Surplus Horses collected in field near 4th Hy Lines.	
"	17-11-18		Section's proceeded to VI Corps mobile veterinary station at LE QUESNOY under 2Lts JACOBS & BRUCE.	
"	18-11-18		No change. Brigade warned that 3rd D.A. would move on 20th.	
"	19-11-18		Orders to march on 20th to LA LONGUEVILLE. Order of march to be as follows HQ- 6th, 23rd, 49th, 130th Bty. Brigade transport in rear.	
"	20-11-18		Brigade marched at 9 AM. Rts BERCHERIES and South edge of BAVAY. Adj. 2 Bty captain did billeting. Arrived and billeted in LA LONGUEVILLE at 11.30 AM. Orders received to march to HARPENT.	
	21-11-18		Brigade marched in following order 23rd, 49th, 130, 6th Bty, at 8.25 AM. Rts MAUBEUGE, ROUSIES, RECQUIGNIES and RoSQ. CRA inspected Bde on the march. Adj. & Bty Captains did billeting. Brigade arrived at [illegible] HARPENT 1 PM.	

Army Form C. 2118.

WAR DIARY or INTELLIGENCE SUMMARY.

(Erase heading not required.)

Place	Date	Hour	Summary of Events and Information	Remarks and references to Appendices
MARPENT	22/11/18		Battalions cleaned up. No change. C.R.A. addressed officers of Brigade on march discipline.	
	23/11/18		All ranks of Brigade walked in German military boots. No change.	
	24/11/18	9:30am	Church Parade in local concert hall. About 160 officers & men of 23rd & 40th Bdes. attended. Singing on TE DEUM in Roman Catholic Church and sang "Now our God be the God" at request of the Curé. CRA inspected Batteries. Orders to march to LABUISSIERE on 25th received.	
	25/11/18	9AM	Brigade marched to LA BUISSIERE. Order of march, H.Q. 49th Bdy. 130th, 6th, 23rd. Route NEUMONT, ERQUELINES, SOLRE-SUR-SAMBRE. G.O.C. Bde. inspected Brigade on the march. Arrived in billets at 11:30 a.m. Orders received to march to BERZEE on 26th.	
	26/11/18	10:20AM	Brigade marched in following order H.Q. 130th Bdy. 6th, 23rd, 49th. Route FONTAINE-VALMONT, THUILLIES, BERZEE. Arrived & billeted at 2:15 P.M.	
	27/11/18		No change. Orders to march to BIOTRAURY on 28th.	
	28/11/18	9:45AM	Brigade marched in following order H.Q. 6th, 23rd, 49th, 130th Bdy. Route GOURDINNE, SOHZEE, TARCIENNE, GERPINNES, BIESME, SERY, arrived & billeted in BIOTRAURY at 3:15 P.M. Orders received to march on 29th to WARNANT.	
	29/11/18	11 A.M.	Brigade marched in following order H.Q. 23rd, 49th, 130th, 6th Bdy. Route ST GERARD STN, GRAUX, BIOUL. Arrived & billeted in WARNANT (2 miles W of Meuse river) (to PURNODE on 30th). Orders recd for Brigade to march to PURNODE on 30th.	

Army Form C. 2118.

WAR DIARY
or
INTELLIGENCE SUMMARY.

(Erase heading not required.)

Place	Date	Hour	Summary of Events and Information	Remarks and references to Appendices
GOOD	30.11.18	11:30AM	Brigade moved off. Order of march HQ 49th, 130th, 6th, 23rd Bty. Route ANHEE. Crossed MEUSE at YVOIR, EVREHAILLES. Bde Inspected by GOC div. at YVOIR. Bivied & billeted at PURNODE at 1 P.M.	

O.D Musgrave
Colonel R.A.
40TH BDE R.F.A.

30.11.18.

40th Brigade R.F.A.

1st to 31st December 1918.

Army Form C. 2118.

WAR DIARY
or
INTELLIGENCE SUMMARY.
(Erase heading not required.)

Place	Date	Hour	Summary of Events and Information	Remarks and references to Appendices
PURNODE	1.12.18		No change.	
"	2.12.18		No change.	
"	3.12.18		No change. CRA inspected Brigade. Orders to march to SPONTIN.	
SPONTIN	4.12.18	10AM	Brigade marched out. Order of march HQ, 49th, 130th, 6th, 23rd Bty. Route DORIENNE.	
		11AM	Arrived and billeted in SPONTIN.	
			Orders to march to MOHIVILLE & SCOVILLE	
SCOVILLE	5.12.18	8.40AM	Brigade marched out. Order of march HQ 130th, 6th, 23rd, 49th Bty. Route EMPTIENNE & ACHET.	
		12 Noon	Brigade arrived and billeted in MOHIVILLE & SCOVILLE.	
			Orders to march to GRANDE ENEILLE, MONTUEVILLE and NOISEUX. Order of march. HQ 6th, 23rd, 49th, 130 —	
GRANDE ENEILLE	6.12.18	8.40AM	Brigade marched out. Route JANNEE, HEURE, BAILONVILLE. HQ 23rd & 130 billeted in GDE ENEILLE, 49th in NOISEUX and 6th Bty in MONTUEVILLE. 130 inspected Bdge. between HEURE & BAILLONVILLE.	
			Orders to march to HOTTON.	
HOTTON	7.12.18	8.40AM	Brigade marched out. order of march HQ 23rd 49th 130th & 6th Bty. Route DEVLIN, FRONVILLE and MONVALEE.	
			Brigade arrived & billeted in HOTTON at 10.30AM.	
"	8.12.18		No change. Church parade.	
			Orders to march to MALEMPRE. Orders changed for Bde. to billet in VAUX CHAVAINE.	
VAUX CHAVAINE	9.12.18	8AM	Brigade marched out. Order of march HQ 49th, 130th, 6th, 23rd & 49th Bty. Route Soy, MORNANT.	
		1 PM	Brigade arrived & billeted.	
"	10.12.18		No change.	

Army Form C. 2118.

WAR DIARY
or
INTELLIGENCE SUMMARY.

(Erase heading not required.)

Instructions regarding War Diaries and Intelligence Summaries are contained in F. S. Regs., Part II. and the Staff Manual respectively. Title pages will be prepared in manuscript.

Place	Date	Hour	Summary of Events and Information	Remarks and references to Appendices
REGNE	11.12.18	9.40 AM	Bde marched to REGNE. Route MANHAY along main road to REGNE. Arrived and billeted at 12.45 P.M. Orders to march to BOVIGNY.	
BOVIGNY	12.12.18	9 A.M.	Bde marched through SALMCHATEAU arrived and billeted at 12.30 P.M. Orders to march to ALDRINGE. Bde to cross frontier at 11.15 A.M.	
GERMANY ALDRINGEN	13.12.18	9.30 AM 11.15 AM	Bde marched out. Head of Column crossed German frontier. Inspected by G.O.C. Div. Orders of march H.Q, 6th, 23rd, 49th, 130th Batteries. Route BEHO. H.Q. 49th & 130 Batteries arrived & billeted in ALDRINGEN, 6th & 23rd Btys in ESPELER at 12 Noon. Orders to march to NIEDEGEN.	
NIEDEGEN	14.12.18	8.40 AM	March continued through SCHIRN, ST VITH to NIEDEGEN. Bde arrived and billeted at 12 Noon, 6th Bty in BEITFELD, KREWINKEL (6th & 23rd & 49th) HERRSBERG (130th). Orders to march to BERTRATH (HQ).	
BERTRATH	15.12.18	9.15 AM	Brigade marched through ST VITH, SCHONBERG and MANDERFELD arrived in billeting area at about 3 P.M. Orders to march to DAHLEM.	
DAHLEM	16.12.18	10.10 AM	Bde HQ moved out. Starting point at LOSHEIM Station passed at 10.45 A.M. Route HALLSHLAG, KRONENBURG, STADT KYLL. Arrived and billeted at 2.30 P.M. in DAHLEM.	
FROHNGAU	17.12.18	9.25 AM	March continued through BLANKENHEIM and TORNDORF to FROHNGAU. Arrived and billeted at 11.30 P.M. Orders to march to KOMMERN.	
KOMMERN	18.12.18	10 A.M.	Bde marched out. Route ENGELGAU, ZINGSHEIM, WEYER, MECHERNICH to KOMMERN. Arrived at 1.45 P.M. Orders to march to EMBKEN (HQ, 6th & 23rd), & PISSENHEIM (49th & 130th).	
EMBKEN & PISSENHEIM	19.12.18	9.45 AM	March continued through SCHWERFERN, BURVENICH, EPPNICH to EMBKEN & PISSENHEIM. Arrived and billeted at 12.30 P.M. Orders to march to final areas in KREUZAU and DROVE.	
KREUZAU and DROVE	20.12.18	9.10 AM	Bde marched out. Route through BERG, THUM, 6th billeted in N. part of DROVE, 23rd Bty in S. part, 49th Bty in W. part and 130th Bty in E. part of KREUZAU. HQ in houses on S.E. of KREUZAU. Final areas of occupation.	
"	21.12.18		No change.	

Army Form C. 2118.

WAR DIARY
or
INTELLIGENCE SUMMARY.

(Erase heading not required.)

Instructions regarding War Diaries and Intelligence Summaries are contained in F. S. Regs., Part II. and the Staff Manual respectively. Title pages will be prepared in manuscript.

Place	Date	Hour	Summary of Events and Information	Remarks and references to Appendices
KRUEZEAU and DROVE	22.12.18		No change.	
"	23.12.18		"	
"	24.12.18		"	
"	25.12.18		Xmass Day.	
"	26.12.18		No change.	
"	27.12.18		"	
"	28.12.18		Demobilisation of Coal-miners & pivotal men began.	
"	29.12.18		No change. M.G.R.A. 2ND ARMY visited Bde H.Q.	
"	30.12.18		No change.	
"	31.12.18		No change.	

[signature] for O.C. 110th Bde, R.F.A.
2.1.19.

40TH Brigade R.F.A

Army Form C. 2118.

WAR DIARY
or
INTELLIGENCE SUMMARY.
(Erase heading not required.)

1st to 31st January 1919

WO 3-3

Instructions regarding War Diaries and Intelligence Summaries are contained in F. S. Regs., Part II. and the Staff Manual respectively. Title pages will be prepared in manuscript.

Place	Date	Hour	Summary of Events and Information	Remarks and references to Appendices
KREUZAU DROVE	1.1.19		No change.	
	2.1.19		No change.	
	3.1.19		No change.	
	4.1.19		No change.	
	5.1.19		No change.	
	6.1.19		Corps Commander inspected all batteries of the Brigade.	
	7.1.19		No change.	
	8.1.19		No change.	
	9.1.19		No change.	
	10.1.19		No change.	
	11.1.19		No change.	
	12.1.19		No change.	
	13.1.19		No change.	
	14.1.19		No change.	
	15.1.19		No change.	
	16.1.19		No change.	
	17.1.19		No change.	

Army Form C. 2118

WAR DIARY
or
INTELLIGENCE SUMMARY.
(*Erase heading not required.*)

Instructions regarding War Diaries and Intelligence Summaries are contained in F. S. Regs., Part II and the Staff Manual respectively. Title pages will be prepared in manuscript.

Place	Date	Hour	Summary of Events and Information	Remarks and references to Appendices
KREUZAU and DROVE	18.1.19		No change.	
	19.1.19		No change.	
	20.1.19		No change.	
	21.1.19		No change.	
	22.1.19		No change.	
	23.1.19		No change.	
	24.1.19		No change.	
	25.1.19		No change.	
	26.1.19		No change.	
	27.1.19		No change.	
	28.1.19		No change.	
	29.1.19		No change.	
	30.1.19		No change.	
	31.1.19		No change.	

A.D. Musgrave
Col. R.F.A.
Commanding 40th Bde. R.F.A.

Army Form C. 2118.

WAR DIARY
or
INTELLIGENCE SUMMARY.
(Erase heading not required.)

40 Bde R.F.A.

Place	Date	Hour	Summary of Events and Information	Remarks and references to Appendices
KREUZRU and DROVE.	1-2-19		No Change.	
	2nd		No Change.	
	3rd		No Change.	
	4th		No Change.	
	5th		No Change.	
	6th		No Change.	
	7th		No Change.	
	8th		No Change.	
	9th		No Change.	
	10th		No Change.	
	11th		No Change.	
	12th		No Change.	
	13th		No Change.	
	14th		No Change.	
	15th		No Change.	
	16th		A drive of civilians took place over the whole Bde. area, starting at 21-15 hrs. 40th Bde searched their own area. The object of the drive was to find out if every firm over 12 yrs Old had an Identity Card, see that there was no civilians moved about in possession of	

Army Form C. 2118.

WAR DIARY
or
INTELLIGENCE SUMMARY.
(Erase heading not required.)

Instructions regarding War Diaries and Intelligence Summaries are contained in F. S. Regs., Part II. and the Staff Manual respectively. Title pages will be prepared in manuscript.

Place	Date	Hour	Summary of Events and Information	Remarks and references to Appendices
10th Bgde			Army Postal Services Ordinary. Number of parcels for the Brigade as under	
	19/4			
	20/4			
	21/4			
	22/4			
	23/4			
	24/4			
	25/4			
	26/4			
	27/4			
	28/4			

A.D. Musgrave
Col. R.F.A.
Comdg. 40th Bde R.F.A.

www.ingramcontent.com/pod-product-compliance
Lightning Source LLC
Chambersburg PA
CBHW080825010526
44111CB00015B/2606